Research Methods in Management

Research Methods in Management

A concise introduction to research in management and business consultancy

Geoff Lancaster

ELSEVIER
BUTTERWORTH
HEINEMANN

AMSTERDAM • BOSTON • HEIDELBERG • LONDON • NEW YORK • OXFORD
PARIS • SAN DIEGO • SAN FRANCISCO • SINGAPORE • SYDNEY • TOKYO

Elsevier Butterworth-Heinemann
Linacre House, Jordan Hill, Oxford OX2 8DP
30 Corporate Drive, Burlington, MA 01803

First published 2005

British Library Cataloguing in Publication Data
A catalogue record for this book is available from the British Library

Library of Congress Cataloguing in Publication Data
A catalogue record for this book is available from the Library of Congress

ISBN 0 7506 6212 3

For information on all Elsevier Butterworth-Heinemann publications visit
our website at http://www.books.elsevier.com

Typeset by Newgen Imaging Systems (P) Ltd, Chennai, India
Printed and bound in Great Britain

Contents

About the Author

Professor Geoff Lancaster MSc, PhD, FCIM, FLCC
Chairman, Durham Associates Group, Castle Eden, Co. Durham, with offices in London and Hull, UK; Bahrain; Jeddah and Dhahran, KSA; Dubai, UAE; Kish, Iran; Muscat, Oman; Doha, Qatar; Lusaka, Zambia and Johannesburg, South Africa. The company was established in 1990 to engage in business consultancy and education. An international division was established in 1994, and the company received the Queen's Award for Exporting in 1999.

Acknowledgements

I am grateful to the following for permission to use their material:

Richard Charlesworth and Peter Morley, London Metropolitan University, for part of Chapter 10 *'Questionnaire Design'* and *'Samples and Populations'*.

David Crowther, London Metropolitan University, for part of Chapter 11 *'Semiotics'*.

John Colby, University of Central England, Appendix V, *'Referencing and advice on presentation'*.

Andy Hollyhead, University of Central England, Advice on Executive Summaries and Reporting.

I am grateful to Frank Withey, University of Huddersfield, for the help he has given in terms of providing assistance in the form of advice on the structure of the text, for sourcing material and for his critical and constructive evaluation.

Hollyhead
Colby

1

Introduction

1.1 Background and major themes

This book was planned and written to fill what was felt to be a distinct gap in the literature on management research. This recognition came about as a result of the author's long experience tutoring undergraduate and postgraduate students completing projects and dissertations for their studies in management. In understanding how to get the best out of this book it would be helpful to trace this background to the development of the book and, in particular, to highlight and explain the major themes in the book and how these serve to differentiate this text from others in the areas of management research and consultancy.

On most undergraduate and postgraduate courses in management, students studying in this area are usually in the final stages of their studies, and are required to research in-depth a selected area of management in order to complete a project or dissertation as part of their assessment and award. Although the precise nature and requirements of this research obviously differ between, for example, individual students, the course requirements and the purpose and level of the research, on many management programmes students are increasingly being encouraged, and in some cases required, to complete their research and produce their projects and dissertations based on managerial issues or problems in a real-life organization.

In the case of students studying part-time, or perhaps through distance learning, the organization on which the research/project is based is often the one in which the student is working. Perhaps understandably where this is the case, both students and their organizations often welcome this approach as there are clearly advantages to both the student and the organization.

In the case of full-time students, although they are not usually employees of a particular organization, here too students are being increasingly encouraged to develop their managerial skills by conducting their final year projects or dissertation for a real life organization. In this case, students might be allocated to selected companies who agreed to provide management problems for students to look at.

As already mentioned, for both full-time and part-time students an increasing trend is for students to complete their project or dissertation work based on a real-life management issue in an organization.

One of the main advantages of this approach is that at the same time as satisfying the academic requirements in most undergraduate and postgraduate programmes to complete an extended in-depth project or dissertation based on research, it helps students to develop their skills and expertise as managers. After all, the knowledge developed on most management courses, it can be argued, only becomes useful when it is applied to the real world of organizations and real-life management issues and problems. In order to facilitate this move towards learning through organization-based management, research students need to acquire skills and knowledge in several key related areas.

Management consultancy skills

First, students need skills and knowledge in how to plan and conduct what is effectively a management consultancy exercise. They need to understand the consultancy process through from how to initiate a management consultancy project with a client, how to conduct a project, and how to implement, follow up and withdraw from the project.

Management research skills

Second, students need skills and knowledge in how to plan and conduct research in management. In particular they need to understand the main approaches to conducting research in this area, for example, techniques of data collection and analysis.

Self development skills

Third, as perhaps a subsidiary, but nevertheless still important need, students also need to understand and appreciate how the application of management research principles and techniques through a management consultancy exercise contributes to their development as managers.

How these areas relate to the structure and use of this book, and why it was felt necessary to write a new text are outlined below.

• *Management consultancy*: Where students and/or managers are going to work on real-life management problems with organizations for their projects and dissertations, they are, as already mentioned, effectively working in a consultancy capacity.

Surprisingly, however, most undergraduate, or even postgraduate courses in management spend very little time on developing the skills and techniques of management consultancy. Admittedly, students are taught skills in, say, marketing research, financial or human resource management, and so on, which can later be used if working in a consultancy capacity, but in the context of many management courses much of what is taught is often conceptual in nature with applications being confined to, for example, case study activities. If students are going to be asked to act as management consultants for companies as part of their studies then it is necessary to address the development of the skills and expertise required for this activity. In fact, there are very few texts available in this area, especially when the consultancy is to be linked to the completion of a project or dissertation as part of a course of studies in management. Generally, the texts available on management consultancy, excellent though many of them are, focus on the practising management consultant rather than on the undergraduate or postgraduate student conducting this work to produce a research project or dissertation. It was felt, therefore, that there was a need for a text which specifically addressed the issues in, and approaches to, using a consultancy-based approach to the process of studying and researching in management, and at the same time, fulfilling appropriate academic criteria. Consultancy then became the first major theme of this text.

- *Management research*: Unlike the management consultancy area, there are literally dozens of excellent texts, designed to introduce students to the concepts and techniques of research in management. Even in the more specific context of researching for an undergraduate or postgraduate dissertation or project on management, again there is no shortage of excellent texts on, for example, how to conduct a research project; qualitative and quantitative methods of research; and approaches to completing student research projects and dissertations. However, many of these texts on management research are often very conceptual in nature and rarely are structured around a consultancy-based approach. The uses and application of the main techniques of management research to real-life management issues and problems centered on a consultancy-type project then became the second theme of the text.
- *Self development*: It is increasingly recognized that, having completed their courses and studies, managers in today's environment will nevertheless need to constantly develop and refine their skills during their careers in management. A major advantage of conducting a research project through a consultancy-type approach in an organization is that it can be a major vehicle, not only for developing the sorts of management and executive skills needed for today's manager, but in addition, can serve to promote self-development through action learning which in turn leads to an understanding of the nature and processes of continued professional development throughout a manager's life in organizations. This idea of self-development, then, is one that runs throughout this text and is, therefore, the third key theme of the text.

1.2 Using this book

The aim of this book is to help you become competent in the process of management and consultancy research activities. In achieving this aim the text encompasses the skills and procedures of consultancy research. These encompass the steps in the consultancy process ranging through from initiating, planning and designing consultancy research projects through to the methods and skills of data collection and analysis. The key processes of implementing and actioning consultancy research findings in client organizations are also covered.

It is envisaged that most readers using this text will be completing a project or dissertation as part of their studies through the practical application of a management consultancy project in a selected organization. The text, therefore, also aims to help develop your management competence and expertize through becoming an active part of the organizational world, thereby acquiring transferable skills needed for personal and professional development throughout your life as a manager.

In Chapter 2, you will be introduced to the importance of managing your development and learning as a manager and, in particular, the importance of self-development and learning through the completion of a consultancy-type project in an organization. Development and learning in this way is, as we shall see, often referred to as 'action learning'. In order to get maximum benefit from the use of the book, it is important to familiarize yourself with the action learning process and principles outlined in this chapter. In addition, in this chapter you will also be introduced to the steps in planning a self-development programme to assess your own personal needs for development as a manager. Because of this, Chapter 2 differs slightly in approach to the subsequent chapters in the book. You will be required to consider your own development needs as a manager perhaps working together with a mentor, or possibly your project/research supervisor. This in turn will require you to consider the key managerial skill areas and your strengths and weaknesses in each of these. You will then be asked to set personal objectives for your self-development as a manager. Finally, having considered your own personal development objectives, you are asked to consider the selection and design of a consultancy-type research project which will help towards the achievement of your identified management self-development objectives.

You may be tempted to omit this part of the chapter on self-development and instead move on to the design of a consultancy-based project and the techniques of management research. However, it is useful to remember that one of the key themes in the book is using management research and consultancy to develop the sort of management and executive skills needed to survive in the complex and ever changing business world of today and the future. The ideas and frameworks developed in this chapter therefore are relevant to all the stages of the consultancy research process from the perspective of self-development and therefore it may be useful to return to this chapter from time to time as you work through the research process.

In Chapter 3 you are introduced to research in management. The chapter compares and contrasts the different theoretical stances in the practice of research; the overall management research process, the different approaches to conducting management research and the relationship between management research, management development and management consultancy. You should use this chapter to familiarize yourself with the main traditions and approaches to conducting research. In some ways, this is the most conceptual chapter in the book, but it is vital to developing your understanding of the main research approaches in management and how they relate to research through consultancy.

Chapters 4 and 5 together explain the nature and process of management consultancy and research encompassing the nature, purposes and issues of this process and the key steps involved. Obviously, when you come to initiate and plan your consultancy project these two chapters are vital to these processes.

Chapters 5–11 encompass the main methods of data collection and analysis in management research. Obviously a key choice in research is the method(s) of data collection. Which of these chapters will prove to be most useful and relevant to your particular research will of course, depend on the choice you make of the appropriate data collection methods. This choice, requires you to be familiar with the alternative approaches to data collection and analysis and therefore, these chapters not only provide this familiarization but also help in selecting and applying the research techniques which are most appropriate for any given consultancy research project. For readers who are conducting more traditional non-consultancy-type management research projects, these chapters can be used as stand alone chapters covering the main methods of data collection and analysis.

In the final chapter of the text – Chapter 12 – we look at the process of moving from data analysis to using this analysis to make recommendations and decisions about courses of action. Because the approach taken throughout the text centers on conducting management and consultancy research, this chapter introduces the key considerations regarding consultancy proposals to clients and how, at the end of a consultancy project, the consultant can disengage from the client system and leave the internal managers in the organization to continue managing on their own. Again, readers who are not adopting a consultancy-based approach may be tempted to omit Chapter 12. However, as the logical conclusion to most management research processes is the determination of recommended courses of action and as this aspect of a management research project is included in this chapter, most of you will find this final part of the book essential reading.

On completion of the book you will be able to:

- engage in management consultancy and research, using a range of appropriate tools and techniques of management research;
- manage a strategic project from its conception to the presentation of an executive report;
- monitor your own development as a manager during the execution of consultancy-type project work.

1.3   Chapter structure/studying each chapter

With the exception of Chapter 1 which for reasons explained in the chapter itself differs slightly from the other chapters, the remaining chapters have a number of common structural elements designed to help you get the maximum benefit out of reading and studying the chapter. The main structural elements include the following:

Learning Outcomes

Each chapter includes a set of learning outcomes designed to highlight what skills and knowledge the chapter is designed to cover and which, on completion of the chapter, you should you have learned.

Activities/activity debriefs

Many of the chapters will, at the appropriate juncture, ask you to undertake some sort of activity. These take a number of forms, but essentially are designed to reinforce the learning process by asking you to apply key concept, provide answers to questions, reflect on key learning points, and so on. Obviously it is up to you to decide whether or not to complete these activities – and indeed how much time and effort you want to devote to them. However, you will find that completing these activities will provide valuable insights and serve to help you understand key concepts and techniques and you are therefore advised to complete the activities. In the Appendix to the book you will find a set of activity debriefs which explain the activities and, where appropriate, provide solutions. Again, how you use the activity debriefs is up to you, but ideally you should try to complete an activity before consulting the corresponding debrief.

References/Glossary

Although the book is designed to be self-contained, as you would expect, you are encouraged to read as widely as possible. To this effect each chapter contains specific references to help you explore and expand your knowledge in key areas. In addition, key words and terms introduced in the chapter are explained in a glossary section at the end of each chapter.

 ## 1.4   The research/consultancy project

Remember that a key distinguishing feature of this book is that the content and structure are based around, and are primarily intended to be applied to, a management-consultancy-type project that users of the book will select and work on. For many, this project will also underpin the completion of a project report or dissertation as part of a programme of studies. Obviously then, the nature and organization of the consultancy project will have a major effect on how this book is used. In particular, major factors influencing the use of the book will include, for example: the choice of consultancy/research topic, the type of consultancy client, the nature of the relationship between consultant and client, and so on. In addition, where the research is part of a programme of study leading to an award of some kind, then the use of the book will also vary according to the precise nature and role of the research project, the level of the award, the time scale, arrangements for supervision, whether the project is individual or group work, reporting procedures, marking criteria, and so on.

Clearly, with so many factors influencing precisely how the book will be best used, it is impossible to prescribe how you should work through and use the various chapters. No doubt, where appropriate, you will be discussing details such as project selection and approval, client selection, precise objectives, methods of working, research framework, timetables and so on with a project/research supervisor. As an overall guide, however, the book links up to the completion of a research project or dissertation together with a planned programme of professional self-development as follows:

- initiating, planning and the consultancy project: including initial discussions with a project/dissertation supervisor;
- design and agreement of research proposal;
- conducting the consultancy project/feedback from supervisor;
- completing the consultancy report;
- planning an ongoing process of monitoring professional self development.

If you are using this book in order to complete an actual research project, then clearly you will have to manage the above mentioned activities within the time allocated to them. How many hours will be required to complete each chapter in the book is suggested below. The remaining time will be taken up by the other activities already mentioned, and together will account for most of the time required to complete a research project. Obviously, allocations and requirements regarding planning study time should be discussed individually with a project supervisor and any client organization according to circumstances.

Chapter 2 Managing your development as a manager The importance of and approaches to manager and executive development. Identifying and planning self development needs	3 hours
Chapter 3 Introduction to research in management The nature, scope and purpose of management research	3 hours
Chapter 4 Management consultancy and research The nature, purposes and issues of consultancy research	3 hours
Chapter 5 The consultancy research process Key issues and steps in initiating, planning, designing and conducting a management consultancy project	3 hours
Chapter 6 Data collection: an overview The range of data collection methods	3 hours
Chapter 7 Data collection: secondary data Meanings, sources and uses of secondary data	3 hours
Chapter 8 Data collection: observational research Techniques, uses and limitations	3 hours

1.5   Concluding comments

In this introductory chapter I have explained the background to the design of the book. In so doing, I have also highlighted the major themes which run throughout. The overall aim of the book is to help you become competent in the process of management and consultancy research activities. I have outlined the nature and content of each chapter, and the role each chapter plays in the development of your competencies in research and consultancy, and I have given some suggestions as to how many hours will be required to complete each chapter in the book, including the activities which are an essential part of each chapter.

Finally, I have added my opinion by way of an acknowledgement regarding the difficulties and frustrations of conducting consultancy-type-based research, and now proffer some suggestions as to how to minimize these.

After many years' experience of this type of research you are warned that the path of such research hardly ever runs smoothly and is fraught with pitfalls for the inexperienced or unwary. There is no doubt that you will make mistakes. You will certainly experience unexpected problems and roadblocks. Who knows, but along the way you may even make some enemies. All research is potentially complex and, at times, frustrating. The only solution to these problems is good research design; a systematic and planned approach; and finally perseverance and patience. Remember that applied/consultancy research in particular, largely because of the challenges it poses, is one of the most satisfying and rewarding ways of learning about management and organizations. You are assured that with perseverance and patience no other element of your learning and studies will potentially contribute more to your self development as a manager, and possibly senior executive of the future, than the activities and skills which are encompassed here. In the next chapter then, you are introduced to the process of managing your development as a manager and the role which a consultancy-type research project plays in this.

2

Managing Your Development as a Manager

Learning outcomes

After completing this chapter you will understand:

- the importance of, and approaches to, management development;
- the different models of management development including self-development, action learning and collaboration with others;
- the process and practices involved in successful, professional self-development;
- how to contribute to your own self-development as a manager using consultancy-type research projects.

Introduction

As you are aware, one of the key distinguishing themes of this book is that of helping develop your competence and expertise as a manager using consultancy-type research. The bulk of the book centers on actually planning, conducting and reporting upon a consultancy project, and although 11 of the 12 chapters in the book focus on how to complete these activities, again, it is important to stress that consultancy type projects and research are among the most useful vehicles for helping to acquire and develop transferable skills needed for personal and professional development throughout a management/executive career. In this chapter, therefore, I introduce the process of trying to ensure the development of a manager/executive focusing primarily on how this can be achieved through a process of self-development. In doing so, I shall also relate this process of self-development to the consultancy research process. As already mentioned, this second chapter uses a somewhat different approach and style to the remaining chapters in the book. In this chapter I shall be taking you through how consultancy-type research projects can contribute to the development of the manager/executive, including how to establish goals for self-development, determining how consultancy-type research activities can help achieve these goals, and the importance of constant evaluation in the process of management self-development. At the same time, and through this process, we are seeking to establish an awareness and receptiveness to the importance of continuing self-development throughout the manager's life.

It is important to note that the concepts and techniques referred to in this chapter are relevant to the whole of the research and consultancy process with regard to using this process as a vehicle for developing the manager/executive. The ideas and frameworks in this chapter then can be used throughout the different stages of conducting a management research and/or consultancy project; from the initial selection of the project, through the research design, data collection and analysis stages; and finally through to the stage of evaluating how the project has contributed to your own professional development. You will therefore, probably need to return to this chapter from time to time throughout the consultancy research process.

 ## 2.1   The importance of continued professional development for the manager

It is tempting to believe that once a professional has been trained, perhaps through completing successfully a course of study, passing the requisite examinations and assessments, and receiving a qualification of some kind, that there is no need for any further training and development, rather the professional can now get on with simply practising and applying his/her skills and knowledge. However, such a belief is misplaced. All of us, including perhaps in some particular ways, the professional manager, need to continue to develop our skills and knowledge throughout our lives (Harrison 2002; Marchington and Wilkinson 2002). Even if we accepted the idea that the newly qualified MBA graduate, for example, was honed to a point of perfection with regard to up-to-date and comprehensive managerial knowledge and skills – again perhaps itself a misplaced idea – in today's rapidly changing environment it would not be long before at least some of this knowledge and skills became outmoded. Quite simply, organizations change, ideas and knowledge change, and the circumstances also change. Over the course of a manager's working life there is no doubt that change will not only be inevitable but may often involve seismic changes in ideas and thinking. Quite simply, then, it is crucial that the effective manager adopts the attitude of an acceptance of the need for continuous professional development over a working life. Even if change were not the order of the day, however, part of the professional development of the manager is continuous honing and refinement of existing skills and knowledge to practical management problems and issues. Again, the manager needs to develop these skills and knowledge on a continuous basis. Managers who are unwilling or unable to accept this need for continuing professional development are likely to quickly find that their skills and knowledge are outmoded and irrelevant to the real world of organizations. In addition, managers who resist change in this respect are unlikely to progress through the management hierarchy to the highest levels of executive activities. If we accept the importance, and need for, continuing professional development with regard to the manager, it raises the issue of how such development is to be achieved.

 ## 2.2   Approaches to professional development: self-development

Once we accept the need for continued professional development for the manager, then we have to consider how such development can be achieved. There are a number of ways in which this can be accomplished that include:

- external training courses/study courses,
- internal training,
- learning on the job/action learning.

These alternatives for the continuous professional development of managers are not of course mutually exclusive. All three approaches may play a part in the development process. In addition, development may be facilitated in a number of ways by using a number of alternative methods and approaches including:

- 'tutoring' by a tutor or trainer,
- learning from others in the organization,
- 'shadowing' in another organization,
- self-development activities.

Again, these alternative methods and approaches are not mutually exclusive. However, it is recognized that perhaps the most effective approach to professional development, particularly where this is to encompass the whole working career of an individual, is that of self-development (Stewart 1999; Morgan 2002).

Self-development moves the emphasis away from someone else being responsible for training, teaching and developing us, to an acceptance of the value and effectiveness of pursuing these activities for oneself. Using self-development to facilitate the development of the manager has the following advantages compared to development that is externally planned and/or imposed. Self-development is likely to

- result in new skills and knowledge being internalized and accepted by the manager,

- reflect the needs of the individual manager,
- facilitate continuous development of the manager throughout the manager's working life,
- represent one of the most challenging but rewarding activities for the individual.

This does not mean that other development activities for the manager are always ineffective or less useful; indeed, there is a real need to integrate other management development and training programmes with self-development ones. However, we can see that self-development not only has many advantages over other approaches to developing the manager, but is essential in a rapidly changing environment where a management career may span thirty years or more. What then, are some of the ways or paths to self-development for managers in organizations? Pedler et al. (2001) suggest that the following are some of the most commonly found routes to self-development within organizations:

- mentoring,
- coaching/counselling,
- appraisal,
- internal rotation, attachment and placement,
- external attachments and placements,
- reading,
- joining special projects,
- committee membership,
- discussion groups, working parties, meetings of professional bodies and institutes,
- learning from one's own job and experience,
- special activities.

Source: Pedler et al. (2001).

Each of these approaches to self-development has its own advantages and uses according to the circumstances and needs of the individual manager, and once again, several of these approaches may be used in combination as part of a self-development programme. In this book of course, I have selected the vehicle of a 'real life' management consultancy research project for the self-development process. In case you are wondering how this relates to the alternative routes to self-development shown above, the consultancy research project in fact incorporates several of these including learning from one's own job and experience, joining special projects, participating in special activities and discussion groups and reading. As I have already said, several of the paths to self-development that have been referred to can be combined in using a consultancy-based research project for self-development. A particularly good reason for using an organizational-based consultancy project for self-development and continued learning is the fact that it affords the opportunity to benefit from the so-called action learning process and principles. It is useful therefore, at this stage, to introduce you to these principles.

■ 2.3 Action learning: process and principles

The concept of action learning was first promulgated by Kurt Lewin (1952) in the United States and later by Revans (1971) in the United Kingdom. In essence, the concept of action learning is simple. As the name implies, action learning is learning by doing things (actions) in real life situations (Kemmis and Grundy 1981; Burns 2000). In some respects, the idea of action learning is a reaction to learning based on teaching by an expert, particularly where such teaching takes place in a classroom. Revans suggested that the most effective way of learning and discovery was by undertaking activities in real-life situations, whereby the individual could learn by reflecting on the effectiveness of actions taken. The key to action learning is to work on real problems, then, observing the effects of one's actions and, through a process of feedback and reflection, to learn from every action undertaken.

There is no doubt that action learning offers a particularly useful way of thinking about learning for the professional manager. After all, management takes place in the real world of organizations, and let us face it, managers and executives are actually paid for taking action. In the context of this book, however, the most important aspect of action learning is the notion that an individual's work and activities undertaken in completing the work as a manager is perhaps the most valuable learning experience possible. This does not mean that classroom learning and theories, and so on, are not useful or important. Often, they provide a framework for understanding and interpreting one's actions and learning from these actions in organizations. Using a real-life consultancy project as the vehicle for learning and self-development as a manager explicitly recognizes the value of the action learning approach. Indeed, in Chapter 8 we discuss in some detail the methodology and ideas of action research as a method of data collection. We shall see that action research – which in turn leads to action learning – is an approach to research involving practical hands-on field research in an organization where the researcher has the objective of solving practical problems in an organization with a view to solving real-world problems. Although action research is a research methodology then, it is based on the principles of action learning, that is, learning by doing. In this way the manager learns for him/herself and therefore is very much in line with the philosophy and aims of this book. Action learning and action research are aimed therefore at helping us develop as better managers through implementing and evaluating action programmes in organizations. The value of action learning in the self-development process for managers and executives is the main reason I have emphasized the completion of a consultancy research project, as well as a more traditional academic style project or dissertation as the vehicle for learning and self-development in this book.

2.4   Working with and learning from others

Although the main thrust of action learning is learning by working on real-life problems in an organization, another key supporting feature of the concept of action learning is the notion of learning from others. Action learning, therefore, is often done by joining a small group that meets periodically, and where members of the group discuss the problems they are working on with others. These small groups are usually referred to as a *set*. Part of the action learning approach to self-development is the assigning of individuals to small groups normally under the supervision of a facilitator (sometimes referred to as a set adviser). As already mentioned, this group should typically meet periodically and members will usually take turns to describe the problems – or the consultancy projects – they are working on, analyse their understandings of these problems with others, consider ideas from other members, decide actions to be taken on the problem, and then report back to discuss and learn from the outcomes of previous actions taken.

Because of the value of learning from sets in action learning, you may be using these throughout your research project. The organization and operation of any such sets is beyond the scope of this book, but will no doubt, where appropriate, be organized by the research supervisor/tutor. Where sets are being used, you will probably be given more detailed information on how the sets will operate including the allocation and role of the facilitator at the outset of the module by the supervisor/tutor. A variety of methods can be used to facilitate the operation of sets in action learning according to circumstances. Ideally, sets work best as a vehicle for action learning where members of the set, together with the facilitator can meet face-to-face. However, as you will appreciate, this may not always be possible, so alternative methods of operating sets, and for collaborating with other course members on project management and problem solving can be arranged at the start of the programme.

2.5   Planning a self-development programme

A self-development programme should be just that. It should be planned for each individual according to his or her requirements, and centre on development activities carried out by that individual. Put another way, each manager will need a different self-development programme encompassing different objectives, activities, evaluation mechanisms, and so on. Remember, the choice of a consultancy-based research project approach that has been highlighted in this book, is intended not only as a mechanism for completing a research project/dissertation, but at the same time, to provide for reasons we have already seen, a powerful vehicle for self-development. In order to gain the maximum development value out of a consultancy-based research project, however, it is necessary for each individual to plan their own programme for self-development as a manager/executive, and in this case how the consultancy research project is to link in with, and support, this programme.

Although an individual can be helped in planning their programme by others including, for example, tutors, trainers, or in the case of action learning, other members of the set, each individual has to take the responsibility for their self-development programmes and activities, which will be unique to that individual (Gibb, 2002). I have listed some guidelines for planning the self-development process that are useful in planning a programme for continued professional development, and how a consultancy-type research project might fit into this. Some of the key steps in planning a programme of self-development are as follows:

Taking stock: identifying individual personal development needs

The first step in planning a self-development programme is for the manager to identify his or her own personal needs for development as a manager. One way of thinking about these is for the individual to assess their own personal strengths and weaknesses as a professional manager. In turn though, this begs the question of strengths and weaknesses – in what respect and in what areas? This question can perhaps best be addressed by considering what constitutes an effective manager/executive, or if you like, what are the skills and attributes required to be an effective manager/executive? Consideration of these skills and attributes can then be used to assess strengths and weaknesses in these areas.

It has long been recognized that the four key functions of the manager encompass *planning, organizing, leading* and *controlling*. To be effective as a manager/executive an individual has to be strong in each of these four functions. A manager, therefore, could assess his or her strengths and weaknesses with regard to these four key functions. However, simply listing these four functions does not give much idea as to the precise skills required of a manager. Mintzberg (1980) was one of the first to begin to provide such detail with regard to managerial activities. He identified three key general roles for the manager, that in turn, were associated with a number of key activities which managers actually perform during their work. Mintzberg's roles can be used to give us clues about the kinds of skills that a manager is likely to need to carry out his or her work effectively. It therefore potentially provides a framework for an individual to assess their strengths and weaknesses with regard to these skills. Mintzberg's three key roles were *interpersonal roles, informational roles* and *decisional roles*. In turn, each of these roles, as already mentioned, is underpinned by a series of activities and in turn skills required of a manager. These are shown below.

Interpersonal role

This role essentially involves developing and maintaining positive relationships with significant others in the organization. The activities that underpin this role include acting as a figurehead, leadership roles and liaison roles.

Informational role

This role pertains to receiving and transmitting information to others inside and outside of the organization. Activities that underpin this role include acting as a monitor, disseminating information, and acting as a spokesperson.

Decisional role

This role, as you would expect, involves making key decisions that affect the organization. Activities that underpin this role include acting as an entrepreneur, taking corrective actions to handle disturbances, allocating resources, and negotiating.
Source: Adapted from Minzberg, H. (1980).

Mintzberg's roles and activities can be used to take stock of the individual manager's strengths and weaknesses with regard to these key roles and activities.

Another approach to taking stock of our strengths and weaknesses as a manager with regard to planning a self-development programme is to identify the key management skills and then assess strengths and weaknesses with respect to these. Bartol and Martin (1998) identify the following three areas of key management skills:

- *Technical skills*: These are skills with reference to, and understanding of, and a proficiency in, a specialized field. For example, the manager may have technical skills in accounting, finance, engineering, manufacturing, and so on.
- *Human skills*: These are skills associated with a manager's ability to work well with others both within a group and as a leader who gets things done through others. Key skills in this area would include the ability to motivate others, and skills of leadership and communication.
- *Conceptual skills*: These are skills related to the manager's ability to consider the organization as a whole and how the organization fits into the wider context of the industry, community and world. Conceptual skills are particularly important at the higher levels of management and, therefore, are particularly relevant to this module as they are essential in areas such as corporate and strategic planning.
Source: Adapted from Bartol, K. M. and Martin, D. C. (1988) p. 15.

These ideas and frameworks about the nature of effective management and the roles, activities and skills required provide a basis for taking stock of individual strengths and weaknesses and thereby enabling objectives and programmes for self-development to be identified. This approach to planning self-development programmes is comprehensively developed by Pedler et al. (op. cit.). They have identified in some detail the attributes and skills required of successful managers that in turn can be used to take stock of strengths and weaknesses with regard to these attributes and skills. Some of these key attributes and skills include the following:

- technical knowledge and skills,
- sensitivity and awareness (of factors affecting the organization),

- problem solving and decision/judgement making skills,
- social skills and abilities,
- emotional resilience,
- proactivity/purposefulness,
- creativity,
- mental agility,
- learning skills.

Source: Pedler et al. (2001).

These schemas can be used to devise a personal development programme. It is unwise and unhelpful to be prescriptive about the precise areas and skills which should be included in a personal strengths and weaknesses assessment, as by definition each individual is different, may have different aims and objectives, be faced with different circumstances, and so on. So long as we remember this, either individually or together with the help of others, we can use these ideas about what constitutes effective management and the key roles, activities and skills required of the effective manager to take stock of our individual professional development need. Having done this, we can then move on to the next step in planning a self-development programme, namely setting personal objectives.

Setting personal objectives

Once the individual has identified managerial strengths and weaknesses, and hence our own personal needs and requirements as a manager with regard to self-development he or she can move to set specific objectives for the self-development programme. As with all objectives, those for self-development should be 'SMART' namely, specific, measurable, actionable, realistic and timed. Objectives may relate to one, or several, of the key areas of activity and skills required to operate as an effective manager and any identified weaknesses in these.

In the context of management consultancy research it should be possible to identify how, and in what areas, a research project will contribute to the achievement of self-development objectives. Indeed, in some cases this contribution may be an important consideration in the selection of the consultancy project itself. In some academic programmes, and especially where the project or dissertation research is recognized as being a key vehicle for developing management skills, these self-development objectives may be part of the research submission to be discussed and agreed between researcher and supervisor at the planning stage of the research.

Determining actions, and activities to achieve objectives

The next step in planning the personal development process is to determine how identified objectives for self-development are to be achieved. The routes to self-development identified earlier in the chapter including, for example, mentoring, coaching/counselling, reading, discussion groups, and so on, illustrate the wide range of alternatives. Again, in the context of this book the emphasis is on identifying how the actions and activities of both academic management research and management consultancy research including the design and implementation of the project itself, will contribute to self-development with regard to the identified objectives.

As part of a self-development programme the management research process should ideally involve the individual in actions and activities which will facilitate the achievement of the previously identified objectives for self-development as a manager. These activities, and how and why they contribute to the identified objectives for self-development, might be part of the research proposal to be agreed upon with a supervisor. If so, the proposal should also contain details of measures and mechanisms for monitoring and evaluating the self-development programme.

Monitoring and evaluating self-development

Self-development requires mechanisms for being able to monitor and evaluate the self-development activities undertaken. Where a management consultancy project is part of the self-development programme there are a number of ways in which this can be achieved including the following:

- discussions with others to evaluate and assess self-development activities with research supervisor, other members of action learning set, and so on;
- keeping logs/diaries, which can be extremely useful, of any activities undertaken during the research and/or consultancy project. This should include, for example, the objectives of the activity, what was done, when, how and with whom, and an evaluation of how effective the activity was with regard to self-development objectives.

2.6 Concluding comments

In this chapter I have emphasized the fact that a management research or consultancy project, besides being an ideal vehicle for completing a project or dissertation, is often a part of an academic programme on management. It is also an extremely useful way for helping the individual manager to develop as an executive and an effective manager in the future. We have seen that there are a variety of approaches to developing management competence and expertise, but one of the most useful and long lasting of these approaches is that of self-development, of competence and expertise. Much of what has been covered in this chapter is relevant throughout the use of a consultancy research project as part of a self-development programme, but is particularly relevant at the commencement of a research project where the individual will need to identify and sometimes agree on how the research project will contribute to their own personal development as a manager and executive.

2.7 References

Bartol, K. M. and Martin, D.C. (1988) *Management*, 3rd edn, Boston, MA: McGraw-Hill.

Burns, R. B. (2000) *Introduction to Research Methods*, 4th edn, London: Sage Publications.

Gibb, S. (2002) *Learning and Development: Processes, Practices and Perspectives at Work*, Hampshire, Palgrave Macmillan.

Harrison, R. (2002) *Learning and Development*, Chartered Institute of Personnel and Development.

Kemmis, S. and Grundy, S. 'Educational Action Research in Australia' AARE Annual Conference, November 1981, Adelaide.

Lewin, K. (1952) 'Group decision and social change', in T. Newcomb and F. Hartley, (eds), *Readings in Social Psychology*, New York: Holt.

Marchington, M. and Wilkinson, A. (2002) *People Management and Development*, London, Chartered Institute of Personnel.

Mintzberg, H. (1980) *The Nature of Managerial Work*, New York: Harper and Row.

Morgan, P. (2002) *Managing Yourself*, Harlow: Pearson

Pedler, M., Burgoyne, J. and Boydell, T. (2001) *A Manager's Guide to Self Development*, Berkshire, England: McGraw-Hill.

Revans, R. (1971) *Developing Effective Managers*, London: Longman.

Stewart, J. (1999) *Employee Development Practice*, Harlow, England: F. T. Prentice Hall.

2.8 Glossary

set A term used in action learning for the small groups that meet periodically for the members of the group to describe and discuss the problems they are working on.

3

Introduction to Research in Management

Learning outcomes

After completing this chapter you will be able to

- compare and contrast the different theoretical stances to the practice of research;
- understand the overall management research process;
- discuss the different approaches to conducting management research; and
- understand the relationship between management research and management development and how these are related to the process of management consultancy.

Introduction

As in many other spheres of human endeavour, research provides a key basis for developing knowledge. In the physical sciences, physicists, biologists, mathematicians, chemists, and so on, have long relied on and used research as a way of helping to define and refine knowledge in their subject areas. It is only comparatively recently that the social scientist has begun to use research for the same purpose. Certainly, research in management is one of the newest areas of research. In this chapter we examine the background to, and the development of, management research, tracing the different approaches to management research, the purposes of management research and some of the particular problems and issues which research in this area gives rise to. In the process we shall also examine the main traditions and approaches to conducting research in general including what is referred to as the different 'philosophies' of research.

3.1   The theoretical antecedents to management research: epistemological versus ontological orientations

Management research raises both theoretical and practical problems not encountered in research in the physical sciences and even the social sciences. Contemporary management research contains certain theoretical strands and antecedents that serve to shape and inform how such research is conducted. Before we look at the different approaches to contemporary management research, we need to consider what some of these key theoretical antecedents to management research practice are, and in particular, the different approaches to theory development and testing in the research process. We start by examining two of the earliest approaches which centre primarily on the development of knowledge and theory but which, in turn, have helped shape approaches to research. These two early approaches are the **epistemological** and the **ontological** schools of thought. Both these schools of thought date back to the Greek philosophers.

Epistemological orientations

Gilbert (1993) suggests that in this approach to developing knowledge and theories, the theories are built on the basis of gaining knowledge of the world. An epistemological approach organizes and explains knowledge in the form of theories. For example, an epistemological approach to a theory of leadership might be based on exploring what we can observe about effective leadership in the real world. By developing our knowledge of effective leadership in this way, we might observe that effective leadership seems to be associated with the possession of certain traits or characteristics on the part of the leader. This knowledge can then be used to form theories of leadership based on the possession of certain traits and their relationship to effective leadership. As we shall see later in this chapter and in several of the chapters that follow, much research and theory building in the social sciences uses the epistemological approach of building knowledge. Admittedly, there are many critics of the limitations of the epistemological approach to developing knowledge (Feyerabend 2004; Cook and Campbell 2004). As Easterby-Smith et al. (2002) suggest, however, this orientation to building theories and knowledge can, and does, result in several approaches or methodologies to the generation of such knowledge. Because of this, there is little doubt that the epistemological school of thought has resulted in a powerful and enduring legacy when it comes to the development of theory and the practice of management research.

Ontological orientations

This approach to the development of theories, Gilbert (op. cit.) suggests, is based on suggestions about the 'nature of phenomena'. For example, an ontological approach to developing theories of leadership would consist of developing views on the nature of effective leadership with or without reference or an attempt to relate these views to a knowledge base. In fact, this represents a very simplified description of what is in fact a variety of ontological approaches in the physical and social sciences. For example, we have the so called 'critical realism' ontology such as that of say Bhaskhar (1989) compared to say the 'interpretative' ontological approach suggested by Sayer (2000). For our purposes at this stage and as you will probably recognize, we have now identified the main distinguishing difference between epistemological and ontological orientations. Specifically, that respectively they represent an empirical versus a conceptual approach to theory building and research and as such are indeed different orientations. As already mentioned, we shall see in some of our methodologies and approaches to management research that both epistemological and ontological orientations survive to influence and shape the nature of contemporary management research.

3.2   Deductive versus inductive research

From our two earliest schools of thought regarding theory development and knowledge building have developed two equally important, but also in their own ways equally contrasting, alternative schools of thought with regard to the methodology of theory and knowledge building namely *deductive* versus *inductive* research methods. In fact these methods of research derive from two alternative methods of thinking (Graziano and Raulin 2004). The differences between these alternative approaches to research are explained below.

Deductive research

Deductive research develops theories or hypotheses and then tests out these theories or hypotheses through empirical observation. It is essentially a set of techniques for applying theories in the real world in order to test and assess their validity. Essentially the process of deductive research is as Saunders et al. point out 'the development of a theory that is subjected to a rigorous test' (2003). Deductive research is the most widely used research approach in the natural sciences.

Gill and Johnson (1997) suggest that the process of deductive research is as shown in Figure 3.1.

Others, such as Robson (2002), add another stage to this process namely that of modifying the theory in the light of findings, but the key steps in deductive research are now explained.

Theory/hypothesis formulation

The first step in deductive research is the generation of theories or hypotheses. These can be generated in a number of ways, for example, the researcher might

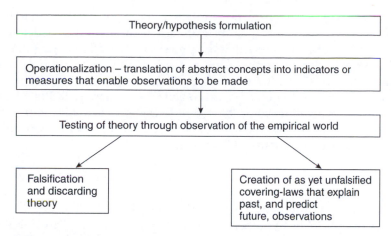

Figure 3.1 The process of deduction
Source: Gill J. and Johnson P. (1997) p.32.

simply have an idea based on, say, previous experience which s/he wants to test out or, for example, the theory or hypothesis to be tested might stem from, say, a literature search bringing together the ideas of others. Yet other sources of theories or hypotheses are those that stem from the desire to work out a solution to a specific problem. You will appreciate that this source of theories or hypotheses is particularly important and relevant in the context of this book which of course centres on consultancy-type research looking at a selected management problem. Most management consultancy projects start with a specific set of problems or issues that the research is designed to address ultimately with a view to making recommendations to resolving the problem or issues. The deductive research method, therefore, is particularly appropriate and relevant to the consultancy-type of research. Because of this, much deductive research can be considered as falling into the category of what is often referred to as *applied research*. We shall be considering the nature and process of consultancy-based research in more detail in the next chapter. In addition, we shall be considering the generation of theories and hypotheses for testing in later chapters when we consider research design in more detail.

Operationalization

Having formulated theories or hypotheses, the next stage in the deductive research process is to *operationalize* these. Essentially, this is the process whereby the concepts in our theories or hypotheses are defined in such a way that they can be measured through empirical observation. As Burns (2000) points out, operational definition is necessary to eliminate confusion in meaning and communication. This means ensuring that we have defined precisely what is to be measured or observed and how this measurement or observation will be carried out. For example, if our hypothesis is along the lines that 'personality traits' are associated with 'effective leadership', then we need to ensure that we have defined and can measure 'personality traits' and what constitutes 'effective leadership'. It is important to stress that the process of operationalizing theories or hypotheses can be difficult as we are often dealing with abstract concepts, which of themselves, are difficult to measure. These, and other aspects of operationalizing theories or hypotheses are considered in more detail in Chapter 5. At this stage, however, it would be useful to begin to acquaint you with this important process in deductive research through our first activity in the book. (See Activities/activities debrief Chapter 1).

Activity 3.1. You have developed the following hypothesis which you intend to test empirically.

Job satisfaction is affected by a person's managerial level.

Which concepts in the hypothesis will need operationalizing, and what might be some of the problems and issues in achieving this?

Theory testing/empirical observation

This stage in the process of deductive research is concerned with the process of measurement and observation such that we can eventually, in the next stage of the process, decide whether our theory/hypothesis can be supported or rejected. This stage of the deductive research process involves identifying and deciding between alternative techniques and approaches for measuring our operationalized concepts. It also includes the selection and design of the research methodologies to be used including, for example, any sampling plan, research instruments, and methods of analysing and interpreting empirical observations and measurements. In many ways, this stage of the deductive research process encompasses most of the activities that will be required to be planned and undertaken in conducting the research and as such several of the chapters that follow are essentially concerned with the design and application of this stage.

Once we have completed this stage in the deductive process then we can move to the final stage of deciding the extent to which our theory or hypothesis has been falsified and the extent to which parts, if any, of our theory/hypothesis remains as yet unfalsified. We refer to this as the falsification and discarding stage.

Falsification and discarding theory

At first, it may seem strange that the aim of the deductive process is to assess the extent to which a theory or hypothesis can be falsified and hence should be discarded. Surely, one might think that the process should be aimed at proving rather than refuting our hypotheses or theories. The idea that the outcome should be falsification and discarding of theories and hypotheses stems from the ideas of Karl Popper (1967) in what is often referred to as his maxim of 'falsificationism'. Simply stated, this maxim is based on the premise that the researcher should aim to refute rather than verify their theories or hypotheses. To the extent that the empirical observations made in the previous step in the process of deductive research do not support our theory or hypothesis, then these observations can be said to falsify and may lead us to discard all or part of our theory or hypothesis. This is the bottom left-hand box in Figure 3.1. That part of our theory or hypothesis which is not falsified through our observations and measurements of the empirical world does not prove our theory as such but rather allows those parts to remain as yet unfalsified theories or hypotheses. This is the bottom right-hand box in Figure 3.1. Clearly, the falsification-ism approach to testing of theory and hypotheses leads to possibly very different approaches to research design, methodology, and techniques of testing theories and hypotheses than where we are using a 'verificationism' approach. For example, how we state hypotheses or theories for testing is very different with a fal-sification as opposed to a verificationism approach. Again, we shall see this when we discuss hypothesis setting and testing in later chapters.

These, then, are the main steps in the process of deductive research. It is a fact that this approach to research represents the main, and some would say, the only justifiable, method of research in the natural sciences. There are those who, in addition, suggest that this is the only truly 'scientific' approach to devel-oping knowledge and therefore should also be the only approach that is used in the social sciences.

However, applying the deductive method in the social as opposed to the natural sciences is not without its problems. For example, measurement can be more problematical. Unlike the natural sciences, research is difficult to control and particularly the factors that can affect research outcomes, that is, the experi-mental method so widely used in the natural sciences is difficult. Again we shall consider some of these problems of the deductive methods of research and research techniques in later chapters but it is partly because of some of the problems and criticisms of the deductive approach to research that our second and alternative approach to research and research methods is almost exactly the reverse of deduction. Not surprisingly, this is known as 'inductive research'.

Inductive research

As already indicated, inductive research essentially reverses the process found in deductive research. Here, the researcher develops hypotheses and theories with a view to explaining empirical observations of the real world. These empiri-cal observations can be based on many factors, for example, they can simply be based on personal experience. Consider your own experiences in this respect. What have you observed best motivates you, or other people, in work organi-zations? Do you have any ideas on this? If so, you could develop your own explanations and theories about what you have observed through personal experience. Alternatively, theories might be developed to explain observed data and information, for example, the researcher might develop theories based on observed patterns of labour turnover. All sorts and types of information and data can be used to develop theories in inductive research. In fact, in the con-text of this book, when considering management research in general and consultancy-based research in management in particular, the inductive approach can be the more appropriate approach to research compared to the deductive method just outlined. Perhaps the greatest strength of inductive research is its flexibility. This research approach does not require the establishment of a- priori theories or hypotheses. On the contrary, we can build our theories based on our observations thereby allowing a problem or issue to be studied or approached in several possibly different ways with alternative explanations of what is going on. It is particularly suited to the study of human behaviour, including of course behaviour in organizations. Inductive research also enables more flexibility in research design including aspects such as sample size and type of data.

Activity 3.2. Using your own experiences in organizations, suggest a hypothesis or theory that might serve to explain a particular phenomenon you have noted from your experiences. In order to help you in this activity, I have included an example for you.

Phenomenon noted: Older employees in an organization seem to find it more difficult to adapt to new procedures.

Hypothesis/theory: In an organization age is a key factor affecting resistance to change.

Now select your own phenomenon and suggest a hypothesis that might explain this.

To reiterate, inductive research and investigations begin from description or observation and then move towards explanation. This approach, then, is initially concerned with observations that then lead to the development of a hypothesis and theories in order to explain those particular observations. In this context, we should note that in many research projects the management researcher, and the consultant researcher in particular, might be required to investigate ideas that stem initially from the observation or more specifically the occurrence of practical and observable issues and problems. The researcher/consultant may then be required or called in to investigate these issues and problems in order to develop theories to first explain, and then perhaps solve these issues and problems. As already stated, the inductive approach to conducting management research, therefore, can be particularly appropriate to management research. Indeed, we shall see when discussing some of the different approaches to, and techniques of, management research that some of the most powerful techniques of management research and consultancy use the inductive approach. The inductive approach is also better suited to the use and interpretation of qualitative data, whereas the deductive method, with its emphasis on measurement, often requires, and can only utilize, quantitative data. Given that management research and certainly management problems can often involve both qualitative and quantitative aspects, more often than not, effective management research often requires a combination of inductive and deductive methods. We may, for example, begin a research project using inductive methods and approaches, by say, first observing and measuring a phenomenon or problem that we wish to explore. This in turn can lead us to develop theories that we can then test using the deductive methods and approach.

3.3   Nomothetic versus ideographic research

The contrast between inductive and deductive research methods has given rise to two alternative categories of research methods. Burrell and Morgan (1979) have referred to these alternatives as the 'nomothetic' versus 'ideographic' methodologies. In fact, these two methodologies are best thought of as the extremes of a continuum of research methods but as Burns (2000) points out, each of these alternatives 'has profound implications for the way in which research is conducted'.

Nomothetic methods are most appropriate to the deductive approach to research in as much as they include the more highly structured research methodologies which can be replicated and controlled, and which focus on generating quantitative data with a view to explaining causal relationships. Perhaps the best examples of nomothetic research methodologies are those that are based on controlled laboratory experimentation. As such, they are obviously better suited to research in the natural sciences. Ideographic research methodologies, on the other hand, are much less structured and are focused more on the explanation and understanding of phenomena with much more emphasis on qualitative data. As such, the ideographic methods are better suited to the inductive research approach and in some ways are better suited to research in the social sciences including, of course, management research. Among the best examples of the ideographic research techniques are those of the previously referred to action research and the related research approach of 'ethnography', both of which are explained in more detail in later chapters.

Both nomothetic and ideographic methodologies can be used in management research, and again will often be used in combination. In addition, specific techniques of research within both methodologies often cut across and combine nomothetic and ideographic approaches. The characteristics of nomothetic and ideographic methods are considered in later chapters when we consider the selection and use of alternative research methodologies.

So far in this chapter we have examined the main theoretical antecedents to the process of and practice of research in general in both the physical and social sciences including some of the main alternative research methodologies. It is important for us to understand these as they serve to shape and direct contemporary research practices including the practice of management research. As such, we have briefly explored some of the implications of these antecedents and major methodological approaches for the process of management research. In the final parts of this chapter, however, we need to focus more specifically on the nature and issues of management research in particular. We shall start the last part of this chapter, therefore, by discussing three main types of research in management, followed by an overview of the management research process. Together, these will serve to set the framework for much of what follows in later chapters.

Finally, in this chapter, we consider some of the problems and issues in management research.

Types of management research

Although there is overlap between them, it is possible to identify or categorize three different types of management research with regard to the primary focus or objective of the research.

Theory building research

First, there is that research which is primarily aimed at developing management theories, and by so doing, improving our understanding and knowledge of the management process. You will now recognize that this type of management research is essentially inductive in nature. For example, it seeks to develop theories based on, observations, experience, intuition and so on. Much academic research in management is of this nature.

Theory testing research

Second, there is that research which is primarily aimed at testing out theories of management. Again, as we have already seen, more often than not this testing involves the process of empirical observations and measurements so as to be able to arrive at the decision as to whether or not, or what parts of a theory can be rejected and which, therefore, can remain as yet unfalsified theories or hypotheses. Again, much academic research in management falls into this category.

Problem centred/practical research

Our third type of research in management is that which is primarily aimed not at building or generating new theories, or adding to knowledge through the testing of theories or hypotheses. Rather, this type of research is primarily aimed at investigating a practical problem, question or issue in a specific organization or management context with a view to resolving the problem and subsequently making recommendations for courses of action. The primary focus of such research, then, is not academic or knowledge building for its own sake, but rather is aimed at investigating and proposing solutions to real-life management problems. This is not to say that this type of research does not potentially add to the body of theory and knowledge about management and indeed some of the most significant contributions to our knowledge and understanding in this area have stemmed from what was essentially problem-centred consultancy-type research. The so called 'Hawthorne Experiments' at the General Electric Company, USA, are a good example (these experiments are explained in fuller detail in Chapter 7). Having said this, for the most part, in the past with consultancy-type research any contributions to theory or knowledge building along the way have been more of a bonus than a primary aim. It is contented here, however, that this is changing. Increasingly, it is being recognized that consultancy-type research, even if it is still primarily problem/application centred, can at the same time be used for theory building and theory testing and hence for knowledge building. As already mentioned, there are plenty of examples of consultancy-type research making substantial contributions in this way. In this book, we continue this tradition, but in so doing, strive to bring even closer together and combine the applied consultancy-type research approach with more academic-type research that is so often the prime focus of most undergraduate and graduate projects and dissertations. In so doing, it is important to emphasize that this means that a variety of research methods and approaches may need to be combined for a particular project according to the circumstances. This is what Gill and Johnson (op. cit.) refer to as 'methodological pluralism' by which they mean that there is no one best research method or approach, but rather 'many methods contingent on the issue being studied'.

The reason for stressing this increased emphasis on combining the different research approaches is because many, and perhaps most, users of this book will be actually undertaking a project or dissertation as part of an academic programme of studies, but based on an applied piece of consultancy-type work in an actual organization. In fact, most MBA dissertations these days are of this applied type. The importance of this, however, is that where such applied/consultancy-based research is set in a wider context of producing a project report or dissertation for academic purposes, such consultancy research needs to go further than simply addressing practical managerial problems and issues in an organization. In addition to identifying solutions and making proposals about real-life organizational issues or problems, where the research is also part of an academic project or dissertation the researcher will also be required to set the content of the normal practising consultants report in an academic or theoretical context. Phillips and Pugh (1987) make a useful distinction between what they refer to as 'what' and 'why' questions in this respect. 'What' questions, they suggest, are questions that the client (organization) wants answered through the research/consultancy, often in the form of recommendations for action 'Why' questions, on the other hand are questions – or perhaps we should call them issues – that are required to be addressed for academic purposes – in our case probably to meet the academic requirements for a programme of study. Consultancy-based research, as part of such a programme of study, combines both 'what' and 'why' questions and therefore involves both inductive and deductive scholarship skills and processes and the combination of a variety of research methods and approaches.

Clearly there are different types of management research according to nature, purpose and context. However, it is useful to describe in broad terms the overall management research process which can now be introduced.

An overview of the management research process

As you will appreciate, the term 'management research' encompasses a wide variety of approaches and types. It is perhaps, therefore, problematical to propose an outline or model of the process of management research that fits or reflects all these possible approaches and types. However, I share the view of

Gill and Johnson (op. cit.) who suggest that despite the potential problems of proposing an overview of the research sequence, such an overview, although admittedly idealized, serves to help understand and appreciate the research process, including where the actual research process detracts from this idealized version. Using a framework proposed by Howard and Sharp (1983), Gill and Johnson suggest that the stages in the research sequence are as follows:

- identification of broad area of research,
- selection/delineation of specific research topic,
- decisions regarding research approach,
- formulation of research plan,
- information collection,
- data analysis,
- presentation of findings.

Source: Adapted from Gill, J. and Johnson, P. (1997) p. 3

Activity 3.3. When considering applied management research (including consultancy research) are there any stages that you would add to Gill and Johnson's stages in the research sequence?

It is important to emphasize that rarely, if ever, is the process of research as smooth as suggested in the sequence above. More often, the process is messy and frustrating with the stages overlapping and often having to be revisited in an iterative manner as the research progresses. All too often there are cases when the research process does not progress at all with what initially appeared to be 'exciting' and 'feasible' research projects. For a variety of reasons, many turn out to be 'non-starters'. Hopefully, if you are just starting your own research project you will not find it too messy or frustrating, but it is as well to post this warning.

Planning and implementing a student research project which is consultancy-based in an organizational setting does, however, give rise to several key potential problems which are common to virtually all projects of this type. The most important of these are now outlined.

3.4 Problems and issues in management consultancy-type research

As already suggested, conducting any type of research project can be messy and frustrating. Some of these problems and issues are common to all types of social research. For example, unlike the natural sciences, in social science research, we have the problem of trying to apply some of the processes and methodologies in settings or situations which are difficult and sometimes impossible to control. Unlike the physicist or chemist the social sciences researcher does not have the benefit of a 'laboratory' in which to conduct his/her research. Similarly, quantification and hence statistical analysis and verification can be more problematical in social sciences research.

In addition, within the field of management research there are particular problems and issues which stem from, and are associated with, particular types or methodologies of management research. For example, the management research methodologies such as action research and ethnographic research techniques give rise to certain special issues and problems only associated with these particular methodologies.

Finally, there are special issues which arise when research is conducted in an organization on a consultancy-type basis. Here, the research involves and indeed is carried out for 'clients' which in turn can give rise to additional problems and issues in conducting research (van der Velde et al. 2004). However, what of consultancy-type management research projects – what special problems and issues for the researcher arise here?

Some of the main problems and issues in consultancy-type management research are the following:

- *Ethical problems and issues*: Conducting management research in general can give rise to ethical problems, but there are some special ethical issues and problems associated with management consultancy-based research.

    Ethical issues in research encompass a set of mores and values for conducting and using research and the researcher must be careful not to violate these. The conduct of research therefore must conform to a set of ethical codes or values. A problem here is that what is considered ethical – and therefore unethical – behaviour can vary from situation to situation; from researcher to researcher; and from culture to culture. There are in fact guidelines for researchers in the social sciences regarding the treatment of ethical issues such as those published in the United Kingdom by the Social Research Association (2002), but in practice the researcher must carefully assess the likely ethical issues associated with any given research programme at the outset of that programme and determine an approach to dealing with them. In other words, ethical issues must be part of the research plan and may affect key issues such as data collection methods; data recording and analysis techniques and reporting research findings. Examples of ethical issues which can and do arise specifically with management consultancy-type research, and particularly where this research is also the basis for a student project or dissertation, include:

    – Whether or not the researcher will reveal to members of the organization the existence of the research study, and if so, which members will be privy to this information;
    – Where the research study is revealed to members of the organization, how much information regarding, for example, the nature and purpose of the research will be revealed and to whom;
    – How much 'power' the researcher will be given, for example, with regard to requiring organizational members to participate in the research, provide information, and so on;

– In the treatment of confidential/commercially sensitive information, for example, how much, and what types, of information can be included, or revealed in any report; whether or not respondents will be identified and so on;

– Related to the above, the extent to which results will be made available to other researchers (and possibly competitor companies) perhaps even through simply lodging a completed thesis in a University library.

● *Access Issues*: Perhaps this is a subset of ethical issues, but another potential problem which arises with consultancy-based research projects concerns that of 'access'. Access in the context of consultancy-based management research encompasses a number of aspects.

First of all, access encompasses initial permission to enter an organization, and this is what Gummesson (2002) refers to as 'physical access'. Obviously, without such permission, management consultancy-type research is virtually impossible. However, if the organization in question is that of the researcher that is, the researcher is employed by the company or perhaps even is the company owner – a situation often found in the case of many MBA students these days – then physical access is much less of a problem. On the contrary, as we shall see, when we consider the initiation of management consultancy projects, often it is the organization itself which initiates the project for the researcher.

Besides this initial access/permission we also have the issue of access to information and people as part of the research design. For example, the researcher and organization have to consider and agree as to what information the researcher will have access to, and on what basis, and who/where the researcher will be allowed access and seek information from as part of the research.

Obviously, access needs to be negotiated and agreed between researcher and the client company, but overall should be such as to ensure that the research objectives can be met. In practice, limitations or problems in access often result in modifications to initial research objectives and programmes.

● *Cultural issues*: Where the consultancy research involves, or cuts across, different cultures as when, for example, the research encompasses say different geographical divisions in a multinational organization, there can be particular problems of methodology and interpretation. Even where the research is confined to one country, internal organizational culture too can be an issue in planning and conducting management consultancy-based research projects. Because this type of research is conducted directly within an organizational environment the researcher must be careful to ensure that the research approach, techniques of data collection and so on are appropriate to organizational systems and procedures.

Activity 3.4. Identify any examples of cultural issues, which you can think of, that might affect the process of management consultancy-based research.

● *Client/consultant relationship issues*: Consultancy-basedmanagement research can give rise to issues with regard to the client's expectations of the consultant, and equally for the consultant's expectations of the client. For example, the consultant may refrain from revealing certain research results that are felt to be not in the client's or consultant's interest. The importance of, and approaches to, the management of such issues are discussed in more detail in Chapters 4 and 5.

- *Conflicting stakeholder issues*: These issues in consultancy-based research projects stem from the fact that a number of parties, or as we prefer to refer to them here, 'stakeholders' have an interest and possibly influence in the research. The most obvious stakeholder with an interest in the research or certainly the research results and recommendations, is of course the organization for which the consultancy research is being conducted. Clearly, the organization may seek to influence the nature of the research, how it is conducted, the objectives and so on. In addition, however, where the research is also the basis for a thesis or dissertation of some kind, there are also academic stakeholders. These stakeholders also have an interest in how research is conducted and its objectives and so on. However, this stakeholder group may have a fundamentally different perspective on these matters and will certainly often have a different set of criteria for judging how effective the research has been. This means that the researcher must often resolve any potential conflicts which stem from trying to meet potentially conflicting aims of different parties. In some cases, this may result in two different reports being produced, one for the organization and its management, and one for the academic research supervisor.
- *Resource and budget issues*: Although, admittedly, not exclusive to consultancy-based management research, given that it is likely that this type of research must be organized around organizational resources and budgets for this activity, there can be problems and issues in terms of having to tailor the research approach and methodologies adopted to these resource and budgetary constraints.

3.5 Concluding comments

In order to understand both the process and nature of contemporary management research, it is necessary to understand some of the theoretical antecedents to research in general. In particular, the management researcher needs to appreciate some of the major alternative schools of thought or models of research. Of particular relevance and importance in this context are the epistemological versus ontological orientations in research, the nature and differences between deductive and inductive research, and the comparison between nomothetic and ideographic research approaches.

The term 'management research' encompasses several different types and forms of research which can primarily be distinguished with regard to the objectives or purpose, and hence the outcomes of the research activities. Management research, therefore, encompasses both theoretical and applied research. Our particular interest in this book, however, is the process of consultancy-based management research.

Although we must be careful, it is possible to model the management research process in general terms, and by so doing, demonstrate the key steps in the process and how they are linked together.

Finally, we need to appreciate that management consultancy-type research in general, and particularly where this research forms the basis of an academic research thesis or dissertation, gives rise to a number of issues and problems not encountered in other types of social research.

3.6 References

Bhaskar, R. (1989) *Reclaiming Reality: A Critical Introduction to Contemporary Philosophy*, London: Verso.

Burrell, G. and Morgan, G. (1979) *Sociological Paradigms and Organisational Analysis*, London: Heinemann.

Burns, R. B. (2000) *Introduction to Research Methods*, 4th edn, London: Sage Publications.

Cook, T. and Campbell, D. T. (2004) 'Popper and falsificationalism' in C. Seale (ed.), *Social Research Methods: A Reader*, London: Routledge.

Easterby-Smith, M., Thorpe, R. and Lowe, A. (2002) *Management Research: An Introduction*, 2nd edn , London: Sage Publications.

Feyerabend, P (2004)' Against method' in C. Seale (ed.), *Social Research Methods: A Reader*, London: Routledge.

Gilbert, N. (ed.) (1993) *Researching Social Life*, London: Sage Publications.

Gill, J. and Johnson, P. (1997) *Research Methods for Managers*, 2nd edn, London: Paul Chapman Publishing.

Graziano, A. M. and Raulin, M. L. (2004) *Research Methods: A Process of Inquiry*, 5th edn, Boston, USA: Pearson Education Group.

Gummesson, E. (2002) *Qualitative Methods in Management Research*, 2nd edn, Thousand Oakes, CA: Sage Publications.

Howard, K. and Sharp, J. A. (1983) *The Management of a Student Research Project*, Aldershot: Gower.

Phillips, E. M. and Pugh, D. S. (1994) *How to get a PhD: A Handbook for Students and Their Supervisors*, Buckingham: Open University Press.

Popper, K. R. (1967) *Conjectures and Refutations*, London: Routledge.

Robson, C. (2002) *Real World Research*, 2nd edn, Oxford, Blackwell.

Saunders, M., Lewis, P. and Thornhill, A. (2003) *Research Methods for Business Students*, 3rd edn, Harlow: Pearson Education.

Sayer, A. (2000) *Realism and Social Science*, London: Sage Publications.

The Social Research Association's Ethical Guidelines (2002): http://www.the-sra.org.uk/index2.htm

van der Velde, M., Jansen, P. and Anderson, N. (2004) Oxford: Blackwell Publishing Ltd.

3.7 Glossary

action research   A set of research methodologies based on monitoring and evaluating the effects of the actions of a planned intervention by the researcher.

applied research	Research which is directed towards a practical aim or objective and is concerned with working out the solution to a specific problem.
deductive research	Research aimed at testing theories and hypotheses through empirical observation.
epistemology	A philosophical approach to theory building which investigates the nature, grounds, limits and validity of human knowledge.
ethnography	A set of research methodologies based on the researcher using primarily naturalist modes of enquiry such as participant observation.
falsificationism	That school of philosophy of science which suggests that scientists must attempt to refute rather than verify their theories.
ideographic methodologies	Research techniques which use less structured research methodologies aimed at generating qualitative data to facilitate explanation and understanding.
inductive research	Research aimed at developing theories and explanations based on observations from the empirical world.
nomothetic methodologies	Research techniques which are based on highly structured research methodologies primarily aimed at generating quantitative data to explain causal relationships.
ontology	A philosophical approach to theory building based on investigating the universal and necessary characteristics of all existence.
operationalize	The translation of theories or hypotheses such that they can be empirically measured and tested through observation.
verificationism	That school of philosophy of science which suggests that scientists must attempt to verify rather than refute their theories.

4
Management Consultancy and Research

Learning outcomes

After completing this chapter you will be able to:

- understand the development and meaning of the consultancy process,
- compare and contrast the advantages and disadvantages of using management consultants,
- discuss the different types, roles and activities of management consultancy approaches,
- understand the different models of consultancy roles,
- be aware of recent developments and trends in management consultancy,
- understand the key professional and ethical issues in management consultancy and research.

Introduction

In Chapter 3 we looked at the background to, and the issues concerning, research in management. In so doing, you were introduced to some of the special issues and characteristics of consultancy management research. In this chapter we look in more detail at the nature, purposes and issues associated with management consultancy research. In doing so, we shall see that consultancy has a long history. Not surprisingly, therefore, there are good reasons why consultants are often turned to for help and advice. We shall see that it is possible and useful to classify management consultancy approaches, particularly as regards the dimensions of task versus process consulting, directive versus non-directive, internal versus external and in terms of the different styles of consultancy. Consultancy practices and approaches have evolved over the years and we shall briefly examine some of these major developments. Finally, we look at the important area of professional and ethical issues in conducting management consultancy research and projects in organizations.

4.1 The consultant and consultancy: development and meaning

The consultant and the process of consultancy has a long and, some would say, chequered history. For example, the Egyptian Pharaohs turned to their priests for advice and help in performing their kingly duties. In fact, kings and queens across the ages have often used consultants. This long history of the consultant and consultancy is reflected in our language. For example, we have 'consultation', 'consultive', 'consulatory', 'consul' and of course 'consult', 'consultant' and 'consultancy'. Websters New International Dictionary (1996) defines a consultant and the process of consulting as follows:

'consultant' (noun) – a person referred to for expert or professional advice
'consult ' (verb) – to ask advice or information of

Essentially then, the consultant throughout history has been used as a source of advice and guidance, usually based on some actual perceived or claimed specialist knowledge, skills or expertise. This essential nature of the consultancy process and the role of the consultant remains unchanged, even today.

If anything, the need for and therefore, the use of, consultants and consultancy, in any number of areas of our lives and activities, has increased. There are many reasons for this, but perhaps the main reason is the fact that in today's society life is increasingly complex. We are beset by a potentially bewildering series of problems and issues that we have to deal with and manage in order to survive, let alone prosper. For example, we all have to deal with and sort out financial issues, we have to manage our health and well-being and to some extent that of our loved ones. We have to make decisions about where to live, what jobs to do, how to travel, and other such. Societies need bridges built, medical operations performed, buildings designed, markets researched, and so on.

This increasingly complex world entails that no one can be an expert in every area and/or have all the skills and information to hand needed to complete every task which we have to perform during our lives. Because of this, we all have occasion to call in the 'expert' from time to time for help and advice. Obviously, such help and advice may involve many different types of experts or consultants being used, and indeed the type of consultants and the areas they consult in are diverse and wide-ranging. For example, we have medical consultants, engineering consultants, tax consultants, architectural consultants, and so on and so forth. You will appreciate, then, that here we are concerned with just one type of consultant or consultancy process, namely, the management consultant and the management consultancy process. Even within this more limited sphere of consultancy activity, as we shall see, there is still a wide variety of types of consultant and consultancy processes. Before we examine these different types of consultant and consultancy processes, however, let us briefly examine why, and when, organizations turn to consultants for help and advice.

4.2   Why organizations use consultants: advantages and contributions

The complexity of the modern world applies as much to organizations and their management as to any other area of activity. In fact, in some ways the contemporary organization and its management is one of the most complex entities that we have to deal with. Organizations are complex systems of interacting activities and processes. Human resources must be combined with physical and financial resources in order to achieve organizational aims and objectives. Managing just the human resources aspect of an organization is complex enough. We have to consider, for example, how to recruit and select human resources, how to motivate them, how to train them, how to lead them, and how to evaluate them. Even within just one functional area of a business then, the manager may find that occasionally they need to draw on additional skills and advice over and above those which they would normally have access to (Biech 1998). In addition, managing organizations is becoming increasingly technical. For example, the contemporary manager might need to understand complex computer systems or intricate tax calculations, and so on. Again, few individuals have all the skills necessary to encompass every facet of management in the modern business organization. The need for the consultant and for consultancy, therefore, has if anything, become more important and pressing (Sadler, 2001). Outlined below are some of the reasons and occasions when organizations turn to consultants for help or instigate a consultancy-type process.

- *Additional skills/experience*: One of the most frequent reasons for instigating a consultancy project, and particular calling in an outside consultant, is when an organization requires additional skills or experience over and above that which they can draw on with their existing management team. As already mentioned, the modern business organization is complex and requires many skills to function effectively. Even the largest organization may not have the necessary skills or experience to deal with a particular problem or to investigate a particular area. The smaller organization, in particular, will often lack all the necessary skills and experience. For example, many organizations do not have, say, marketing research skills, or information technology skills and experience. Where these are required in order to improve organization effectiveness or to address a particular organizational problem, then the skill and experience of an outside consultant may be required (Kubar, 1996); (Rasiel, 1999).

- *A fresh perspective*: Another reason when organizations turn to consultants for help, and again particularly with reference to the use of outside consultants, is when a fresh perspective on a particular problem or aspect of the organization's operations may be needed or considered to be valuable. As in so many areas of life, sometimes we are so close to problems, or have looked at them in a particular way for so long, that we find it difficult to see what the real problem is or how to solve it. An outside consultant can often bring simply a fresh perspective to such problems or issues. In fact, this may be one of the most important benefits of turning to outside management consultants for help.

- *No vested interest*: Our third reason for organizations turning to consultants is where a consultant is used partly or even primarily because they have no vested interest and therefore can be more objective and/or open in their approach to an organizational issue or problem. For example, a consultant who is used to investigate, say, falling sales and market share may be able to look at areas and make proposals which the existing sales and marketing team simply could not because they have, or might be perceived to have, vested interests. Clearly, this particular reason for organizations turning to consultants only applies when either an external consultant is being used or when the consultants come from a different part of the organization than that which is the focus of the consultancy activities.

- *No time*: One of the most scarce and therefore precious commodities for most managers is time. In fact, most managers simply do not have enough time to complete all that is required of them. Since many consultancy projects encompass areas and activities that are outside of the 'normal' line of duty of the manager, many managers simply do not have the time to perform consultancy-type projects and activities especially where they are one-off or special projects. Although we tend to think that using consultants is primarily associated with the use of the external consultant, in fact the use of an internal consultant or consultancy team may also be a way of overcoming the problem of lack of time on the part of the normal management team. Sometimes a consultancy process is employed using an internal consultant, or team of consultants, who will address a particular organizational problem or issue in the form of a special project by clearing time from their usual day to day functional activities and responsibilities. The use of internal consultants in this way to deal with the time problem can entail the internal consultancy team being totally liberated from their normal duties for the period of the consultancy exercise, or perhaps being liberated from part of their duties during which time they work as 'consultants' in the organization.

- *Legal/regulatory/ethical reasons*: In some circumstances, using consultants, and particularly consultants who are required to come from outside of the organization, may be a legal and/or regulatory requirement. For example, in order to examine allegations of wrongdoing, or malpractice on the part of the management of an organization, as part of, say, an enquiry or perhaps even a criminal investigation, it may be obligatory or at least good practice to use a consultant for this process. Even where there are no such legal or regulatory requirements, it may be considered more ethical to use consultants to address an organizational issue or problem. The obvious advantage is that this will help to ensure a more objective report.

These are some of the main reasons why organizations use consultants and particularly why they often turn to outside consultants. It is important to stress, however, that much consultancy-type research is in fact conducted by internal members of the organization acting in a 'consultancy' capacity. Clearly there are differences in the issues and approaches when using internal versus external consultants. We shall consider later in the chapter some of these advantages and disadvantages.

Using consultants or a consultancy-type approach has many potential advantages, but it also has disadvantages and limitations and some of the more important of these are outlined in the next section.

Activity 4.1. Can you think of any administrative/organizational structure arrangements that companies can use when using internal staff to work on one-off 'consultancy' type projects?

4.3 Disadvantages and limitations of management consultants

As many organizations have found to their cost, using consultants, and especially outside consultants or even a consultancy-type approach with internal staff is no panacea to every organizational issue and problem. Among the more important potential disadvantages and limitations of using consultants and/or consultancy-type approaches are the following:

- *Cost*: Admittedly somewhat unfairly, external consultants and consultancy companies have a reputation for being *expensive*. Certainly, when reckoned on a cost-per-day or completed-project-basis, often the external management consultant would be costlier than if the organization had used internal staff. Experience and expertise rarely come cheaply. However, we do have to be a little careful with regard to the high costs of consultants and consultancy in as much as what really matters is value. Very often, using a consultant, or even a consultancy-based approach with an internal team, can often offer better value for money. Certainly, we have to be careful to appraise and monitor the costs of consultancy and consultants, but cost effectiveness can be achieved if, as we shall see in the next chapter, we are careful in the selection of our consultancy team, and in particular, in the planning and control of consultancy research and projects.
- *Resentment/Fear/Antagonism*: Bringing an external consultant or consultancy team into an organization can be a major source of resentment among existing staff. Sometimes this resentment is due to the fact that bringing in an outside team is seen as being something of a slur or insult to the existing internal management team, seemingly implying that the internal team are simply not

up to the task. Often, resentment is more simply based on fear, for example, the existing organizational staff may fear that the consultant may make recommendations which may result in, say, some form of reprimand or even worse, loss of job. Such resentment and fear can mitigate against the successful outcome of a management consultancy or a research exercise. Existing management staff may simply refuse to co-operate with a consultant or, perhaps, even may knowingly distort and pass on false information. Although resentment, fear and antagonism may principally apply to the use of external consultants, in fact, the use of internal staff on consultancy problems and projects may also cause some resentment, fear and antagonism. For example, managers not called upon to be involved in or conduct an internal consultancy project may feel that their services and expertise are not valued or that they may similarly be the focus for some sort of potential disciplinary actions. Again, it is important to recognize the potential for this problem when using consultants and/or conducting consultancy-type exercises and research. As with the issue of cost, the problem can be at least reduced through careful planning and implementation of consultancy projects.

- *Lack of familiarity with organization*: As we have seen, the outside consultant can bring a fresh perspective to an organizational problem, while at the same time, being an outsider, having no vested interests to complicate issues. At the same time, these advantages can be offset by the fact that the outside consultant will lack familiarity with the client organization. This lack of familiarity often means that the consultant must first undergo a learning process before any effective consultancy and research can be conducted. This learning process can extend the time of the consultancy project and is often a major source of frustration for the client who wants his or her problems solved as quickly as possible.
- *Lack of responsibility/accountability for results*: One of the major criticisms of outside consultants is that they lack real responsibility and accountability for results. Certainly, in many cases the responsibilities of the consultant end with the making of recommendations to the client. Implementation and follow up of these recommendations is then left to the client organization. As such, it is often argued that the outside consultant can avoid any responsibility for the effectiveness, or otherwise, of any implemented courses of action.

As we shall see later, professional management consultancy increasingly involves the management consultant in at least accepting professional responsibility for the effectiveness of any agreed or proposed courses of action and often the management consultancy contract will include responsibilities for implementation and follow up. Obviously, if these responsibilities are to be included, then they need to be defined and agreed between consultant and client at the outset. They are, therefore, part of the initiation and agreement processes of consultancy projects. We shall return to these issues when we consider the planning and design of management consultancy research projects in Chapter 5 and in Chapter 12 when we consider more specifically the issues of implementation and follow-up of consultancy research projects.

These then are some of the potential disadvantages and problems with using consultants and/or with using consultancy-based approaches to organizational issues and problems. Again, it is important to remind ourselves that many of the disadvantages and problems can be removed, or at least mitigated against, and the advantages of using consultants and/or consultancy-based approaches can be achieved through effective design and implementation of consultancy.

Activity 4.2. Identify some ways in which resentment, fear and antagonism towards the consultant or consultancy team can be minimized in an organization.

4.4   Management consultancy – types, roles and activities

Although the overall role of the management consultant is, as we have seen, that of providing expertise and advice, within this there are a broad range of consultancy types, roles and activities. It is, therefore, useful to consider and categorize these different activities. In order to categorize management consultancy approaches and activities, however, we need some basis or system for the categorization. You will not be surprised to learn that there are any number of ways in which consultancy types, roles and activities can be classified. Just some of the ways in which this can be done include, for example, the following continuums:

● internal versus external,
● fact finding versus educational,
● ad hoc versus continuous,
● problem/project centred versus exploratory/investigative,
● imposed versus voluntary.

Among, perhaps, the most useful models of different ways of conceptualizing the range of different management consultancy types and activities, however, are those of:

● task versus process models,
● non-directive versus directive,
● consultancy styles.

Each of these is now discussed.

Task versus process consultancy models

Margulies and Raia (1972) used the notion of task versus process oriented roles to classify different types of, and approaches to, management consultancy. Their model is shown in Figure 4.1.

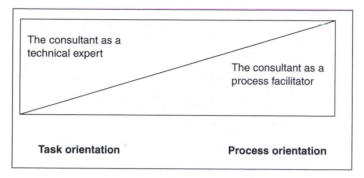

Figure 4.1 The task versus process model of consultancy
Source: Margulies, N. and Raia, A. (1972).

- *Task orientation*: The *task-oriented* approach to consultancy in this model emphasizes the role of the consultant as a 'technical expert'. Here, the consultant assesses problems through collection of data and the application of 'expert' knowledge. The consultant is expected to provide ideas and opinions, design data collection methods, and present this data with expert interpretations to the client. The consultant makes specific and concrete recommendations based upon the data. The relationship with the client is essentially objective, detached and task/problem oriented. Involvement is primarily with the problem to be solved and other parts of the organization are not considered.
- *Process orientation:* In contrast at the *process orientation* end of the spectrum in this model, the role of the consultant is seen as being more of 'problem sensor' and 'facilitator'. Problem solving activities by the consultant focus on the problem solving capability of the organization and creativity. Research and feedback focuses on providing meaningful data that enables the client to use their own interpretation and develop their own solutions. Relationships with clients in this approach are personal, involved and process oriented. Involvement is primarily with people and groups in the organization and consideration is given to other parts of the organization.

Activity 4.3. Give an example of a type of organizational problem or issue that might be approached through a task-oriented consultancy approach and one which might be best approached through a process orientation.

4.5 Non-directive versus directive consultancy models

As the name implies, these models are based on the extent to which the consultant directs problem-solving activities for the client. At the *directive* end of the continuum, the consultant is highly involved in the activity of problem solving for

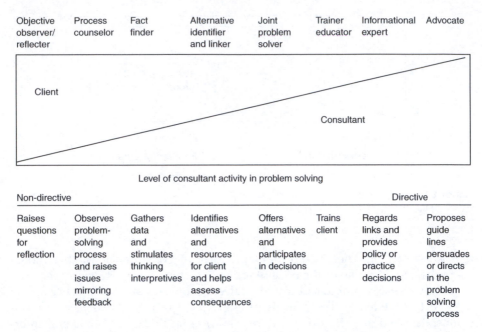

Objective observer/ reflecter	Process counselor	Fact finder	Alternative identifier and linker	Joint problem solver	Trainer educator	Informational expert	Advocate

Level of consultant activity in problem solving

Non-directive							Directive
Raises questions for reflection	Observes problem-solving process and raises issues mirroring feedback	Gathers data and stimulates thinking interpretives	Identifies alternatives and resources for client and helps assess consequences	Offers alternatives and participates in decisions	Trains client	Regards links and provides policy or practice decisions	Proposes guide lines persuades or directs in the problem solving process

Figure 4.2 Description of the consultant's role on a directive and non-directive continuum
Source: Lippitt, G. and Lippitt, R. (1978).

the client, proposing specific guidelines or directions for problem solving. At the other extreme, the *non-directive consultancy* approach simply raises questions for the client to reflect upon in a non-specific directive manner. Perhaps the most influential model in this category is that of Lippitt and Lippitt (1978) who use the continuum of 'non-directive versus directive' consultancy activities to distinguish different alternative roles for the consultant. This model is shown in Figure 4.2. As can be seen, at the directive end of the spectrum the consultant essentially plays an 'Advocate' role in the consultancy and problem solving process with a high degree of involvement in problem solving and direct recommendations to the client. At the other extreme, the consultant acts more as an 'Observer/Reflector' playing an essentially non-directive role in the problem solving process by, for example, simply raising questions for the client to reflect upon. In between these two extremes, as we can see, the roles encompass 'Process Counsellor', 'Fact Finder', 'Alternative Identifier and Linker', 'Joint Problem Solver', 'Trainer/Educator', and 'Informational Expert'.

4.6   Other styles of consulting

The third model of consultancy approaches and roles is less a continuum and more a typology of alternative consultancy styles. The notion of styles of consultancy was first proposed by Blake and Mouton (1983), but has since been developed by Cockman et al. (1992).

Referring to them as 'intervention styles', Cockman et al. (op. cit.) suggest four distinct styles that can be employed by the consultant, namely: 'Acceptant', 'Catalytic', 'Confrontational', and 'Prescriptive'. These are now explained.

- *Acceptant style*: This style of consulting is based on helping the client confront organizational problems by encouraging them to find what is blocking their ability to solve these. It uses the employment of careful listening techniques, and attempts to understand the problem and difficulties from the client's point of view empathetically and providing emotional support. It is essentially a neutral and non-judgemental style, designed to encourage clients to find their own solutions to problems and encouraging them to express their innermost thoughts and feelings about a situation.
- *Catalytic style*: This style of management consultancy centres on helping the client address problems and needs by clarifying existing data and/or gathering additional data. This data is then used to help the client make a diagnosis of the problem. This approach is based on the notion that once clients have the relevant data or information, they themselves will be able to identify options and move towards solutions. Responsibility for solutions and decision making remains with the client. This type of consultancy assumes that either data absence or overload is the main problem to be overcome. Once this has been done, clients themselves will be able to identify solutions.
- *Confrontational style*: This style of consultancy is used where the consultant believes that the clients are part of the problem, and in particular, where there are discrepancies between what clients say or think they do, and what they actually do. For example, where the consultant believes that the problem is essentially one of a discrepancy between approaches, say, to customer satisfaction. Here the client might believe they are providing this when in fact they are not. It is then that a confrontational style may be appropriate. The approach taken is to highlight the discrepancies between the client's stated values and behaviour and their actual values and behaviour. The idea is that once these discrepancies, together with the implications, are pointed out to the client, then the client will begin to move towards a solution to the problem. Obviously, confrontational consultancy styles can be risky in as much as they can alienate the client. The consultant needs to have strong interpersonal and communication skills to utilize this approach.
- *Prescriptive style*: In many ways, this is what many think of as being the *typical* consultancy style. This style of consultancy involves listening to the client's problems, collecting any data required, making sense of and interpreting this data and finally, presenting clients with a solution or recommendation. As Cockman et al. point out, typically, this is the style used by experts and is essentially based on the assumption that the clients themselves do not have the skills, knowledge or objectivity to make an accurate diagnosis or prescription of their own. Although it is perhaps the most traditional model of the consultancy process – in fact in most management/organizational consultancy settings rarely does the client not have some skills, knowledge or the required objectivity to make their own diagnosis or recommendations. The consultant, therefore, has to be careful not to alienate or insult the client by being too prescriptive.

However, the prescriptive style can be useful where quick solutions and decision making are required due to the situation, or where the client's expectations are for specific and definitive proposed solutions.

Source: Adapted from Cockman et al. (1992) pp. 22–24.

These then are three of the most useful and influential models of alternative consultancy approaches and responsibilities. Although they are different, all three models essentially compare and contrast between the more traditional prescriptive solution proposing approaches to consultancy and the increasingly used 'softer' non-prescriptive approaches to consultancy where the consultant helps the client to perceive their own solutions. A key issue for the consultant, however, is to decide which consultancy model or rather more specifically, approach, to use. There is no simple answer to this, as the different approaches are each suited and more suitable to particular circumstances. Even during the course of a particular consultancy project the consultant may use several approaches during the different stages of consultancy. For example, an accepted style of consultancy might be more appropriate at early stages of the consultancy process with clients and a prescriptive style more appropriate for later stages. Many factors affect the choice of an appropriate consultancy approach, and it is impossible and dangerous to be prescriptive about which consultancy approach/style to use and when. Indeed part of the consultant's expertise is in knowing which style of consultancy or intervention approach to use.

Activity 4.4. Try to list as many factors as you can think of which might affect the choice of an appropriate consultancy approach or style.

Because selecting the appropriate consultancy approach and style is so important, here is another activity for you to consider.

Activity 4.5. Considering the four alternative consultancy styles suggested by Cockman et al. which style do you think is likely to be most appropriate to each of the following consultancy situations.

(a) The client has asked an external consultant to come up with proposals for designing and implementing a management information system. The client has no previous experience or knowledge of information systems and is anxious to implement any proposals as quickly as possible. The consultant selected is an international expert in the area of information systems.
(b) The client has asked the external consultant to help make sense of a substantial amount of data that the client already has collected regarding competitors. The client is unsure how to interpret the data with a view to improving the competitive position of the organization.
(c) An external management consultant has been asked to investigate the problem of increased customer turnover. More and more customers are being lost to competitors. After preliminary investigations, the consultant believes that the problem essentially lies with existing management attitudes and systems with regard to customer care.

(d) A management consultant has identified that a major problem in his client organization is conflict between the different functional areas of the business. An additional problem, however, is the fact that there are indications that the different functional managers feel unable to discuss the problem and tend to gloss over this issue.

4.7 Internal versus external consultants

Several times already in this text I have pointed to the distinction between internal and external consultancy. Although I have suggested that there are many similarities to the process for both internal and external consultants, needless to say, there are also differences. For example, some of the advantages and disadvantages of using consultants discussed earlier will differ when using internal versus external consultants. In addition, of course, as you would expect, the internal consultant often needs to approach the consultancy process and faces different problems and issues compared to the external consultant (Scott 2000). It is worthwhile highlighting, therefore, some of these differences, and in particular, it is useful to appreciate some of the main advantages and disadvantages faced by the internal as opposed to the external management consultant.

Activity 4.6. List what you feel might be the main advantages and disadvantages faced by the internal as opposed to the external management consultant.

4.8 Developments in management consultancy approaches and techniques

Perhaps as you would expect, with such a long established activity, approaches to, and the techniques of, management consultancy are constantly evolving and developing, and trends have become apparent in approaches and practices. The main developments and trends are as follows:

- *More powerful tools and techniques*: Today's management consultant has access to a range of much more powerful tools and techniques compared to even ten years ago. In particular, improvements in data collection, storage and analytical techniques. Developments in management information systems, and in particular data manipulation techniques such as data mining, offer powerful analytical tools to the contemporary management consultant.
- *Less prescriptive/softer methodologies*: As we have seen, the traditional model of consultancy roles and styles has in the past tended to be of the prescriptive type, and although this traditional model is still appropriate for many client situations, there has been a gradual movement towards the less prescriptive styles of consultancy with an emphasis more on process interventions which are very client focused. This, in turn, often involves *softer* methodologies and approaches being adopted by modern day management consultants.

- *More professional/ethical approaches and practices*: Although it might be unfair and inaccurate to suggest that in the past many management consultants have been less than professional or ethical, it is fair to say that today's management consultant is more professional than ever and is increasingly aware of some of the ethical issues surrounding the management consultancy process. Many consultants are increasingly required to belong to a professional body or association encompassing and often proscribing their consultancy activities. There is also increased legislation that can be used to seek legal redress against incompetent or unprofessional consultants. Thankfully, however, the major impetus to an increasingly professional and ethical body of management consultants has been an increasing recognition on the part of most management consultants that professionalism and ethical practices make good common sense in the increasingly competitive world of management consultancy. (Pinault and Pollan 2000; Wickham 2004).

Because of the importance of ethical issues in the management consultancy process, these issues are considered further in the last part of this chapter.

4.9   Professional and ethical issues in management consultancy and research

I introduced the notion of the importance of some of the ethical issues associated with management research in Chapter 3. If anything, these ethical issues are heightened when the research is based on, or involves, management consultancy.

I have stressed that management consultancy is not only a process, but is also a profession. As a profession, there is an increasing obligation on the consultant to act, not only professionally, but in particular, ethically. However, management consultancy research often poses difficult ethical dilemmas and problems. Not only does the consultant face, perhaps, a wider range of ethical issues than many of his or her non-consulting management counterparts, but also many of these issues do not have simple solutions in as much as there is inevitably a 'right' or a 'wrong' solution. Frequently, therefore, the management consultant must make valued judgements and use his/her discretion in resolving ethical issues. Sometimes, of course, the professional bodies encompassing the particular area or type of consultancy and consultant will provide guidelines with regard to ethical practices and even a Code of ethics, but rarely if ever do such guidelines or codes encompass every possible ethical dilemma that a practising consultant may face. Indeed, the range of potentially ethical issues and dilemmas in management consultancy is enormous. In fact, it is probably not an over-exaggeration to state that the consultant runs the risk of literally drowning in ethical issues. This can easily be demonstrated.

Activity 4.7 List as many of the possible ethical issues that you can think of that might confront the management consultant.

It would be surprising if you found this activity difficult. How many issues did you manage to come up with in 2 minutes: 5, 10, more? The simple fact is that it is not difficult to think of possible ethical issues with which any management consultant might be potentially confronted during his/her work. Examples would include:

- confidentiality,
- conflicts of interest,
- issues concerning honesty and integrity,
- discrimination,
- responsibilities towards organization,
- responsibilities towards people/individuals,
- issues of competence,
- adherence to moral and legal standards,
- human rights issues,
- organizational versus consultant values and ideologies.

With such a range of ethical issues and dilemmas, it is impossible and indeed dangerous to be prescriptive about how these dilemmas should be solved. The management consultant should have clear ideas about his/her personal values and ethics and be open and honest about these when dealing with clients. The management consultant should place the highest value on objectivity and integrity while maintaining the highest standards of service. The consultant should show regard for social codes and moral expectations of both the culture and organizations in which s/he practices. Confidentiality and client welfare should be respected at all times (Biswas and Twitchell 1999).

4.10 Concluding comments

In this chapter we have explored the nature, purposes and issues in management consultancy research. We have seen that there are good reasons why consultants have been used throughout the ages and are a particular feature of contemporary organizations. Management consultancy within the general purpose of providing expertise and advice, encompasses a broad range of consultancy types, roles and activities. Although there are a number of ways in which these various types, roles and activities may be conceptualized, among the most useful models of different consultancy approaches are those based on task versus process consultancy models, directive versus non-directive consultancy models and the notion of alternative consultancy styles. We have seen that there are also particular issues when it comes to the advantages and disadvantages of internal versus external management consultants. Finally, we have seen that management consultancy processes and activities are evolving and changing. Of particular importance in this respect are more powerful techniques of data collection, analysis and interpretation, a move towards *softer* less prescriptive consultancy approaches focusing more on processes, and finally the increasing importance of ethical issues.

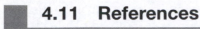

4.11   References

Biech, E. (1998) *The Business of Consulting: The Basics and Beyond*, Jossey-Bass, Pfeiffer. San Francisco, CA.

Biswas, S. and Twitchell, D. (1999) *Management Consultancy: A Complete Guide to the Industry*, London: John Wiley.

Blake, R. R. and Mouton, J. S. (1983) *Consultation: A Handbook for Individual and Organisation Development*, Wokingham: Addison-Wesley.

Cockman, P. Evans, B. and Reynolds, P. (1992) *Client-centred Consulting*, Maidenhead: McGraw Hill.

Kubar, M. (1996) *Management Consulting: A Guide to the Profession*, 3rd edn, International Labour Office.

Lippitt, G. and Lippitt, R. (1978) *The Consulting Process in Action*, California: University Associates.

Margulies, N. and Raia, A. (1972) *Organisation Development: Values, Processes and Technology*, Maidenhead: McGraw Hill.

Pinault, L. and Pollan, S. M. (2000) *Consulting Demons: Inside the Unscrupulous World of Global Corporate Consulting*, NY, Harper Collins.

Rasiel, E. M. (1999) The McKinsey Way, NY, McGraw Hill.

Sadler, P. (2001) *Management Consultancy*, London: Kogan Page.

Scott, B. (2000) *Consulting on the Inside*, American Society for Training and Development.

Websters New International Dictionary, (1996): Trident Press International.

Wickham, P. A. (2004), *Management Consulting: Delivering an Effective Project*, 2nd edn, NY, Prentice Hall.

4.12   Glossary

directive consultancy	An approach to consultancy which is based on the consultant proposing specific guidelines or directions for problem solving to the client.
non-directive consultancy	An approach to consultancy which is based on the consultant raising questions for the client to reflect upon and consider with the client essentially being responsible for proposing solutions.
process oriented consultancy	An approach to consultancy which is based on the consultant acting as problem sensor and facilitator for the client.
task oriented consultancy	An approach to consultancy which is based on using the consultant as a technical expert to make specific and concrete recommendations to the client.

5

The Consultancy Research Process

Learning outcomes

After completing this chapter you will be able to:

- understand the overall process of, and steps in, conducting management consultancy research,
- understand how management consultancy research projects can be identified and initiated,
- appreciate the importance of planning and agreeing upon the consultancy research brief,
- appreciate the importance of designing and agreeing the research plan.

Introduction

As with any complex, and potentially costly activity, it is essential to plan and design how the activity will be completed. In this chapter we shall identify and discuss the key steps and considerations in initiating, planning, designing and conducting a management consultancy research project. During this process, alternatives with regard to the purpose and objectives of the consultancy research must be determined and important decisions made with regard to, for example, the overall direction and focus of the consultancy research, the methods of research and data collection, and alternative methods of data analysis and presentation. In addition, we shall be looking at the important activities of scheduling, resourcing and controlling the research project. Finally, we shall be looking at aspects such as responsibilities for conducting the project, and where appropriate, for implementing and follow-up action programmes.

5.1   Management consultancy and research: an overview

As we have seen, there are many different types of management consultancy and research projects involving and encompassing very different types of management consultancy activities and roles. It is difficult, therefore, and perhaps potentially dangerous to propose an overall framework of the key steps in the management and consultancy research process that can broadly apply irrespective of the type, nature and context of the management consultancy and research being considered. However, so long as we are aware of this problem, it is possible and indeed useful to consider a model of the overall process of management consultancy and research in order that we can consider the key steps and stages in this process.

A generalized model of the process of management consultancy research is shown in Figure 5.1. This model is based on what are suggested as the key steps in most consulting cycles or projects.

It is important that you familiarize yourself with this model as it forms the basis of the content of the majority of the following chapters of the book. In this chapter, in addition to introducing you to an overview of the process shown in

Initiation of the consultancy research project – meeting/identifying the client

Identifying, selecting and agreeing upon the consultancy project/topic

Planning and agreeing upon the consultancy/research brief to include:

- research/consultancy objectives
- timing and funding
- responsibilities and duties
- reporting requirements
- constraints and restrictions

Designing and agreeing the research plan to include:

- research/consultancy objectives
- data and information requirements
- methods of data collection
- methods of data analysis and presentation

Data collection

Data analysis, interpretation and diagnosis

Recommendations, implementation, and actions

Control, evaluation and monitoring

Disengaging from client/project

Figure 5.1 The consultancy process: steps in the consulting cycle

this model, we shall be concentrating particularly on the first stages in the processes in our consulting cycle encompassing: initiating the consultancy research process, meeting and identifying the client, identifying and agreeing the consultancy project/topic, planning and agreeing the consultancy research brief, and designing and agreeing the research plan. I shall also in this chapter be introducing you to the steps to be covered in more detail in later chapters, encompassing: data collection methods, methods of data analysis interpretation and diagnosis, recommendations implementation and actions, control evaluation and monitoring, and finally disengaging/ongoing activities.

5.2 Initiating the consultancy/research process: meeting/identifying the client

Consultancy projects can be initiated for all sorts of reasons and in all sorts of ways. How and why consultancy projects are initiated can have major effects on how the consultancy project is conducted including, for example, methods of data collection, methods of analysis and presentation, implementation and control issues. It is important to consider therefore, the different ways in which consultancy projects can be, and are, initiated.

- *Client initiates project*: Many consultancy projects are initiated by the client. The 'client' is normally taken to mean the person(s) for whom the consultancy is being undertaken and who will often, though not inevitably, be paying for the consultancy. In most circumstances this will mean the organization for which the consultancy project is being commissioned, but of course this will be effected through the management of the organization, and of course may be a specific named individual. The client, therefore, is often taken to mean a specific manager or management team for whom the consultancy is being performed. In fact, very often, identifying the 'client' is not always as straightforward as you might think, and is certainly very often not simply the person or party who has commissioned the project. We shall consider the issue of client identification later in this section.
- *Consultant initiates project*: Often management consultancy projects are initiated by the consultant. This might be the case, for example, where a consultant or consultancy company contacts a potential client and offers their services with regard to some area or aspect of business and business performance. For example, a company might be contacted by, say, an information technology consultancy company offering to look at ways in which IT systems could be introduced and/or improved.
- *Third party initiates project*: Third, we have those consultancy projects that are initiated by a third party. This third party could comprise a manager or function within the organization or could be an outside party. For example, the consultancy project may be initiated at the behest of the board of directors who use either an inside or an outside consultancy team to conduct the consultancy project. In the case of an outside third party, the consultancy here

may be initiated by, say, a government initiative that is aimed at improving industrial effectiveness in certain areas.

How the consultation process is initiated and whether the consultant or consulting team being used is internal or external to the organization will have an influence on the nature of the initial contact between consultant and client. However, irrespective of how the consultation was initiated, there is no doubt that this initial meeting or contact between consultant and client is crucial to the effectiveness of the whole process of consultancy. Consultants often refer to this initial contact stage as *gaining entry*. It is probably not overstating the case to suggest that the effectiveness or otherwise of this initial contact and meeting between client and consultant is probably one of the most crucial steps in the consultancy process.

Activity 5.1. List three key objectives that you feel the consultant should be aiming to achieve with regard to the relationship between the consultant and client during the consultant's first meeting with the client.

The first meeting between client and consultant is extremely important since the consultant, whether internal or external may not be known personally to the client. The consultant can establish an immediate climate of openness and trust, and good communication by taking the following steps.

- *Prepare in advance*: The consultant should find out as much as possible about the client's business, problems and circumstances
- *Use listening skills*: One of the key skills of the consultant, and certainly a skill which is crucial in these initial stages of the consultancy process, is the skill of effective listening. The consultant should be prepared to encourage the client to open up and discuss freely with, initially at least, as few interruptions as possible. Verbal and body language signals are important here, as it is crucial to signal to the client that his or her thoughts and ideas are being assimilated.
- *Be open-minded*: Related to effective listening skills is the attitude on the part of the consultant of being initially as open-minded as possible with regard to the client's problems and business situation. It is often tempting to identify problems or even suggest solutions as quickly as possible. In addition, the consultant is likely to have his/her own ideas as to the client's situation and problems. It is important not to voice these too early in the process.
- *Be client-centred*: It may sound obvious, but the consultant is there to help the client and not the other way around. All too often, however, relationships between client and consultant are clouded or in some cases even soured by the consultant not being sufficiently sensitive and responsive to the needs, feelings and requirements of the client. In fact, the need to be client-centred relates to the whole process of consultancy and should be evident in every stage. However, it is particularly important in this first initial stage of the consulting process and in particular it is important that the consultant starts where the clients are and not where the consultants would like them to be.
- *Be confident but not cocksure*: Remember that the client will only trust the consultant if they have confidence in him/her. It is important, therefore, that

the consultant tries to build this confidence as quickly as possible. Building confidence on the part of the client in turn requires that the consultant also exudes confidence. There is clearly a fine dividing line between demonstrating your confidence to the client and appearing smug or overconfident. It is a good idea at the first meeting with the client to encourage the client to find out something about the consultant so that confidence can begin to build.

Needless to say, building trust and confidence with the client is not possible until we have identified the client. Earlier, I introduced the notion that the client is often taken to mean the person(s) for whom the consultancy is being undertaken and who may be paying for the consultancy. In fact, Cockman et al. (1992) suggest that defining the client too narrowly is often one of the major mistakes made by the inexperienced consultant. They suggest it is more useful to think of a *client system*. The notion of a client system is that in many situations the person or party who has initiated the consultancy project and with whom therefore the consultant initially meets, is often only a part of the system which the consultant will have to become involved with and explore. For example, the production director may have called in a consultant with a view to solving a quality control problem. In addressing this problem the consultant may find that they have to discuss the problem with employees from several different functional areas of the business, for example, the problem may lie, with the purchasing department. Although initially the consultancy client would appear to be the production director or at least the production department, in fact the client system includes other persons/functions in the business. Revans (1980) suggests a useful and relatively simple approach to identifying the real clients or client system which has been adapted by Cockman et al. (op. cit.). This is outlined below. He suggests that the client system can be identified by asking three questions, namely:

- *Who knows?* Any person or party who could potentially provide information or shed light on the consultancy problem is effectively part of the client system and should therefore be involved in the process.
- *Who cares?* Any person or party who has occasion to care about the consultancy problem and its potential solution again is part of the client system.
- *Who can?* Can here refers to who can do something about the solution to the problem. So, for example, if the solution involves additional resources that must be sanctioned by a third party then this party too is part of the client system.

Source: Adapted from Cockman et al. (1992) pp. 10–11.

Activity 5.2. A marketing consultant has been called in to the ACME Trading Company and asked to prepare a consultancy report with regard to the effectiveness of the company's advertising and any recommendations for improvement. Like most organizations, ACME makes use of an outside advertising agency to help plan and execute their advertising. Advertising in the company is also linked with other marketing activities including sales promotion and particularly sales force incentives. Budgets for advertising are determined by the accountancy function and market research is used to evaluate advertising results. Last year there was a particular problem when an otherwise very effective advertising campaign was rendered ineffective due to problems with late delivery of the products being advertised.

Using Revans three questions, who might be part of this consultant's real client or client system?

5.3   The consultancy research project/topic

Initiation

It is vital to identify and agree upon what the consultancy project is to encompass. We can think of this in a number of ways. For example, we could refer to it as the consultancy problem or, perhaps being more client-centred, as identifying the client's needs. In whatever way we refer to this process, it is vital to agree to what the consultancy project/topic is to encompass and include it as early as possible in the process. Essentially, this then becomes the *contract* between the consultant and the client. The term contract here refers not to any legal agreement and document established between consultant and client (although obviously where the consultancy arrangements do have such legal contracts encompassing and including for example terms and conditions, confidentiality, access to information, etc.) rather the term is used here in the sense of both client and consultant arriving at the point where they feel happy to work together, can proceed with reasonable trust by both parties and have agreed at least in outline as to what the consultancy project is to be about and encompass. If anything, the contract is a psychological commitment by both parties, one to the other, to proceed. The contract therefore, requires that any barriers and potential problems between consultant and client with regard to conducting the consultancy have been considered and as far as possible removed or at least minimized. Both consultant and client must at this stage be convinced of the value of the consultancy process. For example, the client should be convinced that they need and can benefit from help and the consultant in turn must be convinced that they can offer the required help. Again, we should remember that very often in many consulting assignments, in the early stages at least, clients can sometimes be suspicious or resentful of the consultants' presence. Unless this is overcome then, there is unlikely to be an effective contract based on mutual openness, trust and honesty. It is impossible to be specific about how to assess when such a contract has been effectively established. The consultant must use his or her judgement, but when both client and consultant are in a position to do so, they can move to the next step of identifying and agreeing upon the consultancy project or topic.

Identifying and agreeing upon the consultancy project

Very often where consultancy projects are initiated by the client there is sometimes little room for discretion with regard to selection of the consultancy topic. This would be the case, for example, where the client not only initiates the consultancy project, but specifies more or less precisely what the problem or issue is and therefore what the consultancy topic is to be. For example, the client may well call in a consultant to conduct a consultancy project to investigate new wage structures to reduce a problem of high levels of labour turnover. Here, the client has already effectively selected the consultancy topic and the consultant is simply required to determine and discuss how the project will be conducted and the topic investigated. In effect, the client selects the consultancy topic from which flow the consultancy brief and the consultancy plan.

In other circumstances, again the client initiates the consultancy process but with less clear or set ideas about the precise nature of the consultancy problem and topic. Continuing the example above, the client may realize that there is a problem of labour turnover but is not sure what may be causing this. In this case, the nature of the consultancy project is more open-ended and therefore both consultant and client may be much more open about the nature and focus of the project. Here, project selection may not only require potentially lengthy discussion between consultant and client but also some preliminary consultancy activities in the form of exploratory investigations as a prelude and input to the selection and agreement of the precise consultancy topic. Continuing our example, in this case the consultant may ask to examine exit interviewer records of past employees with a view to determining the precise consultancy project.

Finally, we have those consultancy projects where the project, regardless of whether the consultancy is initiated by the client or the consultant, is essentially left for the consultant to propose. Leaving the identification of the consultancy project to the consultant in this way may at first sight appear to be an unacceptable and dangerous way to proceed in identifying consultancy projects. However, remember the client still retains the right to turn down and/or amend any proposals made by the consultant. In some circumstances, in fact allowing the consultant to identify the consultancy project may be the most appropriate way to proceed. For example, the client may simply be concerned to, say, 'improve organizational effectiveness' and a major objective of employing or using a consultant may be for the consultant to investigate and recommend consultancy projects to achieve this.

In selecting and agreeing upon the consultancy project, both client and consultant should pay attention to the following criteria for selection:

- *Client needs*: In line with our exhortation for the consultancy process to be client-centred perhaps the most important criterion for project selection is the extent to which there is a real client need for the consultancy work. This heightens the importance of identifying these needs in the initial meetings and discussions between client and consultant. Remember that the client may not always be aware of, be able to articulate or have identified their own real needs. With regard to Cockman et al.'s (op. cit.) styles of consultancy discussed in Chapter 4, 'acceptant', 'catalytic' and 'confrontational' styles are all appropriate to identifying the real needs of the client. On the other hand, the 'prescriptive' style of consulting is more suitable where the client and consultant are convinced that the client's real problems and needs have been identified.

- *Feasibility of the consultancy project*: There is little point in commencing a consultancy project unless the project is feasible. Many factors affect the extent to which a consultancy project is feasible among the most important of which are the following:
  - access to, and availability of, data and information,
  - time available,
  - financial and other support,
  - risk involved,
  - organizational support or barriers,
  - skills, expertise and experience of consultant.

  Most of these considerations in assessing the feasibility of a consultancy project are self-evident. The last one on our list, however, underlines an important point with regard to professional consultancy practice. Simply stated, consultants should not agree to undertake a consultancy project in which he or she has not sufficient skills, expertise or experience – or access to these – to complete the project successfully. It is far better to be honest with oneself and with the client rather than disappoint a client at a later stage, not to mention perhaps becoming embroiled in contractual wrangles. This aspect of assessing feasibility also points us to another key consideration in the selection of consultancy projects, namely the needs and values of the consultant.

- *Consultant needs and values*: Although the management consultant is essentially there to provide a service to a client we must not forget that consultants too are human. They have their own set of value systems, their own needs and wants, their own ways of working and thinking. Where it appears that the client requires a consultancy project to be completed which is not congruent for some reason with the needs, values and ways of working of the consultant, then it is far better for the consultant to withdraw from the consultancy project unless of course the problem can be resolved through further discussions with the client. Where the needs and values of the consultant might potentially interfere with or hinder a consultancy project, the consultant needs to declare these needs and values at the outset and before the contracting stage.

Activity 5.3. Use your experience of organizations to think of examples of possible needs and values, which a management consultant might bring to the work situation and which might have a major effect on how they would conduct a management consultancy project for a client and indeed whether they would work for this client at all.

- *Cost benefit of the consultancy project*: In some ways this is the most important criterion for the selection of a consultancy project and particularly where there may be several consultancy projects to evaluate and choose between. Any consultancy project should provide benefits that outweigh the costs. Sometimes these benefits and costs may be purely financial in nature. For example, we could attempt to compare any projected increase in profits as a result of a consultancy project with the financial costs of that project. However, not all consultancy projects have outcomes that are easy to measure in terms of financial and specifically profit benefits. For example, a benefit of a successful consultancy project might be, say, improved morale among the workforce. While this will undoubtedly have financial benefits to the organization they are often difficult to measure. We could also argue that the client alone should determine the cost benefits of any proposed consultancy project and that if the client decides a project is worthwhile and is prepared to commission it, then it is not the consultant's job to question this. However, as with feasibility and the consultant's needs and values where the consultant feels that a project is not worthwhile for the client, then the professional obligation of the consultant is to point this out to the client, perhaps even suggest the abandonment of a proposed project.

Assuming that at this stage both consultant and client are happy to continue and have broadly agreed to the consultancy project then the next step in our consulting cycle is to begin to move towards a more detailed and formal set of plans for the consultancy project and research, again which both client and consultant must agree upon. Essentially, this involves fleshing out the nature, purpose, methodology and responsibilities involved with the consultancy project. Most clients will insist on agreeing upon, at the very least, to what the consultant will be required to do, the timescale for the assignment and how much it will cost. However, agreement on just these areas is not sufficient for an effective management consultancy process. In particular both consultant and client need to agree to the *consultancy/research brief* and the *consultancy/research plan*. Only then and on the basis of these two key documents can the consultant proceed to action the next stages of the consultancy process. We shall now consider each of these vital stages and documents.

5.4 Planning and agreeing the consultancy/research brief

As already mentioned, once both client and consultant have agreed upon the general area for the consultancy project/research, then both client and consultant must proceed to develop and agree upon the consultancy/research brief. This involves fleshing out what service or activity the consultant will carry out, the timescale and costs. However, the consultancy/research brief should provide details with regard to the following key areas.

- *Research/consultancy objectives*: These need to be as detailed and as comprehensive as possible. Ideally the objectives of the research/consultancy should be couched such that they are Specific, Measurable, Actionable, Realistic, and Timed. (The so-called SMART criteria).
- *Timing and funding*: The consultancy/research brief should include details of timing not only for the completion of the consultancy project but also for any staging post activities in between, such as the submission of preliminary

reports. Agreeing to timings at the outset can minimize problems at a later stage. In addition to agreeing to timing, the consultancy/research brief should include details of funding including not only overall funding for the project, but again timings, allocations and any administrative/regulatory provisions with regard to funding and budgets.

- *Responsibilities and duties*: Responsibilities and duties of all parties to the consultancy process should be outlined in advance. This of course includes not only the responsibilities and duties required of the consultant but also of the various members of the client system. Included with responsibilities and duties should be the necessary authority which accompanies these. Responsibilities and duties should, where appropriate, encompass activities concerned with implementation and action plans and with controlled evaluation and monitoring. Finally responsibilities and duties should specify the details of any disengagement plan and/or continuing and ongoing activities required of the consultant.
- *Reporting requirements*: This element of the consultancy/research brief relates not only to whom the consultant or the consultancy team will report but also to the methods of reporting.
- *Constraints and restrictions*: This should encompass areas such as confidentiality, any activities, methods of working and other such that are not to be used, and any agreements regarding the use of findings/information elsewhere and for other purposes.

We can see then that the consultancy/research brief effectively delineates most of the key areas and activities that will constitute the consultancy research project. We would reiterate the need for both the consultant and client to discuss and agree to this brief. We have also indicated that ideally the research brief, and the research plan which flows from this and which will be considered next, should be written documents. This is not to suggest that they should be inviolate and inflexible and indeed often both research brief and research plan may need to be amended during the conduct of a consultancy assignment. By having a written document, however, both parties can assess what changes need to be made from the initial plans and with what implications.

5.5   Designing and agreeing to the research plan

Having agreed upon the consultancy/research brief the consultant can now turn to designing the research plan, again which should be written and agreed upon with the client system. The following are the key elements of the consultancy research plan.

- *Research/consultancy objectives*: There is no mistake here, research/consultancy objectives should appear both in the consultancy/research brief and in the subsequent research plan here. Data and information requirements, methods of data collection and methods of data analysis, interpretation and presentation, that is, the subsequent elements of the research plan all flow from and

must be consistent with the research/consultancy objectives. It is useful therefore for them to appear again when considering the research plan for the consultancy project.

- *Data and information requirements*: Careful and professional planning of the
  consultancy project up to this stage should enable the consultant to have a
  very good idea about the types and nature of data and information required.
  Data comes in all sorts of forms and types. It can include *soft* qualitative data
  through to *hard* qualitative data. Obviously, the type of data required will
  depend upon the specific research/consultancy project but it will also depend
  on what is available, cost and budgetary constraints and technical issues. A
  key part of the consultant's skills and toolbox is in understanding the different types of data and which to collect.
- *Methods of data collection*: Once we have determined data and information
  requirements we can then identify, select between, and specify the most appropriate methods of data collection. The different methods of data collection
  are so important that they are considered in more detail in several of the subsequent chapters.
- *Methods of data analysis, interpretation and presentation*: This last part of the
  research plan involves determining which methods of data analysis will be
  applied and how this data will be interpreted and presented to the client.
  Quantitative methods of data analysis may involve a variety of statistical techniques. In the case of more qualitative data different methods of analysing and
  interpreting data will need to be used. It is important to remember that the client
  does not want data but rather an analysis of that data which makes sense and
  relates to the client's needs identified earlier. Making sense of data collected,
  therefore, often needs to be a joint process between consultant and client. Data
  may also be interpreted and made use of with regard to existing knowledge
  and in particular theories and models. Once the consultant and the client have
  agreed upon the research plan then essentially the subsequent steps in the consultancy cycle involve the actions required to complete the consultancy project.

5.6   Completing the consultancy cycle

You may think that up to this point our consultant has not actually done any
consulting. In fact with the preparation and agreement of the research brief and
the research plan, in some ways perhaps the most important and difficult stages
of the consultancy project have been completed. Although not exactly 'paint-
ing by numbers', at this stage, the consultant can simply get on with the remaining stages of the consultancy project. As shown in Figure 5.1 these stages
encompass the following steps, each of which will be considered in more detail
in subsequent chapters.

- *Data collection*: Needless to say, this stage involves the consultant or someone contracted or charged by the consultant to actually collect data and information to be used to complete the consultancy project. The methods of data

collection will have been planned, specified and agreed upon in the research plan of course, which in turn, remember, stems from the agreed-upon consultancy/research brief.

- *Data analysis interpretation and presentation*: At this stage both client and consultant, often working together must make sense of the data. This requires that the appropriate techniques of analysis be selected and applied and that the information is diagnosed, interpreted and presented such that it is most useful to the client.

- *Recommendations, implementation and actions*: Although not part of every consultancy project, very often the consultancy/client contract will be such as to expect the consultant to make recommendations. In some cases the consultant will be expected to take responsibility for implementation and action programmes.

- *Control, evaluation and monitoring: disengaging from client/project*: The final stages of a consultancy project involve someone assessing how successful, cost effective and so on, the consultancy project has been. Sometimes this will be done by the client, sometimes by the consultant as part of the consultancy brief and sometimes by both parties. Certainly, effective control, evaluation and monitoring of consultancy projects is useful if only in planning the next project. Finally, both consultant and client must decide how, when and on what terms the consultant is to disengage from the client and/or any follow up work that the consultant may be asked or required to do.

5.7 Concluding comments

Effective consultancy and research requires systematic planning and implementation. In this chapter we have looked at the key steps in what constitutes a systematic approach to planning, implementing and completing management consultancy projects. In many ways the effectiveness or otherwise of consultancy projects is established very early on in the process of consulting. Failures, for example, to identify the client, to establish an early open and trusting working relationship between client and consultant, and failure to systematically develop and agree upon the research brief and plan condemn most consultancy projects to almost certain failure. In this chapter we have concentrated on these first steps in the consulting cycle, detailing what the steps involve, what needs to be included and how to complete these steps successfully. We are now in a position to move to the implementation of the consultancy brief and plan starting with data collection methods.

5.8 References

Belman, G. M. (2001) *The Consultants Calling: Bringing Who You Are to What You Do*, San Francisco, CA, Jossey-Bass/Pfeiffer.

Block, P. (1999), *Flawless Consulting: A Guide to Getting Your Expterise Used*, 2nd edn, San Francisco, CA, Jossey-Bass/Pfeiffer.

Clark, T. (1995), *Managing Consultants: Consultancy as the Management of Impressions*, Open University Press.

Cockman, P. Evans, B. and Reynolds, P. (1992) *Client Centred Consulting*, Mardenhead, McGraw Hill, pp. 9–11.

Cope, M. (2000) *The Seven Cs of Consulting: Your Complete Blueprint For Any Consultancy Assignment*, Financial Times/Prentice Hall.

Czerniawska, F. (2003) *The Intelligent Client: Managing your Management Consultant*, Trafalgar Square Books.

Freedman, R. (2000) *The IT Consultant: A Commonsense Framework for Managing the Client Relationship*, Pfeiffer.

Lee, K. (2003), *Consulting into the Future: Key Skills*, Trafalgar Square.

Markam, C. (1997) *Practical Management Consultancy*, The Institute of Chartered Accountants.

Revans, R. W. (1980) *Action Learning – New Techniques for Managers*, London: Kogan Page.

Salacuze, J. J. (2000) *The Wise Adviser: What Every Profeesional Should Know About Consulting and Counselling*. Praeger Paperback.

Weiss, A. (2002) *How to Establish a Unique Brand in the Consulting Profession: Powerful Techniques for the Successful Practitioner*, Pfeiffer.

Weiss, A. (2001) *The Ultimate Consultant: Powerful Techniques for the Successful Practitioner*, Pfeiffer.

Wilson, J. (1999) *Consultancy*, Hodder & Stoughton.

5.9 Glossary

client system	all those persons or groups who might provide information, care about or be affected by the proposed solutions with regard to a consultancy project.
consultancy/research brief	A detailed agreement between consultant and client, preferably written, which encompasses agreement with regard to: research/consultancy objectives, timing and funding, responsibilities and duties, reporting requirements and constraints and restrictions.
consultancy/research plan	A detailed agreement between consultant and client, preferably written, which encompasses agreement with regard to: research/consultancy objectives, data and information requirements, methods of data collection, methods of data analysis, interpretation and presentation.
contract	A term used by consultants to denote that point where both client and consultant have agreed to proceed with a consultancy project and where there is an understanding as to what the consultancy project is to be about and will encompass.
gaining entry	The term used by many consultants to refer to the initial contact/meeting stage between consultant and client.

6

An Overview of Data Collection: Approaches, Methods and Techniques

Introduction

Virtually every management research project will involve some type of data collection. Once the research or consultancy topic has been selected and the terms of reference agreed upon through the brief, then, the research plan will encompass the approaches to, methods of, and specific techniques to be utilized for data collection.

The usual problem for the management researcher or consultant when it comes to data is not the lack of it, or at least the potential for it, but rather the potential abundance of it. Quite simply, unless the researcher is careful s/he is likely to end up overloaded with data that sometimes they have little idea what to do with. Above all, the researcher should resist the temptation to collect everything in sight. Data collection must be well planned and managed if the researcher is not to become hopelessly overwhelmed and the data become a barrier rather than an aid to the research project. Planning and managing data collection systematically requires an understanding of the different types of data allied to the different approaches to, methods of, and specific techniques of data collection. Provided the researcher knows what sort of data is required, it is then that we can proceed to select between the different approaches, methods and techniques of data protection, and plan the data collection process accordingly.

 ## 6.1   Data, information and decisions

Data is the raw material of problem solving and decision making. Graziano and Rawlin (2004) highlight the importance of data in research methods suggesting that effective data collection is pivotal in the research process.

Activity 6.1. Suppose that our consultancy-type research project has the objective of investigating a perceived problem of lack of motivation among the company's management. Briefly outline four areas or aspects of the company's operation about which the company might need data in investigating this problem.

Data provides the basis for beginning to address and investigate research and consultancy problems. Data, however, is different to *Information* and the difference is important. Ultimately, the management researcher is interested in information rather than data. However, information stems from raw data and as such data is essential to the problem-solving process. The researcher must know not only what data is required, but also the principal methods, approaches and techniques for collecting data such that the most appropriate data collection techniques can be used. What then are the principal types of data, how may we classify data and data collection methods, and what are the principle ways and techniques of collecting data as part of a consultancy research exercise?

 ## 6.2   Types of data

Data comes in a wide variety of shapes and forms. When it comes to types of data, we can distinguish between the following major categories:

Primary versus secondary data

Amongst others, Saunders et al. (2003) suggest that one of the most fundamental distinctions between types or categories of data is that of **primary** versus **secondary data**.

Primary data does not actually exist until and unless it is generated through the research process as part of the consultancy or dissertation or project. As we shall see, primary data is closely related to, and has implications for, the methods and techniques of data collection. For example primary data will often be collected through techniques such as experimentation, interviewing, observation and surveys.

Secondary data, on the other hand, is information which already exists in some form or other but which was not primarily collected, at least initially, for the purpose of the consultancy exercise at hand. In fact, secondary data is often the start point for data collection in as much as it is the first type of data to be collected. Because of this, and the importance and potential value of secondary data, we shall consider this type of data and its collection in the chapter that follows. Although not strictly a research methodology in its own right, secondary data and its collection, is important enough to warrant a full chapter. We shall see that there are good reasons for this. We shall also see that secondary data comprises both internal and external data sources encompassing internal company information such as databases, reports, company analyses and so on, and external data sources such as published reports, government surveys, competitor information and increasingly, internet and web-based sources of information. Kervin (1999) also distinguishes between 'raw' secondary data where there has been little, if any, processing and 'compiled' secondary data which has received some degree of selection or summarizing.

Activity 6.2. Try to think of any reasons why secondary data might be collected and assessed before collecting any primary data.

Qualitative versus quantitative data

Our second major category of data types relates to the extent to which data is number-based or otherwise in this respect it is conventional to distinguish between *quantitative* and *qualitative* data.

Ghosh and Chopra (2003), in their 'Dictionary of Research Methods' define these two types of data as follows:

> Qualitative data is data in the form of descriptive accounts of observations or data which is classified by type.
> Quantitative data is data which can be expressed numerically or classified by some numerical value.

Quantitative data is often thought of as being more objective and scientific than its qualitative counterpart and is therefore associated with the more traditional scientific approaches to research as used in the physical sciences and discussed in Chapter 3. Because quantitative data is in the form of numbers, it can often be analysed using standard statistical techniques to, for example, test validity. Quantitative data of course implies that what is being measured or researched can be quantified in the first place. It is therefore only applicable to phenomena that can be quantified and measured.

Qualitative data on the other hand, relates to data that cannot be subjected to quantitative or numerical analysis. It is therefore associated with phenomena that cannot be, or is difficult to quantify.

In the past, qualitative and quantitative data have been seen not only as different types of data but essentially from different perspectives or approaches with regard to data and research methodology. Oakley (1999), for example, is not saying anything unusual when he suggests that qualitative and quantitative research and data are essentially different paradigms. He compares and contrasts them as shown in Table 6.1.

The dichotomy between quantitative and qualitative research stems essentially from the notions of what constitutes *scientific* as opposed to *non-scientific* research methodologies. The natural sciences that are primarily concerned with phenomena that are quantitative in nature have, not surprisingly, advanced knowledge in their subjects through the application of quantitative research techniques to the extent that in some quarters only quantitative data is felt to have any real value and validity. In the social sciences, however, much of what the researcher is concerned to measure and evaluate is qualitative in nature and, therefore, qualitative research techniques are more appropriate. Increasingly, it is recognized that there is much overlap between qualitative and quantitative data and research techniques and that at the very least each type of data can make valuable contributions towards the development of knowledge or in the solving of specific problems (Hakim 2000). The overlap and similarities between qualitative and quantitative research are illustrated well by Blaxter et al. (2001) and illustrated in Table 6.2.

We can see that there are as many similarities as there are differences between qualitative and quantitative research and therefore, what at first sight appears to be dichotomy between them is less clear-cut than at first sight it appears.

Table 6.1   Qualitative versus quantitative research

Qualitative paradigms	Quantitative paradigms
• Concerned with understanding behaviour from actors' own frames of reference	• Seek the facts/causes of social phenomena
• Naturalistic and uncontrolled observation	• Obtrusive and controlled measurement
• Subjective	• Objective
• Close to the data: the 'insider' perspective	• Removed from the data: the 'outside' perspective
• Grounded, discovery-oriented, exploratory, expansionist, descriptive, inductive	• Ungrounded, verification oriented, reductionist, hypothetico-deductive
• Process-oriented	• Outcome-oriented
• Valid: real, rich, deep data	• Reliable: hard and replicable data
• Ungeneralizable: single case studies	• Generalizable: multiple case studies
• Holistic	• Particularistic
• Assume a dynamic reality	• Assume a stable reality

Source: Oakley, A. (1999).

Table 6.2 Similarities between qualitative and quantitative research

- While quantitative research may be mostly used for testing theory, it can also be used for exploring an area and generating hypotheses and theory.
- Similarly, qualitative research can be used for testing hypotheses and theories, even though it is mostly used for theory generation.
- Qualitative data often include quantification (e.g. statements such as more than, less than, most, as well as specific numbers).
- Quantitative approaches (e.g. large-scale surveys) can collect qualitative (non-numeric) data through open-ended questions.
- The underlying philosophical positions are not necessarily as distinct as the stereotypes suggest.

Source: Blaxter et al. (2001) p. 65.

Activity 6.3. To what extent do you feel the fact that qualitative research is concerned with phenomena or events that cannot readily be measured, and does this mean that such research is not scientific?

 ## 6.3   Methods of data collection

If quantitative versus qualitative and primary versus secondary represent the first broad categories of data types and data collection, the researcher can now distinguish between various research approaches, again, with a view to selecting those which are most appropriate. Determining the research approach to data collection is often referred to as the *research methodology*. Although there are several facets to the design and categorization of research methodologies a major distinguishing feature between different research methodologies is indeed the different approaches to data collection. Unlike our categories of primary versus secondary and quantitative versus qualitative data types, however, when it comes to types of research approaches for data collection there exist several models or taxonomies of classifying the various research methodologies. Examples of taxonomies of methods of data collection include those of Becker (1998), Gill and Johnson (2002) and Seale (2004). Although these taxonomies of data-collection methods have differences, the following represent the major alternative research methods with regard to data collection.

- secondary data collection,
- case studies,
- experimentation,
- observation/ethnographics,
- interviews and surveys,
- action research.

These, then, represent the major approaches or methodologies of data collection that the researcher may use. They encompass the full continuum from what was referred to in Chapter 3, at one extreme, as nomothetic methods of which, for example, experimentation is probably the best example, through, at the other extreme, to what we referred to as ideographic methods like action research. Because these are, in our view, the major alternative techniques of data collection, we shall be considering each of them in more detail in the chapters that follow in order to explore in-depth the meaning of, approaches to, uses of and advantages and limitations of each of them. We shall see that within each major category of research methodology there are also a variety of research techniques and instruments that again the researcher can choose from. For example, we shall see that when it comes to surveys, the researcher can choose between a number of specific research techniques and instruments for collecting survey data such as, postal questionnaires, or more open-ended face to face interviewing techniques. We cannot, encompass every single possible research instrument and technique but we shall be considering some of the most important and useful ones in the context of consultancy research.

As a prelude to examining the various research methods of data collection, however, we need to consider some of the issues related to data and data collection in general. Related to this, we also need to consider some of the key criteria in evaluating and selecting between our alternative methods of data collection.

6.4   Issues in data collection

Irrespective of the method(s) of data collection there are a number of issues with regard to data and data collection with which the consultant/researcher needs to be familiar. The most important of these issues are now discussed.

The purpose of data: research objectives/hypotheses

Earlier in this chapter a distinction was made between 'data' and 'information'. It was suggested that this distinction is important. It is, and it is now reiterated.

Data, remember, is 'raw'/'untreated' facts, opinions, and so on. What the consultant researcher and client want, however, is information. Information is data that has been collected, interpreted and communicated in a form which is suitable for problem solving or decision making. Orna and Stevens (1995) make an interesting distinction between information and knowledge, suggesting that information is what we 'transfer knowledge into' when we want to communicate it to other people.

The consultant should always remember the distinction between data and information when planning and conducting the data-gathering process. In particular it affects the type of data required, the method(s) of collection and finally, and perhaps most importantly, the techniques of data analysis and interpretation. All data collection, then, starts with the identification of the problems or issues to be addressed by the research/consultancy and the information required to do this. The consultant can then specify the data requirements and begin to consider and evaluate between the different methods of data collection. This is why the importance of designing, negotiating and agreeing upon the research/consultancy objectives as the first step in the consultancy/research brief has been stressed. Having said this, objectives obviously vary with regard to both, what they encompass and how specific or general they are. For example, some objectives will be broad and not specify in any detail the research problem. This may be the case, say, when the nature of the consultancy research is more investigative in nature. The most precise and focused types of research objectives are those which are specified in the form of a hypothesis which is to be tested or more specifically supported or refuted by the research project.

Beginning the data collection process with statements of hypotheses is of course a central feature of the so-called *deductive* research method that was introduced in Chapter 3. You will recall that deductive research is based on developing hypotheses and then testing out these hypotheses through empirical observation. As such, we said that essentially this research approach is a set of techniques for applying theories in the real world in order to test and assess their validity. At this point, it might be useful to remind yourself of the process of deductive research and the role of theory/hypothesis formulation in this sort of research as highlighted in Chapter 3. Hypothesis formulation and testing, you will recall, is the usual and the accepted approach to research in the physical sciences. In the social sciences, however, again as we saw in Chapter 3, sometimes the deductive method of research of which hypothesis formulation and testing is such a central part, is inappropriate or not possible. This would apply to much consultancy-based research. Having said this, there are distinct advantages to couching consultancy research objectives in the form of hypotheses which can then be supported or refuted through an appeal to the facts based on data collection and analysis. Where research objectives are couched in the form of hypotheses, then this will almost certainly begin to tell the researcher what data is required and begin to delineate the most appropriate research design and methods of data collection. As we shall see, couching research objectives in the more specific form of hypotheses to be tested would tend to suggest some sort of experimental or perhaps survey methodology of data collection so as to enable the hypotheses to be tested. You might be tempted to think that it would be preferable in fact, if all research/consultancy exercises could be conducted around a specific set of hypotheses in as much as this is much more likely to avoid the problem of data and information overload for the researcher, compared to where the researcher starts without a hypothesis. As already mentioned, in many consultancy/research projects it is not possible or appropriate to start with hypotheses. In such situations the consultant/researcher can still try to set specific objectives for the research, which in turn, will help to guide data collection. There may, however, be situations where the consultant/researcher may have to settle with a general statement about what the project is investigating and the problems to be resolved and therefore with only vague or unspecified objectives. In situations where it is not possible or appropriate to start with hypotheses, or where it is difficult even to formulate detailed objectives for the research, then at the very least the researcher/consultant should think carefully about what the project is investigating and the problems/issues to be resolved. This will at least begin to focus data requirements and the selection of appropriate methodologies and hence minimize inappropriate and potentially costly data collection.

Finally, we should note that some consultancy/research projects will start, not with hypotheses or even objectives but rather with data collection itself. In fact, an equally valid approach to research methodology is collecting data first and then using this data to produce theories or hypotheses. This is the so-called *inductive* approach to research methodology considered in Chapter 3.

It is important to recognize that this is a valid approach to data collection in its own right and is certainly, therefore, not to be considered 'a second class citizen' only to be used, for example, where it has not been possible to frame hypotheses or even set specific objectives.

Criteria for effective data: data quality

In addition to considering the purpose of data and its relationship to research objectives and any hypotheses, another key issue in data collection relates to what we have termed here *the quality of data* and in particular what constitutes effective data in the context of a research/consultancy exercise. Perhaps as you would expect, data can, and does, vary enormously with regard to quality and the researcher must understand, therefore, what constitutes the different dimensions or criteria for assessing the quality of data.

Overall, effective data provides the basis for the information required to meet the objectives of the research project. Underpinning the seemingly simple perspective as to what constitutes effective data are several potentially complex dimensions or criteria of quality when it comes to assessing data. Of particular importance with regard to dimensions or criteria of data quality are the dimensions of what researchers refer to as *validity, reliability,* and *generalizability*.

- *Validity*: Validity relates to the extent to which the data collection method or research method describes or measures what it is supposed to describe or measure. Ghosh and Chopra (op. cit.) define validity as 'an absence of self contradiction'. Clearly, validity as a dimension or criteria of data quality is crucial. After all, if a research methodology or instrument does not measure or describe what it is supposed to, then at best it is possibly meaningless and at worst misleading. If we are attempting to measure attitude, for example, then it is important that our approach to data collection actually allows us to measure this dimension of behaviour. Although this sounds obvious, in fact validity is a complex concept and there are many different dimensions to, and types of, validity including for example: 'content validity', 'predictive validity', 'concurrent validity', 'construct validity', 'face validity', 'internal and external validity', and 'statistical validity' (Burns 2000; McBurney and White 2004). Most methodologies and instruments will enable us to assess the extent to which they are likely to be valid as a method of data collection, though again, there are several dimensions to such assessments. Overall, as already stated, the researcher must assess the extent to which an approach to the collection of data will produce data that is valid.

- *Reliability*: Reliability relates to the extent to which a particular data collection approach will yield the same results on different occasions. Perhaps we should point out, of course, that this assumes that there are no real changes in what is to be measured or the circumstances of such measurement. Where data is unreliable then we obviously have to be careful in carrying research results from one situation to another.
- *Generalizability*: Generalizability is essentially another dimension of validity quality in data and relates to the extent to which results from data can be generalized to other situations. Generalizability with regard to data is particularly important with regard to two aspects of data.

The first is where data has been collected on the basis of a sample. As we shall see in later chapters, sampling is often used in the generation of data in the process of research and consultancy projects. The researcher must know, or be able, to measure/assess the extent to which results from the sample will also be present in the wider population from which the sample is drawn. Generalizability, therefore, is related not only to the methods of data collection and the circumstances thereof, but also to issues such as sample design and sampling method, etc.

The second, and related aspect to generalizability, is the extent to which the data and results of a particular research project can be generalized to other situations. This, of course, is crucial in developing theories and particularly in the deductive approach to research.

In fact, all three of these dimensions of data quality very much stem from the need within the deterministic model of research to produce results that are *scientific*, and *reproducible*. As Easterby-Smith et al. (2002) point out: 'the notions of validity, reliability and generalisability were in fact originally developed for use in the physical sciences and particularly where quantitative data was being collected'. However, as they also point out, these dimensions of data quality are just as relevant and therefore can also be applied and interpreted in the context of more qualitative research methods and techniques. Their ideas are shown in Table 6.3 linked to the notions of inductive versus deductive research approaches which were considered in Chapter 3.

These are the three key criteria or dimensions for the quality and effectiveness of data. There are, however, a number of other dimensions that can also have an important effect on data quality. These include:

- *Sampling and measurement errors*: Both types of errors can, and do occur in data collection with perhaps obvious potential effects on validity, reliability and generalizability.
- *Data recording, storage and retrieval*: Issues in data recording, storage and retrieval can have important effects on data quality. The researcher must give careful consideration as to how data will be recorded and stored. Sometimes

	Deductive research	*Inductive research*
Validity	Does an instrument measure what it is supposed to measure?	Has the researcher gained full access to the knowledge and meanings of informants?
Reliability	Will the measure yield the same results on different occations (assuming no real change in what is to be measured)	Will similar observations be made by different researchers on different occasions?
Generaliz- ability	What is the probability that patterns observed in a sample will also be present in the wider population from which the sample is drawn?	How likely is it that ideas and theories generated in one setting will also apply in other settings?

Figure 6.1 Questions of reliability, validity and generalizability in deductive versus inductive research methods
Source: Adapted from Easterby-Smith et al. (2002) p. 53.

for example, data recording, storage and retrieval can prove problematical. An illustration would be where, say, the researcher is collecting data through personal interviews. An ideal way of recording, storing and retrieving data from the research might be to use, say, a voice recorder while conducting the interviews. However, the use of a voice recorder might inhibit some inter- viewees in terms of being more guarded about what they say, thereby affect- ing the quality of the data collected. On the other hand, dispensing with the voice recorder and using, say, handwritten notes during the interview might encourage interviewees to *open up* more during the interview, but would be much more difficult to retrieve subsequently, and the act of recording hand- written notes might slow down and affect the spontaneous nature of the inter- view. Ethical issues would, of course, be a consideration if the interviewer was to use a voice recorder without letting the respondent know this before- hand. The researcher must, therefore, give careful consideration as to how data is to be captured and recorded and how it is to be stored and retrieved.

- *Preparation for data gathering*: Data quality can also be affected by the extent to which the researcher has prepared for the data-gathering process. In particular, is the preparation required to ensure that the researcher is famil- iar with the necessary research and measuring instruments being used. An otherwise faultless data-collection design methodology may suffer simply because the researcher has not prepared sufficiently in advance in terms of applying and administering the research instruments for data collection.

6.5   Choosing between data collection methods

A key decision is the selection of the research methodology and techniques. The researcher needs to understand not only which alternative methodologies and techniques are available, but also the main criteria in selecting between them for a particular research project. This in turn requires an understanding of the characteristics, uses, advantages and disadvantages of the main alternative research methodologies and techniques of data collection. You might be wondering then, since we have not yet considered the major alternative research methodologies in detail how we can at this stage usefully introduce the issue of how to evaluate and choose between these alternatives. In fact, although the final choice of research methodologies does indeed require the researcher to be familiar with the characteristics of the alternative methodologies, it is possible and useful at this stage to outline the key criteria when selecting between these alternatives. These are now outlined:

Objectives/purpose of research

The most important factor affecting the selection of the research method is the objectives and purpose of the research. We have seen, for example, that according to the nature of the research/consultancy project, we may want or need to answer a particular set of questions, or address a particular set of problems. This in itself will begin to suggest what methods or techniques are most appropriate.

Researchers' skills and expertise

Although a professional/experienced researcher should be able to use any of the alternative research methodology and data-collection techniques it is probably unrealistic to expect a single researcher/consultant to be an expert in every method and technique of data collection. Although we must be careful not to select a methodology simply and only because we are familiar with and experienced in it, common sense dictates that the researcher should be careful about using research methodologies and techniques in which they do not have the necessary degree of expertise or skills. Lack of skills and expertise, where it is decided that a particular research methodology would be the most appropriate, can be potentially overcome by the consultant tapping into additional expertise where appropriate.

Cost/budgets

Again, realistically, the researcher/consultant needs to consider the costs of any proposed research methodology. Often the largest costs of a consultancy project are associated with, and stem from, the data collection process. Sometimes, the most effective research methodology in quality and potential value for decision making in terms of the data collected may be rejected in favour of a slightly less effective research methodology which is cheaper.

Time

In a similar way to costs/budgets, the researcher consultant must also consider the time available for the research/consultancy project. Some approaches to data collection such as, for example, large-scale surveys can take considerable time. Again, considerations regarding the quality of the data that might be collected through the different research methods sometimes have to be moderated by the amount of time available.

Availability

Quite simply, certain types of data are often more readily available, and therefore easier and cheaper to collect, than others. Secondary data in particular, because it is by definition already available, is easier and cheaper to collect. In some situations the data may simply not be available at all. This could, for example, be due to say, the sensitivity of the data required, confidentiality, and so on. Obviously, it is pointless delineating data requirements and selecting appropriate methods of data collection when the data is simply not available.

Consultants' preferences/values

We saw in Chapter 5 that consultants, whether internal or external to the organization, bring their own preferences and value systems when it comes to how to approach consultancy and research projects. While the professional consultant should be careful not to let these preferences and values dictate entirely the research methodology selected, of itself there is nothing wrong, and indeed it can be helpful, for the consultant to select between two equally valid and cost effective research methodologies, that suits the researcher's preferences and value systems.

Client preferences/values

Considering the need for consultancy research projects to reflect and support the needs of the client, a key factor in selecting between alternative research methodologies, is the preferences and values of the client. These could relate to those of the individual manager or management team for whom the consultancy is being conducted or to the values or culture, systems and procedures of the organization itself. It may well be that although the best system of data collection might be through observation, the client may feel strongly that they do not want this type of research methodology to be used in their organization or department. If the client fundamentally disagrees with the researcher consultant with regard to what is felt to be the most appropriate research methodology, then this will need to be discussed and agreed during the contracting stage of the consultancy process. In some circumstances the consultant has to decline or withdraw from a consultancy project because a suitable research methodology cannot be agreed upon between client and consultant.

Ethical, legal and other issues

In selecting between alternative research methodologies, both the consultant and client may be required to consider and assess a range of other issues. One of the most important of these is any ethical issues related to the choice of research methodology and data collection techniques. As we shall see later when we consider the methods of data collection in more detail, some of these methods raise quite distinct and important ethical issues such as, for example, whether or not respondents should be informed that they are being researched (Wysocki 2004). Similarly, there may be legal issues surrounding research methodology and particularly and increasingly these days, issues pertaining to the collection, storage and uses of data. Many countries now have legislation pertaining to these issues. In the UK for example, such areas are encompassed by the provisions of the Data Protection Act. Although ethical and legal issues are among the more important of our list of considerations and criteria for selecting between research methodologies, there may be others according to the circumstances of the particular research and consultancy project. It is impossible to cover every one of these other possible issues. Suffice to say that the consultant and client together must carefully consider what these other issues and criteria might be according to the particular consultancy and research assignment.

Using more than one method

As already mentioned, a particular management research project may require and involve more than one method of data collection. We might start, for example, with say secondary research followed by observation and finally focus on group interviews and a large-scale survey. The use of several methods of research is common in business research projects. Not only is this because the different research methodologies may be used for different facets of the project, but in order to verify the quality of the information being collected, and in particular its validity and reliability. Where two or more methods are combined for this purpose we refer to this as **triangulation**.

The use and combination of several research methodologies in the process of conducting a particular project, for whatever reasons, serves to remind us that different research methodologies, types of data, and orientations for management and consultancy research are not mutually exclusive, and certainly not dichotomous. Both qualitative and quantitative research, as we have seen, can be used together. Secondary research will often serve as a prelude to primary research. Experimental research may be used in combination with focus groups and surveys, and so on. The different research methodologies and techniques are simply a set of tools that the researcher can use to address the particular consultancy and research problems.

6.6   Concluding comments

One of the most important stages of the research and consultancy process is to
determine the most appropriate methods of research methodology and data
collection. Data provides the basis for information and ultimately problem solving and decision making. We can usefully distinguish between primary and
secondary data and qualitative versus quantitative data. However, we must be
careful to note the similarities as well as the differences between the different
types of data and data-collection methods. There are many ways of identifying
and classifying methods of data collection and in this chapter we have identified six main alternative research methodologies for data collection which will
now be considered in more detail in the chapters which follow. Irrespective of
the methods of data collection selected, there are a number of issues regarding data and data collection with which the consultant/researcher needs to be
familiar. These issues include building data collection methods around research
objectives and hypotheses and the alternative approach of building hypotheses
around data already collected. When considering data and organization for its
collection, the researcher also needs to consider the issues of validity, reliability and generalizability. The researcher must also consider how errors can be
introduced into data, how data is to be recorded, stored and retrieved, and how
to prepare for data collection. Finally, we have considered the issues and the
criteria in selecting between alternative research methodologies.

6.7   References

Becker, H. S. (1998) *Tricks of the Trade: How to Think About Your Research While You're Doing
    It*, Chicago: University of Chicago Press.
Blaxter, L. Hughes, C. and Tight, M. (2001) *How to Research*, 2nd edn, Buckingham: Open
    University Press, p. 65.
Burns, R. B. (2000) *Introduction to Research Methods*, 4th edn, London: Sage Publications.
Easterby Smith, M. Thorpe, R. and Lowe, A. (2002) *Management Research: An Introduction*,
    London: Sage Publications.
Ghosh, B. N. and Chopra, P. K. (2003) *A Dictionary of Research Methods*, Leeds, UK: Wisdom
    House Publications.
Gill, J. and Johnson, P. (2002) *Research Methods for Managers*, 3rd edn, London: Sage
    Publications.
Graziano, A. M. and Rawlin, M. L. (2004) *Research Methods: A Process of Enquiry*, 5th edn,
    Harlow: Pearson Education Group, p. 77.
Hakim, C. (2000) *Research Design: Successful Designs for Social and Economic Research*, 2nd
    edn, New York: Routledge.
Kervin, J. B. (1999) *Methods for Business Research*, 2nd edn, New York: Harper Collins.
McBurney, D. H. and White, T. L. (2004) *Research Methods*, Belmont, USA: Wadsworth/
    Thomson Learning.
Oakley, A. (1999) 'People's way of knowing: gender and methodology', in S. Hood,
    B. Mayall, and S. Oliver, (eds), *Critical Issues in Social Research: Power and Prejudice*,
    Buckingham: Open University Press, pp. 154–77.

Orna, E. and Stevens, G. (1995) *Managing Information for Research*, Buckingham: Open University Press.

Saunders, M., Lewis, P. and Thornhill, A. (2003) *Research Methods for Business Students* 3rd edn, Harlow: Pearson Education.

Seale, C. (ed) (2004) *Social Research Methods: A Reader*, London: Routledge.

Wysocki, D. K. (ed) (2004) *Readings in Social Research Methods*, 2nd edn, Belmont, USA: Wadsworth/Thomson Learning.

6.8   Glossary

data	Data is comprised of the raw unprocessed details and facts pertaining to the issue or problem being explored.
generalizability	The extent to which the patterns and results observed in a research project can be applied to other situations outside of the specific research study.
hypothesis	A set of assumptions often couched in the form of tentative propositions which are subject to verification through subsequent investigation.
information	Information is data that has been arranged, interpreted and assessed in such a way that it is useful for problem solving and decision making.
primary data	Primary data is data that is collected for the first time for the purpose of a particular study (consultancy project) at hand.
qualitative data	Non-numerical data which cannot be mathematically, statistically, or both - interpreted and analysed.
quantitative data	Quantitative data is data in the form of numbers which can be interpreted and analysed mathematically, statistically, or both ways.
reliability	The extent to which a data collection or measurement technique yields the same results on different occasions.
research methodology	The general category of research approach being used in a research/consultancy study and which relates particularly to the approach to data collection.
secondary data	Information which is already collected and available in some form to the researcher.
triangulation	The process whereby several methods of research and data collection are used such that the findings from one type of study can be checked against the findings derived from another type.
validity	The extent to which a data collection or measurement technique measures what it is supposed to measure.

7

Data Collection: Secondary Data

Learning outcomes

After completing this chapter you will be able to:

- understand the value and importance of using secondary data in the completion of business research projects,
- classify and explain the different sorts of secondary data and the main sources of such data,
- understand how to evaluate the reliability and validity of secondary data,
- describe how existing data can be identified and collected,
- discuss the developments in the collection and analysis of secondary data.

Introduction

Once the research topic has been selected and the terms of reference for the academic business research or consultancy project have been agreed upon through the project/consultancy brief and the plan, then we are in a position to begin the research/consultancy project itself beginning with the process of collecting data. In this chapter we start the process of looking in detail at the ways of collecting data in the process of conducting consultancy research. We shall be concerned in this particular chapter with collecting data which already exists, either inside the organization itself or is held external to the organization. We shall see that most organizations have a wealth of such data which they can draw on and analyse in seeking to address consultancy issues and problems. We shall also see that it is to this existing data that the consultant should turn to before considering the need for further data that will have to be collected for the first time. Finally, we shall see that there is a plethora of existing data that a consultant can turn to and utilize. Such data is, if anything, more abundant than ever in today's information age and in addition developments in data and information technology systems are enabling much speedier and detailed access to already available data.

■ 7.1   Secondary data: meaning and scope

The completion of academic or consultancy business research will normally require the collection of data. This data is then analysed and used to assess the area on which the project is focused with a view to using this to solve problems, explore issues, and ultimately make recommendations. In Chapter 6 you were introduced to the different categories or types of data. Specifically, we distinguished between primary and secondary data and qualitative and quantitative data. In this chapter we shall be looking at secondary data: the different types, its collection and how to evaluate and interpret secondary data.

As the term implies, secondary data is essentially *second-hand* in as much as it is not new data collected specifically and primarily for the purpose of the consultancy being conducted. Very often, there is so much secondary data available that could potentially be used in a consultancy research project that the problem for the researcher is in sorting through and evaluating exactly which secondary data to use, and how to assess its usefulness. Perhaps somewhat confusingly, in fact secondary data should be examined before any data is collected for the first time by the researcher. If, and only if, existing data cannot be used to meet the objectives and requirements of the consultancy project, then the researcher should turn to the collection of new data. The reason for this use of secondary data first is perhaps obvious, but nevertheless is worth underlining. Essentially, we use secondary data before collecting new data because the collection of new data is generally much more expensive and time consuming. In addition, of course, it makes little sense to begin to collect such expensive new data if the data needed, or at least some of it, has already been generated within the organization or by some outside body or organization. We shall consider the advantages and uses of secondary data in more detail shortly, but first we need to distinguish between the two main types or categories of secondary data namely *internal secondary data* and *external secondary data*.

Internal secondary data is data that already exists within the organization in some form or another. It is important to recognize that such data may in fact be in a different part of the organization such as, for example, a different division, location, and so on. Much internal secondary data is data that is generated as part of the normal operation of the organization's business and activities. For example, most organizations have some sort of data within the organization on the various functional activities of the business including:

– sales and marketing data,
– production data,

– personnel data,
– financial data.

Increasingly, as we shall see later, often this internal secondary data is part of, and is accessed and analysed through, the company's management information system. In addition to this data from the company's operating activities and records, we also have internal secondary data that stems from previous research and data gathering activities conducted within the organization. For example, a company may already have on record data about the researcher's area of interest from previous research studies. Finally, in terms of internal secondary data, we have the more general types of data which stem from, for example, other documents and records such as company reports, internal memos, in-house magazines and so on. We shall consider the sources, uses and developments with regard to internal secondary data in more detail later in the chapter.

External secondary data includes all data which again already exists but which has been collected outside of the organization. As such, by its very nature, this type of data has been collected by another party. The range and types of external data available to the researcher/consultant these days is so extensive as to be potentially bewildering. There is a real danger here of information overload. Different researchers have in fact generated a range of classifications for secondary data including not only the internal and external classification mentioned here, but also classifications of secondary data encompassing raw secondary data, compiled secondary data, documentary secondary data, survey-based secondary data, and secondary data compiled from multiple sources (Hakim, 1982; Dale et al. 1988; Bryman, 1989; Malhotra, 1993; Kervin, 1999; and Robson, 2002). Again, we shall consider some of the major sources and types of external data available to the researcher/consultant in more detail later in the chapter, but perhaps one of the most useful and comprehensive categorizations of secondary data, we feel, is that of Saunders et al (2003) who distinguish between three major categories or types of secondary data as follows:

– 'documentary' secondary data,
– 'multiple' source secondary data,
– 'survey' secondary data. (Saunders et al. (2003) pp. 189–94)

Uses of secondary data

Although all data is intended to provide information for analysis and decision making, secondary data can be used in several ways in the context and conduct of a research/consultancy project. Admittedly, it is rare for secondary data alone to provide all the information needed to address a consultancy/research problem. The following are the ways in which secondary data can be used in the management research process.

● *Identifying the problem/setting objectives*: A major use of secondary data in the business research process is in helping to identify the problem and more specifically helping to define research objectives or even hypotheses. Used in this way, secondary data is in fact being used as exploratory research and will help shape any subsequent primary data collection processes. There is no doubt that this is a major use for secondary data in helping to verify the findings of a business research project.

- *Developing an approach to the problem*: Perhaps an extension to problem identification, secondary data collection is often used to define and refine the approach to a consultancy/research problem.
- *Formulating the appropriate research design*: Secondary data is often used, for example, to identify and isolate key variables so that the most appropriate research design can be used to investigate these variables further.
- *Answering certain research questions*: Although I have already said that it is rare for secondary data alone to provide all the answers to a consultancy problem, it can and often does resolve certain research questions and may in some cases even be used to confirm or refute some hypotheses.
- *Helping interpret primary data*: Often, secondary data can help provide additional or different insights into data collected through primary data-collection methods. In this context, it is important to stress that secondary and primary data types are not mutually exclusive. The research will often need to combine each type of data in resolving a research/consultancy problem.

Activity 7.1. Write down some examples of how secondary data could be used in a consultancy project in your own organization or one with which you are familiar. Try to be as specific as possible.

7.2   Planning secondary data collection

Although virtually every secondary data collection exercise will be different according to, for example, the circumstances of the data-collection procedure, the research objectives, the amount of existing data available, cost and time considerations and so on, there are a number of issues and steps which any secondary data collection exercise will encompass. These issues and steps can be usefully thought of as a number of key questions which the researcher must address when it comes to collecting secondary data. These questions are, in fact, similar to those encountered in the more traditional academic research exercise when considering completing a dissertation or project of some kind. Jankowicz (1991) suggests that the following are the key questions when planning secondary data collection.

What to look for

The first question Jankowicz suggests is the question of 'what to look for'. In all data collection, including secondary data, the researcher must determine what data to look for. The answer to this question serves to shape all that follows including types of data, sources of data and so on. Data requirements, remember, stem from the consultancy research objectives and will normally therefore be specified in the research brief and research plan discussed in Chapter 5. Again, remember that we have suggested that secondary data is often used in preliminary or exploratory research, and thus has an input to determining what to look for. Wherever possible, however, the researcher should ideally have a good idea of what they are looking for through data collection and therefore what data, in this case, secondary data, to look for. Remember the danger is always one of information overload or perhaps worse still, by not being selective and focused in determining what secondary data to look for, collecting data which is inappropriate and hence not relevant. An example will serve to illustrate the problem and the importance of deciding what to look for.

Suppose that the consultancy research centres on the problem of devising and implementing more customer-responsive systems in an organization. Suppose also that the consultant then wishes to explore any relevant secondary data that will help in resolving this problem. Although the broad subject matter and focus, therefore, for the project has been identified, the researcher will quickly find that there are any number of secondary data sources that might potentially encompass or at least touch on the identified problem. For example, there are likely to be government reports on marketing and customers, journal and other academic references to customer responsiveness, syndicated reports on marketing and customer orientation, and so on. Very quickly the researcher will be looking at very many fields, sub-fields and subsequent sources of information on the subject being researched. The researcher, therefore, has to quickly focus on identifying the most relevant subject matter and hence secondary data. For example, if the nature of the organization is, say, a small entrepreneurial business selling services to business customers, then the researcher can begin to focus on potential sources of secondary data that are only relevant to this type of situation. Instead of collecting all the secondary data therefore, which is relevant to customer response systems, the researcher focuses only on those sources that primarily relate to small entrepreneurial businesses marketing services to business-to-business (B2B) customers.

Starting with a broad topic area and beginning to focus or distil the topic so as to be able to identify more precisely what to look for in secondary data in this way is referred to by Howard and Sharp (1983) as a 'relevance tree' approach to identifying data requirements. The danger of this approach is that the researcher may exclude data that may appear tangential to the main thrust of the research, but which in fact, if included, would be extremely relevant and useful. In other words, it is possible to miss relevant secondary data with this approach. There is no simple answer to this, the researcher must steer a fine line between collecting too much secondary data and too little.

Where to look

Having identified what to look for in secondary data, the second question in Jankowicz 's framework is to determine 'where to look' for secondary data. We have already classified the two main alternatives when it comes to where to look for data, namely 'internal' versus 'external' data sources. With respect to internal secondary data sources it was suggested that we have data from normal operating systems and activities, data from previous research/consultancy studies, and finally data from more general internal sources such as, company reports, memos and so on.

With respect to external secondary data, the following represent just some of the potential sources:

- government publications,
- trade and industry publications,
- trade and other libraries,
- online indexes and catalogues,
- published indexes and catalogues,
- commercial research organizations.

Clearly then, just as with the question of deciding what to look for, when it comes to deciding where to look, the researcher is beset with a multitude of potential sources of data. Again, the nature of the research problem and objectives should serve to guide the researcher as to where to look for information but again there is a fine dividing line between being tempted to look at everything that might potentially be useful, and focusing too narrowly on certain sources, simply because we are familiar with them or they are readily available. We shall be considering this 'where to look' question in more detail later in the chapter when we look at both internal and external secondary sources in more depth.

How to look

The third and final question in Jankowicz's framework for conducting business research returns us to our distinction between data and information. As has already been emphasized, ultimately the researcher is interested in information rather than data. Again, if the researcher is not careful with respect to how they look for secondary information, there is a danger that they will be swamped with data with little information. When looking for secondary data, therefore, it is important to always bear in mind the following questions when considering how to look for data:

- What do I need to know? The more clearly the researcher can answer this question, the less likely they are to waste time looking for secondary data sources which will not provide useful information.
- How will I know when I have found it? The researcher who knows when they have found the data they are looking for, again, is less likely to waste time continuing to search for secondary information.
- How accurate and detailed does the data need to be? The researcher must determine in advance what degree of accuracy and detail is required from the secondary data.

These, then, are some of the major considerations in planning and conducting secondary data collection. We now return to a more detailed look at some of the types and sources of secondary data by using our primary distinction between secondary data types and sources, namely internal and external.

Activity 7.2. An organization has initiated a consultancy project centring on how to improve its new product development systems and processes. How might Jankowicz's framework and in particular the three key questions for conducting business research help the consultant plan the secondary data collection process?

7.3   Internal secondary data

If secondary data in general is cheaper and faster to access than most types of primary data, then internal secondary data must represent the cheapest and most easily accessed type of secondary data. For perhaps obvious reasons, it is internal secondary data to which the researcher/consultant should usually turn to first when considering data collection. This can help avoid costly and potentially embarrassing situations. The author has personally experienced a situation where a company actually commissioned expensive market research when a similar market research report on the same market/topic already existed in a different part of the organization. By the time the researchers realized that a similar survey had been conducted only some months earlier, the research had already been commissioned, completed and paid for.

As we shall see, internal secondary data has become even more important in recent years as companies have developed better management information systems including better ways of collecting, storing, analysing and accessing internal secondary data. Databases, and data mining, which we shall explore shortly, have helped considerably to add value to internal data sources.

In addition to being generally the cheapest and easiest to collect category of data, internal secondary data also has the following potential advantages compared even to external secondary data sources.

- *More focused/pertinent to a particular organization*: Obviously, internal data relates specifically and indeed stems from the organization's own activities and operations. By definition, therefore, it is likely to be more pertinent and more relevant in analysing these activities and operations.
- *Confidentiality less of a problem*: Internal secondary data is likely to cause fewer problems with regard to issues of confidentiality and therefore access. Admittedly, not all internal secondary data will be openly available to the consultant or student researcher even where this person might be an internal employee of the organization, but generally there are fewer problems with this aspect when it comes to internal data.

The major types and sources of internal secondary data, identified earlier were the company's own operating records from its own day to day activities and operations; previous research records and reports, if any; and more general company information such as, company reports, internal memos, publicity and PR announcements and other such. Remember, as with all secondary data, these types of internal company data will normally comprise data that is initially being collected, analysed and stored for reasons other than the purpose of the research/consultancy project being conducted. Admittedly, very often such data may focus on precisely the same areas and aspects that the researcher is interested in, so for example, if the consultancy project concerns exploring rates of labour turnover in an organization and the reasons for this, the personnel department records may well contain data on precisely this area of company operation. Often, though, the researcher will need to interpret even internal secondary data carefully when considering it for what is essentially another use. Increasingly, though, companies are using information and communication technologies to develop internal data information systems in such a way as to be more readily usable for a variety of purposes. Specifically, companies have turned to developing and using management information systems and particularly databases and data mining so as to enable them to make much better use of existing internal data.

Management information systems: databases and data management

An increasing number of companies now have *management information systems* (MIS) that can provide a potentially rich source of internal secondary data to the researcher/consultant. The main function of an MIS is to provide internal managers with the information they need in order to make better decisions. Admittedly, such information systems are usually designed more for the normal operating procedures and activities of an organization. However, the MIS can be used by the consultant to access all sorts of data and information. At the very least, normally an MIS will include data on the transaction processing systems of the organization such as, production data, marketing and sales data and so on. Companies are increasingly beginning to recognize that one of the most important assets they have is data. As a result, companies now have much more effective *database* and database management systems.

As already mentioned, developments in information and communications technology have provided a major boost to the growth and importance of databases. In fact, databases often comprise both internal and external data, but the contemporary database in particular has enabled much more effective access to, and use of, internal data. In the past, it was often the case that internal data was not always collected and stored in the organization. Where it was, it was often in a form, or in such amounts, that it was of little use for consultancy projects. Both access to inexpensive and powerful computers, coupled with much more powerful programmes for analysing and manipulating data have meant that databases are now much more powerful and relevant to consultancy and research projects. Internal databases can now help the consultant to explore organizational problems and to refine, for example, primary research objectives.

In addition to more powerful computers and information technology, the recognition of the importance and value of data in organizations has led to the development of much more effective systems of data organization and management. For example, data can now be much more effectively interrogated by the researcher to reveal patterns or relationships between different aspects of the company's operations. Interrogating data in this way is referred to as *data mining*. Lancaster et al. (2001) show how database management and data mining in particular are enabling the marketer to develop new and more powerful insights into their customers which can then be used to develop more competitive marketing strategies. However, data mining can potentially be used in any functional area of a business and can be particularly useful in the context of research/consultancy project for an organization.

Another development in using internal company data is so-called *data warehousing*. In the past, often data from different functions and parts of a business have been held in separate databases. Data warehousing involves designing the data system in an organization such that information from different functions and parts of the business may be brought together into one central system for further analysis and interpretation. In this way, data from different parts of the business can be cross related and correlated.

Finally, companies and database managers are now much better at ensuring that internal databases contain up-to-date and accurate information. You will appreciate that a database that is out-of-date or inaccurate can be at best irrelevant, and at worst positively dangerous. Regularly maintaining databases is referred to by database practitioners as *database cleaning*.

Overall, then, internal secondary data is not only important and useful, but as a result of technological developments in recent years has become even more so. Most consultancy research projects are likely to make extensive use of this type of data but now what about the sources and uses of external secondary data!

Activity 7.3. In the context of your own organization or one with which you are familiar how might the following aspects of data management help provide more useful internal secondary data? Try to think of specific examples.

– data mining
– data warehousing
– database cleaning.

■ 7.4 External secondary data

When it comes to external secondary data, as we have already seen, the researcher/consultant has even more choices to potentially choose from. Here we shall use the categorization of external secondary data developed by Malhotra (op. cit.). Malhotra distinguishes between published external secondary data sources, syndicated sources, and computerized databases and categories of external secondary data are now explained.

Published external secondary sources

When it comes to published secondary data sources, Malhotra suggests that the contemporary researcher/consultant has a myriad of potential data sources. Below are listed just some of these:

- academic books and journal articles,
- conference papers,
- bibliographies,
- published market reports,
- directories and indexes,
- national government publications,
- local government publications,
- trade association reports,
- research and professional body reports,
- newspapers and magazines,
- company annual reports,
- chamber of commerce reports,
- industry publications.

Within some of these data sources there are often in turn, a further myriad of publications and data sources, for example, national governments publish all sorts of potentially useful data including, for example, census data, business statistics, economic extracts and so on. We can see yet again the importance of having some idea of what we are looking for and where to find it.

Syndicated sources

Malhotra's second major category of secondary data sources are the so-called *syndicated sources* of external secondary data. At first glance it might appear that these types of data are more akin to primary data in as much as they are collected and sold by commercial research organizations using primary data collection techniques. However, the reason they are referred to as secondary data sources is that syndicated research is not initially collected for the purpose of solving a particular consultancy research problem for a client, but rather center on the collection of more general non-client-specific data which can be then be purchased and used by a consultant/researcher in investigating or exploring their own particular problem or consultancy project. Syndicated data sources are used extensively in marketing research problems but are not exclusive to just the marketing arena. Using a marketing example however, many syndicated secondary data sources in marketing are based on collecting data through surveys or consumer-panel data. The organization providing the syndicated data will establish and conduct the survey or consumer panel and then offer the data collected to different firms that subscribe to the syndicated data-provider's services. Continuing our example, a branded goods manufacturer might want data on, say, brand preferences and purchasing patterns for a particular product.

Rather than collecting this data through primary research this company might purchase this data from a supplier of syndicated data. Many syndicated secondary data providers operate to provide panel or survey data in this way.

Computerized secondary data databases

Although syndicated secondary data is often collected, analysed and extracted through computerized databases, Malhotra's third type of database is increasingly being used in its own right as a major source of external secondary data in management and consultancy research. Needless to say this increase is primarily due to the developments in information and computing technology which have enabled much greater access to, and use of, computerized databases from secondary external sources. More recently, we have seen the advent of web-based data and databases which again are growing in importance. The following are some of the major advantages of computerised secondary databases.

- The date can be more up-to-date as it is relatively easy to enter new data on a computerized database as and when it becomes available.
- Often databases can be accessed almost instantaneously and increasingly improved search protocols and technology allow more comprehensive and simpler data access.
- Database secondary information costs are often low compared to other secondary data types.
- Increasingly, data can be accessed at any time and in any location with the development of mobile technologies and the growth of the worldwide web.

Computerized databases can be classified into two types, namely **online databases** or **off-line databases**. Both are now used extensively for accessing external secondary data. Many data providers, including the ones listed in our secondary sources of published data, now provide such data either directly online and/or through CD Rom disks. The contemporary researcher/consultant must be familiar with the relevant computerized databases and how to access and use them.

Again Malhotra (op. cit.) provides a useful classification of different types of computerized databases, namely 'bibliographic', 'numeric', 'full text', 'directory' or 'special purpose' databases as shown below.

- *Bibliographic databases*: These consist of citations to articles in journals, newspapers, research and technical reports, government publications and so on. Many of these databases provide summaries or abstracts of the material contained in them. Essentially, as the term implies, bibliographic databases are effectively a library index that the researcher can use to access existing secondary material pertaining to the area of the consultancy project. There are literally dozens of bibliographic databases available to the researcher in the United Kingdom one of the most extensive bibliographic databases available is that of the British Library site which contains information on over 16 m books and periodicals, 700,000 newspaper titles, 300,000 manuscripts, over 4 m maps, 1.4 m music scores and over 200,000 photographs. An example of a research bibliographic database is the so-called REGARD database funded by the Economic and Social Research Council (ESRC).

- *Numeric databases*: As you would expect, these comprise numeric and statistical information. Both commercial and government sources provide such numeric databases. An example is Euromonitors Global Market Information Database (GMID). This database comprises eight fully searchable data-hubs encompassing, for example, statistical data on 109 countries worldwide: statistics on retail market sizes – volume and value for 330 consumer products across 49 countries worldwide and forecasts, again encompassing volume and value, plus demographic and economic data for 49 countries. Information such as census-based numeric databases conducted by governments in different countries is also available to the researcher.
- *Full text databases*: Again, as the term implies, these databases comprise the complete text of the source documents stored on the database. The databases may encompass journal articles, market research reports, newspaper and periodical articles, company annual reports and so on. The Euromonitor market reports for example comprise nearly three-quarters of a million full pages of text encompassing all the market research reports conducted and published by Euromonitor.
- *Directory databases*: These are databases which produce information with regard to organizations, services or even individuals. They are essentially sophisticated address books, but also help provide a map for a researcher wishing to contact or gain further information about a particular individual organization or topic. Kelly's business directory and Kompass in the United Kingdom are examples of directory databases. There are even directories of databases. These consist of directories that provide information on databases, what they contain, how to access them and so on. Examples of directories of databases would include Gale Research Company's *Encyclopaedia of Information System and Services* and Cuadra Associates Inc *Directory of On-Line Databases*.
- *Special purpose databases*: These are databases that concentrate on providing information on very specific and focused areas. A good example would be the so-called PIMS database developed by the Strategic Planning Institute in Cambridge, Massachusetts. This database provides information on over 2,000 businesses with regard to their strategies and their profitability. In fact, it details the profit impact of market strategies – hence PIMS – for the companies in the database. More and more special purpose databases are becoming available to the researcher. Again directories of databases are a good way of finding out what is available and which might be relevant. (Adapted from L. K. Malhotra (1993).)

The internet

Increasingly, of course, external secondary data including the range of online databases just outlined are being accessed using the internet. Because the web is now such a huge source of data, however, again the problem is distinguishing between useful and useless sources of data. The researcher therefore must know which sites are likely to be most relevant and useful for a particular consultancy/ research exercise and how to search these. Examples of key sites for social science researchers are shown in Appendix II. However, remember that this is just a small selection of the vast range of sites available.

In order to help search for data on the web, web designers have developed *internet gateways*. Internet gateways are sites that focus on certain areas and material within the site is edited by the gateway operators to ensure that it is appropriate to the information area listed.

In addition, increasingly, most search engines use **Boolean operators** and syntax. We need not concern ourselves with the technical underpinning of Boolean operators, but essentially it means that a web search can be made more precise by combining key words and one or more of the operators 'AND', 'OR', 'AND NOT'. An example of the way in which these operators can be used to refine web searches for data is shown in Figure 7.1 below which is taken from the Economic and Social Research Council's website on how to refine a search of their database.

Finding too many records?
  Try narrowing your search by:

- Using AND to combine terms, e.g. social AND exclusion.
- Use phrase searching and connect terms using underscore, e.g. social exclusion.
- Use the advanced search option and restrict your search to a section of the record, e.g. title.
- Exclude words or phrases by using NOT.

NB: AND will automatically be used to connect terms unless you type in a connector, e.g. if you type social exclusion the search will be social AND exclusion, but if you type social NOT exclusion then AND will be overridden by NOT.
  Not finding enough records?
  Try broadening your search by:

- Using OR to combine terms, e.g. forest or woodland.
- Using truncation – type the stem of a word followed by an asterisk to find any other endings, e.g. econ* will retrieve economy, economics, economist etc. Be careful, however, as truncation can retrieve unwanted results: e.g. car* will find cars but will also retrieve carnation and carnage.

NB: If you switch on truncation by adding an asterisk in the search all the terms in that search will also be truncated. For example, econ* AND forest will retrieve economics, economist etc, but will also retrieve forestry, forester and so forth.

Figure 7.1   Refining a websearch using Boolean operators
Source: http://www.regard.ac.uk\regard\help\tips\singletips\basic

Activity 7.4. You are a consultant wanting to find out what might be available on the worldwide web in relation to a consultancy project which you are currently conducting. The project centres on the area of 'Social responsibility in business'.

Conduct your own web search to try and identify useful secondary sources of data on this topic.

7.5   Criteria for evaluating secondary data

As we have seen and indeed emphasized several times, the researcher is potentially inundated with sources and types of secondary data. In this respect I have tried to indicate how to minimize the problem of information overload and the costs of time and effort wasted implied by this. In addition, the researcher must know how to evaluate secondary data. As you will appreciate, secondary data will differ with respect to how accurate, how detailed, how appropriate and it is, so on. The researcher, therefore, needs to establish a number of criteria when choosing between alternative secondary data sources and evaluating secondary data when it has been collected from these sources. Stewart (1984) proposes a set of common criteria that can be used for both purposes with regard to evaluating secondary data as follows:

Methodology

Stewart suggestes that secondary data should be evaluated having due regard to the methodology used to collect the data. Aspects such as the sampling procedure, sample size, response rates, procedures used for field work and data analysis and reporting should, where possible, be assessed. Essentially, here we are checking the reliability and validity of the data, concepts with regard to data that were covered earlier.

Error/accuracy

Stewart's second criterion is related to the specifications and methodology and indeed an outcome of these is the degree of error or perhaps it should be accuracy of the data from a secondary source. Often it can be difficult to evaluate the accuracy of secondary data as the specifications and methodology may not be given in enough detail and of course someone else, in any event, has conducted the research. Where the researcher has worries about the accuracy of the data then wherever possible the data should be verified by using several sources and/or by conducting triangulation research.

Date of data collection

By definition, secondary data is already out of date in as much as it relates to events and circumstances that have already occurred. Admittedly, forecasts using secondary data are future oriented, but remember that these too are based on past data. It is important for the researcher to consider when the data was collected, the time lag between data collection and publication, and as a result whether or not the data is still likely to be useful and relevant. This is a problem, for example, with much census data that, in the United Kingdom, is only collected every ten years.

Purpose of data collection

Again, by definition, secondary data is data that was collected with some other purpose or objective than that which the researcher/consultant now addressing this data is concerned with. The researcher must assess the extent to which data collected with another purpose or specific objective in mind is appropriate and relevant to the researcher's situation or problem.

Nature: content of data

Stewart's fourth criterion relates to the fact that sometimes data that is otherwise valid, accurate and current is not relevant and useful because of the nature or content of the data. For example, the measurement categories used in the data or, the relationships examined by the data may be inappropriate to what the researcher is interested in. For example, the data may consider the relationship between, say, levels of salary in an organization and motivation. However, motivation may have been defined and measured in a way that is inconsistent or inappropriate with how the researcher considering the secondary data wishes to measure motivation.

Dependability/source credibility

Finally, in evaluating secondary data, Stewart suggests that the researcher must consider the expertise, credibility, reputation and overall trustworthiness of the source. Generally speaking, official sources of secondary data such as, government reports, are often considered to have more dependability/source credibility than many commercial sources of secondary data. However, even governments often have *hidden agendas* in terms of what data they present and how they present it. Dependability and source credibility is increased when we know the provider of the data in some way; where details of the data collection specifications and methodology are given, where the data is from an original rather than an acquired source, and where the provider of the data is prepared to be identified. (Adapted from Stewart (1984).)

These then are Stewart's criteria for evaluating secondary data sources. Other criteria which can be used include in addition: costs and benefits, difficulty or otherwise of access, and control over data quality (Stewart and Kamins, 1993; Denscombe, 1998).

7.6   Concluding comments

In this chapter we have examined the value and importance of using secondary data in the completion of consultancy research projects. Data collection in most projects will usually start with secondary data. This is because such data is usually cheaper, faster and easier to access. Secondary data comprises two major categories of data, namely internal and external secondary data.

Secondary data has a number of uses in the process of consultancy research ranging from helping identify the problem and setting objectives through to helping interpret primary data and making recommendations.

Effective planning of secondary data collection is important and the researcher should assess what they are looking for, where to look and how to look for such data.

Internal secondary data comprises data generated and available within the organization and it is this data which should be considered first. Increasingly, MIS and databases and their management are helping to provide more useful and pertinent internal secondary data.

External secondary data come in a myriad of types and form a wealth of sources. The main categories of this type of data encompass published external secondary sources, syndicated sources and computerized databases. The use of computerized databases, and especially online databases is expanding tremendously. The internet and the worldwide web in particular are now important sources of secondary external data for the consultant/researcher.

All secondary data, but perhaps external secondary data in particular, should be assessed and evaluated with regard to criteria such as accuracy, dependability, validity, reliability and perhaps above all, its relevance and usefulness to the research/consultancy project at hand.

7.7   References

Bryman, A. (1989) *Research Methods and Organisation Studies*, London: Unwin Hyman.

Dale, A., Arber, S. and Proctor, M. (1998) *Doing Secondary Analysis*, London: Unwin Hyman.

Denscombe, M. (1998) *The Good Research Guide*, Buckingham: Open University Press.

Hakim, C. (1982) *Secondary Analysis in Social Research*, London: Allen and Unwin.

Howard, K. & Sharp, J. A (1983) *The Management of a Student Research Topic*, Aldershot: Gower.

Jankowicz, A. D. (1991), *Business Research Projects for Students*, London: Chapman & Hall.

Kervin, J. B. (1999) *Methods for Business Research*, 2nd edn, New York: Harper Collins.

Lancaster, G. A., Massingham, L. and Ashford, R. (2001) *Marketing Fundamentals*, Oxford: Butterworth Heinemann.

Malhotra, N. K. (1993), *Marketing Research an Applied Orientation*, New Jersey: Prentice Hall.

Robson, C. (2002) *Real World Research*, 2nd edn, Oxford,: Blackwell.

Saunders, M., Lewis, P. and Thornhill, A. (2003) *Research Methods for Business Students*, 3rd edn, Harlow: Pearson Education Ltd.

Stewart, D. W. (1984) *Secondary Research: Information Sources and Methods*, Beverley Hills: Sage, pp. 23–33.

Stewart, D. W. and Kamins, M. A. (1993) *Secondary Research: Information Sources and Methods*, 2nd edn, Newbury Park, CA: Sage.

7.8 Glossary

bibliographic databases	Databases which contain references to summaries or abstracts of published materials in journals, magazines, newspapers, market and technical reports and government documents.
Boolean operators	A system of syntax which can be used to refine searches on the web.
database	An organized store of data in an organization.
database cleaning	Procedures whereby a database is regularly checked and maintained to ensure that data is up-to-date and accurate.
data mining	The process of analysing and manipulating data to provide insights into a company's operations.
data warehousing	systems for ensuring that data from different parts of the organization are collected and analysed in a central database within the company.
directory databases	Databases containing information on individuals, organizations or services.
external secondary data	Data which already exists but which has been produced by sources external to the organization.
full text databases	Databases which contain the complete text of the source documents in the database.
internal secondary data	Data which already exists within the organization in some form or another.
internet gateways	Sites that edit sources of information so that the researcher can be directed more immediately to what is relevant and appropriate data.
management information systems	Systems which are designed to collect, store, interpret and utilize information for management decision making.
numeric databases	Databases which contain primarily numerical and statistical information.
off-line databases	Data which is accessed through diskettes and CD Rom disks.
online databases	Databases which consist of a central data bank which is accessed via a computer or terminal via a telecommunications network.
relevance tree	An approach to identifying and delineating research problems so as to more accurately delineate data requirements.

special-purpose databases   Databases which focus on specialist/selected areas only.

syndicated sources   Organizations that collect and sell secondary data to different organizations that subscribe to their services.

8

Data Collection:
Observational Research

Learning outcomes

After completing this chapter you will be able to:

- discuss the nature and purpose of observational research in primary data collection,
- describe the major approaches to conducting observational research,
- understand the advantages and disadvantages of observational research,
- discuss how to plan and conduct observational research,
- assess the key issues in using observational research to gather primary data.

Introduction

This is the first of my chapters that encompass techniques of primary data collection. This chapter covers observational research techniques for collecting primary data. Observation is an important and useful way for generating primary data particularly in the social sciences, including management research and consultancy. We shall see that observational research methods range from the relatively simple non-participative techniques that involve, for example, recording events, activities and so on in an organization, through to potentially complex techniques where the data gatherer/researcher becomes a participant in the processes and activities being observed. We shall be considering how to plan and approach observational research including some of the ways in which data based on observation can be gathered and recorded. We shall also be considering some of the key issues in observational research ranging from ethical issues related to, for example, whether or not the researcher informs those being observed that observation is taking place, through to some of the methodological issues in observational research such as the fact that being observed may change the behaviour of the observed and the problems of the observer remaining objective during the process of data collection.

8.1   The nature and purpose of observational research

Observational research has a long and increasingly distinguished history, particularly in the social sciences. In the most general sense, observational research comprises collecting primary data through looking and noting. As you would expect with such a general description, the nature, scope and types of observational research vary enormously. We shall group observational research into a number of key categories using first of all the extent to which the observations are systematic or relatively unstructured and second, the extent to which the observer is a participant or remains an outside observer. However, we must then query the background to this approach to data collection.

As already mentioned, observational research has a long history. In the physical sciences, among some of the most notable applications of observational research would include, for example, Sir Isaac Newton's observation of the apple falling which, it is said, led eventually to Newton's laws of gravity and motion. Similarly, the observations of the medieval astronomers led to significant developments in our knowledge about the universe and its workings. Observational techniques in the social sciences, in any systematic sense, that is, have something of a shorter but no less distinguished history. In particular, as we shall see later, observational research has long been a major tool of data collection in the fields of sociology and anthropology but has now become one of the major tools of research in management and organizations. In the area of management and organizational research one of the earliest uses of observation as a research methodology was the study by Charles Booth in the United Kingdom in the nineteenth century. Booth used observational techniques, in conjunction with other techniques, to study the working people of London in the 1880s. It was probably, however, during the 1950s that the potential value of observational research as a method of data collection in the management/organizational field began to be recognized and there have been many now classic studies in the area of management research using this technique. Examples would include Roy's (1952) study of work in a machine shop; Gouldner's (1954) research into aspects of bureaucracy in a gypsum mine; Lupton's (1963) study of output restriction by employees in two manufacturing plants; the extremely influential research of Minzberg (1973) with his observational-based research on management activities in organizations; Benyon's (1973) extended studies of events and problems at the Ford Halewood plant over a 5-year period; and, more recently, the observational research of Rosen (1991) that was conducted in a Philadelphian advertising agency. As a method of data collection, observational research continues to grow in importance. So what explains this increasing use of observational research, particularly in the area of management and organizational research and, more specifically, what are the advantages of observational approaches to collecting primary data? The following represent some of the major suggested advantages associated with observational research techniques.

- First of all it is suggested that observational techniques, unlike, say, interviews and surveys, rely not on what people say they do or feel, and so on, but rather on actual observations of what they do (Bryman 1989; Delbridge and Kirkpatrick 1994).
- A second advantage claimed for observational research is that as a technique it can often generate data and findings which would have been impossible to discover by any other means. In particular it is suggested that observational research can help identify subtle and otherwise hidden issues and problems in an organization, because with observational research the researcher is able to shift attention to any behaviour which seems most interesting and relevant (Graziano and Raulin 2004).
- Third, particularly where the researcher participates in the activities being performed, observational research allows much richer and detailed data to be generated than, say for example, using secondary data or even primary data-collection methods such as surveys and questionnaires (Robson, 2002).
- Finally, and particularly relevant to a consultancy-type student research project, participant observational research, in particular, is very well suited to research within the researcher's own organization (Saunders et al. 2003).

There are also several disadvantages and limitations of observational research for generating primary data, especially where the research is poorly planned and executed. We shall look at these major disadvantages and limitations as we work through this chapter and particularly when we consider the design and implementation of observational research methodologies, and some of the issues associated with the use of this group of research techniques in data generation. First we need to look in more detail at the range and types of observation techniques.

Activity 8.1. Identify four areas of organizational research/consultancy upon which observational research techniques might be particularly well suited to gathering data.

8.2 Observation approaches and techniques

There are many different approaches to and techniques for using observational methodology to generate primary data. For example, the researcher could *observe* activities in an organization by passively noting the activities involved in working a piece of machinery or performing some function. These activities could then be recorded in some form or other as they take place. You will recognize, no doubt that in one sense, time and motion, and organization and methods studies are a form of observational research. In another approach to using observational techniques, the research may involve the observer actually becoming part of the group or activities being observed with no prior decisions about what are to be observed or even for what purposes. Here, the observer may simply observe events taking place in the group and then write this up at a later stage for further analysis. In the same way, the recording methods used during observational research can vary from simple mechanical observation and recording devices, like the number of times an operative presses a particular button, through to the use of diaries, and even complex case studies. We can identify which approaches and techniques to use in any given situation, using a number of key dimensions. These key dimensions regarding different approaches are outlined below.

Direct versus indirect observation

Although the majority of observation approaches and techniques involve some form of direct watching, listening or otherwise observing the behaviour of subjects, in fact, it is possible to use indirect observation. For example, an effect or an activity, although not personally observed, may be reported to the *observer* by someone else, either orally or in writing. Sometimes, indirect observation can be conducted through the analysis of internal organizational documents. In this sense we can see that some forms of indirect observation actually overlap and blur with the techniques and approaches to secondary data collection outlined in Chapter 7.

Structured (systematic) versus unstructured (unsystematic) observation

Observational research approaches can be distinguished by the extent to which they are structured or as they are sometimes referred to systematic as opposed to being unstructured and therefore unsystematic.

Structured/systematic observational research involves the researcher specifying in advance, and often in some detail, precisely what is to be observed, how the observations will be recorded and possibly even how the observations will be analysed and interpreted. Obviously, structured observation can only be carried out where the researcher knows in advance precisely what is being measured, and why, and also where what is being observed is amenable to being structured in this way. For example, if the researcher was concerned to generate data regarding operative activities in a particular production process the observational research could be structured in advance so as to determine which activities are to be measured, and how they are to be recorded. Structured observation can help to reduce, or even remove, the potential for observer bias, hence increasing the reliability of the data. On the other hand, structured observation can be restrictive and lead to important data being missed because this is not part of the pre-structured observation process.

Unstructured/unsystematic observation is where the observer, at least initially, observes or monitors all aspects that might seem relevant to the problem at hand. For example, if the researcher is unsure of what might be causing high labour turnover in an organization, the observation may encompass all phenomena that might relate to this problem in the organization with a view to making sense of the observations made in this respect at a later date. Unstructured observation can be useful where the precise nature of a problem in an organization and therefore, possibly the objectives for the research itself, have yet to be formulated precisely. Unstructured observation, therefore, can be used to develop hypotheses as well as explain phenomena in its own right. The more unstructured the observation, the greater the potential for observer bias, but also the more flexible data collection can be with less danger of potentially significant data being missed.

Clearly, *structured versus unstructured* is a continuum, and this is a matter of more or less structure. In addition, an observational research data collecting exercise may combine both highly structured and less structured approaches and techniques.

Denscombe (1998) suggests the following advantages and disadvantages of more systematic approaches to observational research (See Table 8.1).

Revealed versus unrevealed observation

Our second dimension for approaches to observational research relates to whether individuals being observed are made aware of this or not. On the one hand, the researcher may reveal at the outset that the respondents are being observed. In some cases this may simply involve the observer declaring their presence. In other circumstances, in addition to this, the observer may give comprehensive details of the reasons for the observations, the methodologies being used, how the data will be interpreted and used, and so on.

On the other hand, the researcher may not reveal that respondents are being observed at any time during the observation, depending on the ways in which the observations are being made. Disguised observation of this type may involve, for example, hidden cameras, *disguises* of one form or another, for example, pretending to be just another employee, acting out another role and so on. The advantage of unrevealed observation is that it helps avoid the problem of people behaving differently when they are aware that they are being observed. The argument is that simply the process of being observed can have an effect, and therefore change the behaviour of those being observed. It can be argued that for ethical reasons respondents should always be informed when they are being observed, irrespective of the purpose of the investigation. In practice, the choice between revealed versus unrevealed observation can be a real dilemma. For example, it may be more ethically sound and indeed in line with the value system of both organization and consultant to reveal the observation process, but by so doing, it may be impossible to access certain types of data or even conduct the research at all once the subjects know that they are being observed or know the true nature of the research.

Table 8.1 Advantages and disadvantages of systematic observation

Advantages of systematic observation	Disadvantages of systematic observation
• *Direct data collection.* It directly records what people do, as distinct from that they say and do. • *Systematic and rigorous.* The use of an observation schedule provides an answer to the problems associated with the selective perception of observers, and it appears to produce objective observations. The schedule effectively eliminates any bias from the current emotions or personal background of the observer. • *Efficient.* It provides a means for collecting substantial amounts of data in a relatively short time-span. • *Pre-coded data.* It produces quantitative data that are pre-coded and ready for analysis. • *Reliability.* When properly established, it should achieve high levels of inter-observer reliability in the sense that two or more observers using a schedule should record very similar data.	• *Behaviour, not intentions.* Its focus is on overt behaviour; describes what happens, but not why it happens. It does not deal with the intentions that motivated the behaviour. • *Oversimplifies.* It assumes that overt behaviours can be measured in terms of categories that are fairly straightforward and unproblematic. This is premised on the idea that the observer and the observed share an understanding of the overt behaviour, and that the behaviour has no double meaning, hidden meaning or confusion associated with it. As such, systematic observation has the in-built potential to oversimplify; to ignore or distort the subtleties of the situation. • *Contextual information.* Observation schedules, by themselves, tend to miss contextual information which has a bearing on the behaviours recorded. It is not a holistic approach. • *Naturalness of the setting.* Despite the confidence arising from experience, there remains a question mark about the observer's ability to fade into the background. Can a researcher with a clipboard and observation schedule really avoid disrupting the naturalness of the setting?

Source: Denscombe (1998) pp. 146–8.

Whether or not the observer reveals to respondents that they are being observed has many implications not only for techniques for data collection through observation, but also with regard to issues such as the validity and reliability of any data collected plus, of course, ethical issues. These issues are important and, therefore, will be considered in more detail later in the chapter.

Natural versus contrived settings

This dimension concerns the extent to which the observation takes place in the natural setting of the phenomena being observed, or in a contrived and therefore largely artificial environment. Natural observation would involve the observations being made, say, in the normal work setting for the individuals being observed, with no special or different arrangements being made because of the observation. At the other extreme, observations can be made in a virtually totally artificial environment. For example, if we were observing the effect of different lighting levels on production efficiency we could carry this out in a controlled *setting* outside of the normal work situation. In this type of setting, observational research blends into experimental research.

The more natural the setting in which observation takes place, the more likely it is that the observations will capture data that reflects the true phenomenon. On the other hand, contriving the observational environment and setting can enable the researcher to more precisely investigate the relationships between different phenomena and may help, therefore, in establishing causation. In addition, a more contrived observation environment means the observer does not have to wait for phenomena to occur naturally and therefore this approach can be less time consuming and expensive.

The naturalness or otherwise of the setting for observation approaches is also related to our dimensions of structured versus unstructured observation and revealed versus unrevealed observation. Obviously, some of the more structured approaches to observation which involve, for example, the researcher using clipboards to record data, tend to add to a more contrived, as opposed to natural setting. Similarly, revealed observation, through its possible effects on changing patterns of behaviour, may also be considered to add to a more contrived situation.

Participant versus non-participant observation: ethnographic research

Although each of the dimensions for describing different approaches to observation research which we have considered so far are important, one of the most important dimensions is the extent to which the observation, or more specifically the observer, acts as a participant or as a spectator.

Within the field of observational research, some of the most useful and important research studies, including many of those highlighted earlier in this chapter, have been based on full participant observation. The extent of participation on the part of the observer/researcher is a key issue in what has come to be termed **ethnographic research**. Primarily, and initially developed by the sociologists and anthropologists in particular, ethnography is literally writing about people, ethnographic research is research that involves participating and often *living* with the people being researched. The main feature of ethnographic research is that the researcher is involved, or participates, in the activities that are the focus of the research (van der Velde et al. 2004). For example, the anthropologist researching the habits and customs of a long-lost tribe found in the jungles of the Amazon may approach observational research of this tribe by actually living with the tribe and joining in their lives and activities. Ethnographic research aims, through this participation, to gain better insights by providing a description of the world from the point of view of the observed. Ethnographic research, based on complete participation has increasingly been used in researching organizations. Minzberg (op. cit.) for example, found that through participant observation he was able to identify what managers actually did as opposed to what they might otherwise have claimed they do, and which in fact the formal organization impelled them to do. When combined with unrevealed observation, participant observation can be a particularly powerful observational technique in as much as not only does the researcher join the observed and therefore share their experiences, feelings, fears and so on, but because the observed are not aware they are being observed, the researcher may be better able to elicit data which otherwise would be unavailable. Unrevealed participant research, therefore, involves the researcher becoming a complete participant. Again, this raises both methodological and ethical issues.

At the other extreme, the observer can act merely as a spectator to what is being observed. Here, the researcher does not become involved in any way with those being observed or with their activities.

In ethnographic research the extent to which the researcher participates or observes is a continuum. In fact, Gill and Johnson (2002) by combining the dimensions of revealed versus unrevealed, (or as they term this dimension 'overt' against 'covert' research) with our dimension of participant against non-participant observation, propose a taxonomy of ethnographic research types as shown in Figure 8.1.

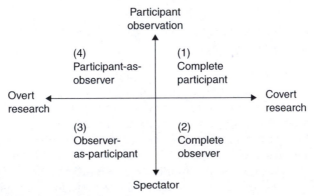

Figure 8.1 A taxonomy of field roles
Source: Gill and Johnson (2002) p. 149.

Techniques of data collection and recording

Our final dimension with regard to observation research centres on the specific types of technique used to collect and record data during an observational research exercise. This dimension is therefore not one of a continuum as some of the others have been, but rather a collection of techniques that the observational researcher can draw from and utilize when it comes to collecting and recording observational data. The techniques selected will be determined by the circumstances of the particular research exercise and not least by the dimensions already discussed with regard to the choice of approach to the observational research exercise. With this in mind, some of the main alternatives for collecting and storing observational data include:

- mechanical and/or electronic means, for example, video cameras/CCTV, work templates, machine and activity meters and voice recorders,
- written materials and records, for example, clipboards, diaries, work and time sheets,
- observation followed up by written case notes.

There is no single best method of capturing and recording observational data and the researcher invariably has to adapt or devise an individual approach to a particular observational research project. For some observational research there may be 'off the shelf' coding schedules available such as, for example, those available for recording certain types of group interactions (Mullins 2002). There are advantages and disadvantages to using off-the-shelf packages and the researcher must carefully consider the extent to which any available packages are suitable for the observation exercise being planned (Walker 1985). As far as is possible, the researcher should try to devise methods of capturing and recording data in advance so preparation is all-important. Wherever possible the researcher should try to avoid the process of collecting and recording observed data influencing what or who is being observed.

Activity 8.2.
(a) Under what circumstances might the researcher/consultant consider approaching observational research in a totally artificial environment?
(b) Under what circumstances might the researcher/consultant use unrevealed observation?
(c) Under what circumstances might the researcher/consultant decide to become a complete participant during observational research?

8.3 Planning and implementing observational research

There is no single method of planning and implementing observational research. Different situations will demand different approaches. However it is possible and useful to make a number of general observations that can serve as guidelines when planning and implementing observational research. The following are some of the key steps and considerations in this process.

Determining if observation is an appropriate method

The first step is to decide whether or not observation is an appropriate method for collecting data as part of a consultancy/research exercise. In this respect, the researcher needs to reflect upon the objectives of the research and the circumstances of the research/consultancy project. While conducting observational research does not rule out using other methods of data collection, time and costs constraints mean that there is an opportunity cost whenever selecting between the different ways of collecting data. The researcher should choose the most appropriate and cost-effective methods. Observational research has several distinct advantages over other methods of data collection. In particular, it is very useful for conducting preliminary research investigations and for generating further hypotheses. Observational research is particularly suited to identifying subtle and otherwise hidden issues and problems in an organization. More structured observational techniques can be particularly useful where the researcher knows precisely what is to be observed/measured and where observational schedules can be used.

Determining what data is required

This step in planning and implementing observational research is of course common to all data collection methods. We have noted, however, that when it comes to observational research in particular, sometimes the researcher will know precisely what is to be observed, and why and will therefore have a clear idea of what data is required. In other circumstances the researcher will have no prior or even clear ideas about what is to be observed, and why. In this situation it is not possible or even desirable to determine in advance precisely what data is required. Between these two extremes it can be useful for the researcher to think about which aspects are going to be observed or investigated and who is to be observed.

Determining what/who is to be observed

Irrespective of the extent to which the researcher knows precisely in advance what observational data is required in planning and implementing observational research, the researcher should consider what, and where appropriate, who is to be observed.

In this respect we can distinguish between observing Content/Process and Interaction.

- *Content/Process observation*: Sometimes, the researcher will be interested in primarily observing content or process of activities and systems in an organization. For example, the researcher might be interested in observing how meetings are conducted in an organization. Content/process observation would involve the researcher collecting data relating to the conduct and content of meetings. In this example, the researcher might need data regarding, for example, where people were seated in meetings; the existence or otherwise of written agendas; who spent most time speaking; how the chairperson dealt with interruptions and so on.

- *Interaction observation*: This type of observation focuses on observing the interactions between individuals or groups in the organization. Here the observer is specifically interested in the behaviour of individuals and groups. Interaction analysis involves the researcher determining which interactions are to be observed and measured and which individuals or groups will be included. Many noteworthy observational studies in the management area have used interaction analysis. For example, Bales' (1950) famous study of the behaviour of individuals in groups used an interaction observational approach. Bales devised a method of classifying or coding interactions between individuals in his groups by identifying in advance which group activities he wanted to observe and then devising a method for recording and measuring these.

Determining the approach to the observational research

Having considered what, and who, is to be observed the researcher must now select between the different approaches to observational research. This involves the researcher making decisions about the key dimensions regarding different observational approaches and techniques outlined earlier in the chapter. The researcher must determine the extent to which the observation is to be structured or unstructured, revealed or unrevealed, natural or contrived and participant or non-participant. In addition, the researcher must select the most appropriate techniques of data collection and recording ranging between mechanical and electronic means, clipboards, diaries, worksheets, or observation followed by written up case notes.

These then are the main considerations and steps in planning observational research. When it comes to implementing observational research, the following additional issues must be considered.

Gaining access and permission

All research and consultancy that is conducted within an organization raises the issue of gaining access and permission. Usually, any access and permission required will have formed part of the earlier discussions and contract agreement between client and consultant. However, observational research in particular can give rise to heightened issues and problems with regard to access and permission. This is particularly true of ethnographic type observational research activities where, as we have seen, the researcher becomes part of the group or processes being observed. Where participatory observation is to be used, then, it is vital to ensure that all necessary access and permissions have been cleared and established in advance.

Piloting observational research and techniques

Often, in using observational research it can be extremely useful to pilot a selected approach to the observational study and the techniques of data collection decided upon. Very often, what might appear to be the most suitable approach and techniques turn out to be not right for the particular task. With observational research, the researcher has to adapt tried and tested methods and approaches to the particular task. For example, a technique of observational research that may have worked well for another researcher and was well documented, may need adaptation in another context. Piloting an observational approach will help indicate any problems in the selected approach and any modifications that may need to be made. Piloting the selected methods and techniques of observational data collection may not always be possible where, for example, the researcher wishes to utilize unrevealed observational research techniques or where the phenomena being observed is a one-off observation exercise.

Careful preparation

All techniques of data collection are more effective with careful preparation. Observational research, in particular though places extra onus on the researcher to be well prepared. We have already considered the importance of planning in advance what is to be observed and why, and the selection and planning of data collection methods and techniques for observational research. Observational research will require the researcher to carefully plan the details of the observational approach including, for example, any necessary charts, grids, checklists, recording devices, and so on, which will be used during the observational research exercise. Very often the researcher will have only one chance to make and record the observations.

Activity 8.3. Are there any situations or reasons where it would not be possible or appropriate to pilot proposed observational research techniques?

 ## 8.4   Other issues in observational research

Objectivity versus subjectivity

As observational research involves the observer in noting and recording what is taking place, the technique raises the issue of the extent to which even the observations and their interpretation at a later stage, might be affected and influenced by the doings of the observer. This is particularly the case when the observation is based on participant observation techniques and where the observational approach is relatively unstructured. Here, there is particular potential for the observer's predispositions, predilections and value systems to affect the data collection. Even when observing seemingly straightforward events and activities, different observers may observe an event differently. For example, two observers watching a fight start in a club may have very different perceptions of what happened and who started it. With observational research subjectivity may be easily introduced into the process of data collection. This in itself does not preclude observation as a justifiable technique of data collection, and it can often provide insights and data that no other method could do, although we need to remember that there is this potential for subjectivity, both in designing observational research methodologies and particularly in interpreting the results of observational research. Observational research is an approach to data collection where both researcher and interpreter need to be aware of the potential for subjectivity and the factors, both with regard to the researcher and the contextual factors, within which the research is conducted, which may affect the data collected and its interpretation.

Observational reactivity: the observed

It is now an established fact that knowing that one is being observed can affect the behaviour of the observed. This has come to be termed **observational reactivity**. One of the first studies to establish this in the area of management research was the Hawthorne Studies comprehensively reported by Greenwood and Wrege (1986). These studies demonstrated the fact that the work groups in the study knowing they were being observed altered their behaviour. The researcher using observational techniques needs to be aware of the potential for this effect, both in observational research design, and also in interpreting observational data. Attempting to eliminate observational reactivity on the part of those being observed is one of the main arguments used in support of unrevealed approaches to observation. Sometimes it may be so crucial to avoid any potential for observational reactivity that even otherwise strong ethical or practical arguments for revealing an observational research exercise to those being observed may be ignored.

Observational reactivity: the observer

The potential for changed behaviour as a result of observation not only applies to those being observed but also to the observer. This can be a particular problem in ethnographic research and particularly where this involves full participation on the part of the observer. For example, if the observer actually joins the group being observed, being a member of this group may over time lead to changes in the behaviour of the observer and ultimately to their perception and interpretation of what is being observed. Anthropologists refer to this phenomenon, somewhat crudely, as *going native*. What matters is not so much avoiding this phenomenon and sometimes it is beneficial to a research exercise, but it is something that the researcher needs to be aware of both in planning data collection and in its interpretation.

Ethical issues

Several times in this chapter I have referred to the ethical issues that surround observational research. In particular, we have seen that unrevealed observational research can give rise to major ethical issues for the researcher. The nature, importance and approaches by the researcher to these ethical issues will vary enormously according to the nature of the research and the specific circumstances. With observational research in particular, it is very important for the researcher to consider any ethical issues which may arise and how to best deal with these in a professional and competent manner.

Methodological issues

A major methodological issue is the extent to which observational research and data can be used to develop theories thereby extending and enhancing our wider knowledge of phenomena. This goes back to the issues considered in Chapter 2 and, for example, inductive versus deductive developments of theory. It is often argued that because observational research often concentrates on relatively limited and unstructured observations involving open participant observation, it cannot be used to collect data so as to enable the deductive development of theory. If this assertion is correct, this means that observational research findings cannot be generalized to situations outside of the situation and circumstances under which the observation data was generated. There are issues in generalizing from observational research and particularly where, for example, this observation takes place only within one organization, and is effectively a case study. Although it is possible to introduce a degree of scientific rigour within observational research with regard to sampling, data collection and analysis, much observational research is in fact situation specific. This does not necessarily decrease the importance and value of observational research, but we do need to be aware of its limitations with regard to the development of theory and more in generalizing from observational research findings.

Activity 8.4. List any reasons you can think of where 'going native' on the part of the observer might be advantageous.

 ## 8.5   Concluding comments

Observational research is now an established approach to collecting data in the area of organizations and management research. It is concerned with collecting primary data through looking and noting. There is now a rich history of this type of research being used to generate significant and valuable findings in the area of management in organizations.

   Observational research has many advantages over other techniques of data collection. In particular, it generates data based on what people or systems actually do rather than what they say, or it is claimed they do. There are several possible approaches to conducting observational research depending on the extent to which the research is structured or unstructured, revealed or unrevealed, natural or contrived, and participant or non-participant. Within these approaches specific techniques of data collection and recording range from mechanical or electronic means through to observation followed up by written case notes. Effective observational research requires the researcher to pay careful attention to the steps in planning and implementing such research, commencing with an assessment of the extent to which observation is an appropriate method through to determining the specific methods and techniques of data collection and recording to be used.

Finally, when considering using and planning the implementation of observational research, the researcher needs to pay careful attention to a number of other issues ranging from practical issues such as gaining access and permission through to more conceptual and methodological issues such as observational reactivity and the development of theories from observations.

8.6 References

Bales, R. F. (1950) *Interaction Process Analysis: A Method for the Study of Small Groups*, Cambridge, MA: Addison-Wesley.

Benyon, H. (1973) *Working for Ford*, Harmondsworth: Penguin.

Bryman, A. (1989) *Research Methods and Organization Studies*, London: Unwin Hyman.

Delbridge, R. and Kirkpatrick, I. (1994) 'Theory and practice of participant observation', in P. Wass and P. Wells (eds), *Principles and Practice in Business and Management Research*, Aldershot: Dartmouth, pp. 35–62.

Denscombe, M. (1998). *The Good Research Guide*, Buckingham: Open University Press.

Gill, J. and Johnson, P. (2002) *Research Methods for Managers*, 3rd edn, London: Sage.

Gouldner, A. W. (1954) *Patterns of Industrial Bureaucracy*, New York: Free Press.

Graziano, A.M. and Raulin, M.L. (2004) Research methods: A Process of Enquiry, 5th Edn, Harlow, Pearson Education Group.

Greenwood, R. G. and Wrege, C. D. (1986) 'The Hawthorne Studies', in D. A. Wren and J. A. Pearce (eds), *Papers Dedicated to the Development of Modern Management*, Academy of Management, pp. 24–35.

Lupton, T. (1963) *On the Shop Floor*, Oxford: Pergamon.

Minzberg, H. (1973) *The Nature of Managerial Work*, New York: Harper and Roe.

Mullins, L. (2002) *Management and Organizational Behaviour*, 6th edn, Harlow, Financial Times: Prentice Hall.

Robson, C. (2002) *Real World Research*, 2nd edn, Oxford: Blackwell.

Rosen, M. (1991) ' Breakfast at Spiro's dramaturgy and dominance' in P. Frost, L. Moorc, M. Louis, C. Lundberg and J. Martin (eds) *Reframing Organizational Culture*, Newbury Park, CA: Sage, pp. 77–89.

Roy, D. (1952) 'Quota restriction and goldbricking in a machine shop', *American Journal of Sociology*, 57, pp. 427–42.

Saunders, M., Lewis, P. and Thonhill, A. (2003) *Research Methods for Business Students*, 3rd edn, Harlow: Pearson Education.

van der Velde, M., Jansen, P. and Anderson, N. (2004) *Guide to Management Research Methods*, Oxford: Blackwell Publishing.

Walker, R. (1985) *Doing Research: A Handbook for Teachers*, London: Methuen.

8.7   Glossary

ethnographic research

A research approach which involves the observer Sociology participating and often *living* with the people being researched.

observational reactivity

A reaction on the part of those being observed whereby their actions and behaviour are influenced by the process of being observed.

9

Data Collection: Experimental, Quasi-experimental and Action Research

After completing this chapter you will be able to:

- understand the meaning and relevance of experimentation in the generation of primary data,
- discuss the key factors to consider when using this research methodology in the social sciences,
- compare the different approaches to designing experimental research methodologies including the techniques of laboratory experimentation, tests and field experiments,
- discuss the steps in designing experimental research,
- understand the limitations of classical experimentation in social science research and the ways in which quasi-experimental, and particularly action research can be used to overcome these.

Introduction

As we have seen, research methods can be divided into deductive versus inductive approaches. In the deductive research methods we can further distinguish between experimental versus non-experimental approaches to data collection. In this chapter we shall look at the range of experimental methods to collecting primary data. We shall consider the nature and purpose of experimental research designs and the application of these in the social sciences and in management consultancy research in particular. Although primarily associated with the physical sciences, we shall see that experimental research can have a major potential role to play in the social sciences, including our business management and consultancy research. We shall also see, however, that there are difficulties in applying true experimental research design in organizations and that, partly because of this, researchers often use quasi-experimental research designs for data collection in this area. Of particular interest and application to research in organizations, is the quasi-experimental research approach known as action research. We shall, therefore, consider this particular methodology in more detail.

9.1   The nature and purpose of experimentation: classical experimentation

Irrespective of the precise design of a particular experiment, with all the possible variations, all experimentation is concerned essentially with relationships between selected variables and in investigating cause and effect (Babbie 2001; McBurnie and White 2004; Pawson and Tille 2004; Wysocki 2004).

In so-called classical experimentation, these relationships and the establishment of cause and effect involve the use of comparison between a *control group* and an *experimental group*. Conditions for the experimental group are then manipulated by the experimenter by applying some condition or variable to the experimental group and then comparing the effects of this on the experimental group with the control group where no conditions or variables have been applied. The effect on the experimental group is therefore compared to the control group with a view to establishing the relationship between the condition or variable applied to the experimental group, and in particular the nature, if any, of causation.

A simple example will serve to illustrate this classical approach. Let us assume that the researcher is interested in investigating the potential effect of using a more democratic style of leadership on motivation in an organization. If the researcher decided to use an experimental design to investigate this issue, the start point would be to establish an experimental and a control group. The experimental group would be the group with which the more democratic style of leadership was used. In the control group, no changes would be made and therefore the presumably less democratic style of leadership being currently used would remain unchanged. The researcher would then seek to measure the effect of the more democratic style of leadership on the experimental group by comparing the outcome with the control group.

This, then, represents essentially the essence of the classical experimental approach. However, in order to generate reliable and valid data, the experimental approach requires consideration of three key factors that underpin the process of effective experimentation. Denscombe (1998) identifies these three key factors as 'controls', 'identifying causal factors' and 'observation and measurement'. These three factors are now explained.

Controls

Given that experimentation involves comparing a control group and an experimental group, obviously effective experimentation requires that the experimenter can control the situation and influences on both the control and the experimental group. The extent to which this control is effective determines the extent to which the researcher is able to identify and assess the range of variables that have any influence and ultimately the establishment of cause and effect. For example, if we wanted to experimentally assess the effect of fluoridated toothpaste on the health of teeth, we could select two groups, one the control group and one the experimental group; with the experimental group being given fluoridated toothpaste and the control group non-fluoridated toothpaste. If, say, the experiment was to be carried out over a 12-month period, at the end of this period we could then assess the health of the teeth of the two different groups in our experiment. Obviously, if we want to be able to establish the effect of our fluoridated toothpaste then we have to be able to control the circumstances and the environment of both control and experimental group. So, for example, in the experimental group we have to be able to control, or at least determine, the amount of fluoride being administered over the experimental period. Similarly, with both control and experimental group we need to be able to control, or again at least assess other factors which may affect the health of the subject group's teeth. Unless we can do this, we cannot draw any reliable and valid conclusions from our experimental study. This principle of control, then, is central to all experimental design. However, in the social sciences, and particularly where we are investigating relatively open social systems such as an organization, control can be difficult and sometimes impossible to achieve.

Denscombe (op. cit.) suggests five ways of introducing control into the design of experimental studies. The first way, Denscombe suggests, is to try to systematically 'eliminate' factors one by one from the experiment. For example, if we were investigating the factors affecting operative fatigue on a particular piece of machinery, we might start by eliminating mid-morning and mid-afternoon work breaks and observing the effect on operative fatigue. Given that this is the only variable altered, then it would be reasonable to assume that any observed changes in operative fatigue were due to the removal of these work breaks. Working through factors one at a time in this way is essentially a way of achieving some degree of control over factors affecting control and experimental group.

Denscombe's second way of trying to achieve control is by 'holding factors constant'. Here, variables that cannot be eliminated from the situation that might affect the outcome are held constant as far as possible. For example, if we are examining factors affecting the motivation of employees in a given situation, we might examine the effect of, say, wage increases on motivation by changing just this factor while holding all the other factors that might affect motivation constant. Clearly this can pose severe difficulties for the researcher in social science experiments. In the physical sciences, factors can be held constant to a much greater extent because the experiments can be carried out under laboratory conditions where it is much easier to hold factors constant. However, there are well-known examples of where the organizational researcher has effectively created 'laboratory type settings' for experimental research on human behaviour, in organizations. The Hawthorne Studies, mentioned in Chapter 7, are a good example of this. Here, the researchers were interested in exploring the effect of lighting on worker output in a particular part of the company's operations. In the experimental group all other factors, other than the lighting, were held constant while the lighting levels alone were varied in a special area set aside for this purpose in the factory where the other variables that might affect productivity could be controlled. We shall return to the use of laboratory-type experimentation in consultancy research later in the chapter. It is not impossible to hold factors constant in this way; it is simply more difficult than in the physical sciences.

Denscombe's third way of trying to achieve control when using experimentation in management/organizational research is what he refers to as 'balancing groups'. For example, if we are investigating the relationship between absenteeism at different levels in the managerial hierarchy, but we also feel that another factor, say social class, may also be a determining factor of rates of absenteeism, we can attempt to control or remove the possible effect of age by using control and experimental groups which have a similar spread of socio-economic groups.

Denscombe's fourth way to achieving control is more a question of mathematical or statistical methodology than anything else. Specifically, the researcher can attempt to ensure that as far as possible a large enough sample is chosen and that this sample is 'randomly selected' for both experimental and control groups. In this way, it is hoped to eliminate any stray individual effects that might affect the outcome of the experimental phenomena being explored.

Denscombe's fifth approach to control is in fact perhaps the most frequently used approach to exercising control in experimental methodology in the social sciences, and returns us to the start point of our discussion of control, and that is the use of 'control groups'. As already pointed out, the experimental process itself is based upon having a control and an experimental group. As far as possible, both control and experimental group should be both randomly selected and as similar as possible with respect to key characteristics. The researcher can then introduce the experimental factor, the subject of the investigation, to the experimental group with no changes being introduced with respect to the control group. The researcher can then assess the effect of the experimental factor on the experimental group by measuring the differences between the control group and the experimental group at the end of the experiment. (Adapted from M. Denscombe (1998): pp. 44–6.)

The extent to which control is possible, or sometimes even desirable, depends upon the setting for the experimental research. I have already suggested that laboratory type settings enable a much greater degree of control but can be difficult to achieve in the real world of organizations. As already stated, we shall return to the use of laboratory experiments later in the chapter, but we shall also be considering other types of settings/approaches to experimentation in organizations including the use of standardized tests and field experiments. We shall also be considering quasi-experimental methods.

Identifying causal factors

Remember, the experimental method has as its objective investigating the relationship between variables, and more specifically establishing cause and effect. Although sometimes it is useful simply to establish that two or more factors are linked in some way, as you will appreciate, it is much more useful to establish which of these factors is responsible for causation. In experimental research we refer to this relationship between variables in the experiment in terms of the notion of *dependent* and *independent variables*.

As experimentation is primarily concerned with establishing cause and effect, it is essential that the experiment is designed in such a way that the researcher can investigate and establish which are dependent and independent variables. The most important implication of the distinction between these two types of variables is that the researcher will be concerned to vary only the independent variables when conducting an experiment, observing the effect if any, of these variations on the dependent variables. Ideally then, the researcher must have a clear idea at the outset of which are dependent and independent variables, and may even have ideas with regard to not only the nature of these relationships and effects, but also their magnitude. Often the researcher will state these ideas in the form of a hypothesis that can then be tested by an appeal to the facts.

Observation and measurement

The third element, in Denscombe's key factors underpinning experimentation, is the processes of observation and measurement. Investigating relationships between factors requires the researcher to make observations. Sometimes these will comprise relatively unstructured assessments of the relationship between dependent and independent variables, with these relationships being expressed in terms such as 'an apparent link', 'the results would seem to suggest or indicate'. Much observation and measurement in experimental research, however, is based on much more definitive and often quantitative measurements stating or expressing relationships between dependent and independent variables with terms such as 'there is a 90% chance that the major factor in increasing motivation at work is levels of salary'. As with observation, or indeed as with in fact all data collection methods, the researcher needs to determine how results are to be observed and measured. This can affect how, in this case, the experiment is structured and conducted, and the extent to which experimentation as a methodology is valid at all.

Activity 9.1. Propose a hypothetical organizational issue or problem that might be investigated through the application of an experimental approach.

For your proposed issue or problem, outline how you would attempt to achieve control in applying the experimental approach.

9.2   Structuring experimental research design: key steps

Of all the techniques of primary data collection, experimental research requires systematic and structured procedures with regard to research design and the collection of the data. The following represent the key steps in systematic experimental research.

Establishing the questions/formulating hypotheses

The first step in experimental research is to establish the questions or problems the research is attempting to address. As mentioned earlier, the more specifically these questions or problems can be stated the better. The design of the subsequent stages of the experimental approach stems from the questions or problems to be addressed. In experimental research in particular, the research questions or problems will be expressed in the form of a *hypothesis* which is to be tested through the research.

Experimentation to support or refute hypotheses is well established in the development of science and knowledge (Black 1999; Bechhofer and Paterson 2000; Hakim 2000). A hypothesis represents a statement reflecting a set of assumptions, usually regarding the relationships between one or more factors, sometimes additionally couched in terms of cause and effect, which can then be tested, or more specifically, supported or refuted by the collection of evidence or data.

Often, hypotheses will be couched so that they can be tested through quantitative statistical technique. Various statistical tests for association are available with perhaps the best known of these being the **Chi-squared test**. Where quantitative statistical techniques are to be used, then the hypothesis will normally be couched in terms of the so-called **null hypothesis**. A null hypothesis is a hypothesis that is stated in such a way that it can either be supported or rejected through analysis of data. Using the Chi-squared test, for example, a null hypothesis will either be supported or rejected by comparing the observed versus the expected data. Where the null hypothesis is rejected through the data then the data supports the **alternative hypothesis**. For example, suppose the researcher were investigating the relationship between the quality of after sales service and the location of purchase, the null hypothesis might be, for example, that *after sales service and location of purchase are not related*. We could then test this hypothesis by collecting data on the quality of after sales service by location of purchase, say perhaps mail order versus retail. The Chi-squared test compares the recorded or *observed* data, in this case regarding quality of service and location of purchase, with that which would have been *expected* had location of purchase and quality of service been assumed to have been independent. By comparing the observed and expected frequencies the Chi-squared test enables the researcher to see whether the assumption or *null hypothesis* is supported or rejected by the data. If the data does not support the null hypothesis we reject this hypothesis in favour of the alternative hypothesis that claims that location of purchase and quality of service are not independent. Admittedly, somewhat confusingly then, it is support for the alternative hypothesis and in turn then the rejection of the null hypothesis which is evidence of inter-relationships.

Identifying/specifying independent and dependent variables

Not all experimental research is based around statistically testable hypotheses, and sometimes the experimental research may centre rather on relatively ill-defined sets of assumptions as evidenced in the statement of the research questions or problems. At the very least, however, there should be some sort of tentative hypotheses. Irrespective of the manner in which hypotheses are expressed, for all experimental research the researcher must identify and distinguish between what were referred to earlier in the chapter as 'dependent' and 'independent variables'.

A key step in the experimental research design, therefore, is to identify the particular phenomenon or factor whose variation we are trying to explain or understand, the *dependent variable* (e.g. variations in the level of motivation) and the particular phenomenon or factors which the researcher is suggesting explains or causes changes in our dependent variable (e.g. in continuing our example, say, money). This is the 'independent variable'.

The researcher should always try to specify the phenomena or factors whose variation the research is attempting to explain or understand and those phenomena or factors the researcher is suggesting might cause or explain these variations.

Operationalizing variables

In order to assess variations in both dependent and independent variables, it is necessary to what is called *operationalize* them. Operationalizing a variable is defining it in terms of the actual procedures to be used to measure or manipulate it (Kerlinger 1992). Although the process of operationalizing experimental variables can be extremely complex, essentially the process relates to ensuring that the researcher can observe and measure any variations in the dependent and independent variables and also that the researcher is able to systematically vary or manipulate the incident or magnitude, and so on, of the independent variables.

For example, if we are investigating a hypothesis which relates to the relationship between, *managerial success* (the dependent variable) and *intelligence* (the independent variable) first of all we must define and refine our terminology with respect to our dependent and independent variables such that we are able to be quite clear about what, in this case, managerial success and intelligence mean, and how to measure them. In addition, we must be able to vary the independent variable (in this case intelligence) so as to observe the effect of these variations. Operationalizing experimental variables often confronts the researcher with one of the most difficult and challenging elements of experimental design. Although we need not concern ourselves with the issues here, operationalizing experimental variables can have major implications for the extent to which research results can be generalized to a range of situations or settings.

Experimental control

This step in the design of the experimental research is concerned with how to try to achieve control in the experimental process. We have looked at the importance of, and the approaches to, introducing controls into the design of experimental research earlier in this chapter. To remind you, we used Denscombe's framework (op. cit.) which suggests that control in experimentation can be achieved by means of: eliminating factors, holding factors constant, balancing groups, random selection and the use of control groups. In addition, the setting or context for the research will also have a major affect on the degree of control that can be achieved. In particular, there are major differences with respect to control between experimental research that is carried out in *laboratory* settings and those that are conducted in the field – not surprisingly known as field experiments. Again, we have touched on laboratory experiments with regard to the degree of control that can be exercised earlier in the chapter. The term laboratory here of course may not mean the same thing as in the physical sciences, it may, for example, simply comprise an area set aside by the researcher from the normal environment of the organization where the experimental research can be conducted. The Hawthorne experiments mentioned earlier, which were laboratory experiments, were carried out in this way. Field experiments on the other hand, are those where the research takes place in the actual work/organizational environment/setting. In fact, most so called field experiments are not true experiments in the real sense of the word, but are usually quasi-experiments, an approach to which we shall return shortly. With the importance of control in the experimental method we might be tempted to think that wherever possible only laboratory experimentation should be used as it affords a much greater degree of control than can usually be achieved with field experiments. However, there is a downside to laboratory experiments, namely the fact that by their very nature, laboratory experiments especially in organizational and management research tend to be unnatural and artificial. In fact, some argue that because of this artificiality, laboratory experiments are of little or no use in the area of management and organizational research. Bryman (1989) a protagonist of this argument goes so far as to suggest that the results of the ensuing findings of laboratory experiments in management research 'have little validity beyond the confines of the laboratory'. While not going so far as this, it is true that great care needs to be taken to try to minimize the degree of unnaturalness or artificiality of the conditions surrounding any laboratory research in management and organizations, particularly when it comes to interpreting the findings of this approach to experimental research (Graziano & Raulin 2004). On the other hand, of course, with field experiments it is often difficult and sometimes impossible to control all the variables that might affect the research.

Experimental methodology and data collection

The final elements in the structuring of experimental research design concerns the selection and design of the specific experimental methodology and means of data collection to be used. The experimental approach to research that we have outlined here is essentially a strategy for research rather than a specific method. When it comes to the details of experimental methodology and data collection design there are very many alternatives. The specific method chosen will depend upon many factors, some of the key ones being: the nature of the precise research objectives, the problems or questions being investigated, the nature of the phenomenon of variables being investigated including how they are to be measured and how the data is to be analysed and assessed once it has been collected including techniques of quantitative and statistical analysis.

These are the steps in structuring experimental research design and some of the key ideas underpinning the experimental approach. However, we have also seen that true experimentation in the classical sense is difficult and sometimes impossible in organizational settings. In addition, where the researcher can overcome some of these difficulties through, for example, the use of laboratory-type experiments, there is the problem of artificiality. Because of this, often in management and organizational research, the researcher will use a quasi-experimental approach. It is to this category of quasi-experiments for collecting data on management issues and problems, and particularly the use of so-called action research, to which we now turn our attention.

Activity 9.2. For your issue/problem selected for Activity 9.1 earlier:
(a) State the issue or problem in the form of a hypothesis that could be tested through experimentation.
(b) Identify independent and dependent variables.
(c) Briefly explain how you might operationalize the experimental variables.

9.3   Quasi-experimentation

Because of the problems of achieving control in experimentation in organizational settings, allied to the fact that, as we have seen, control achieved through laboratory settings raises problems of artificiality, the researcher may instead use a variation on true or classical experimentation, usually referred to as *quasi-experiments*. Most field research that uses some of the experimental methodology falls into the category of quasi-experimentation. The aim of quasi-experimentation is still to analyse and assess causal relationships between independent and dependent variables but to explore these relationships in a real-life field setting where full experimental methodology and particularly control cannot be applied (Campbell 1969). With quasi-experimental methods there is usually less or even no control over the independent variables and a lack of equivalence between experimental and control groups. Because of this it is often difficult therefore, to control extraneous factors that may affect the phenomena being investigated. However, this disadvantage is offset by the fact that quasi-experiments are less artificial and therefore perhaps potentially more representative of real-life situations and issues. One of the best comparisons of true experiments versus quasi-experiments is that provided by Gill and Johnson (1997) and shown in Table 9.1.

Table 9.1   True experiments versus quasi experiments: a comparison

True experiments	*Quasi experiments*
Entail the analysis of the direct intervention of the researcher	Entail the analysis of events that have naturally occurred without the intervention of the researcher, that is, after the fact
Incidence of the independent variable due to the manipulations of the researcher	Incidence of the independent variable occurs naturally
Entail pre- and post-treatment, measurement and comparison of the dependent variable in both the experimental and the control groups	Entail pre- and post- treatment, measurement and comparison of the dependent variable in both the experimental and the control groups
Entail physical control over extraneous variables through assignation of subjects to equivalent experimental and control groups	Since analysis entails naturally occurring events, prior assignation of subjects to control and experimental groups problematic. Instead, control and experimental groups are identified in terms of the incidence of the independent variable and cannot be exactly matched
Strengths: High internal validity	*Strengths* High ecological validity. Avoids problems associated with experimental artefacts; can have high population validity
Weaknesses Low ecological validity; often population validity is limited	*Weaknesses* Loss of control over extraneous variables

Source: Adapted from Gill and Johnson (1997) p. 60.

There are many advantages to quasi-experimental approaches to data collection and research in organizational settings but the most important of these is the fact that it retains many of the advantages of the true experimental approach such as the potential for exploring causality, and the opportunity for replication while, at the same time being less artificial. As with true experimental research, quasi-experimental research can be conducted using many alternative methodologies and research designs. For example, a widely used quasi-experimental research design used in management and organizational research is that of the so-called *ex post facto research* method where the researcher starts with an observed phenomenon and then sets out to deduce what factors could possibly account for the phenomenon observed. In other words, in this approach the researcher works backwards from the effect to find the cause. Another very popular technique is that of the *non-equivalent control group design* which allows the researcher to compare groups which 'already exist in the natural environment and therefore may not be truly equivalent at the start of the study' (Graziano and Raulin, op. cit. p. 295). Many organizational and management problems and issues are suitable for this type of quasi-experimental research and indeed it can be a highly successful approach particularly for consultancy-type research. Another example of quasi-experimental research is where the researcher conducts, say, a before and after research project. For example, a group of managers who have attended a leadership course could be researched with respect to their managerial behaviour and skills, and so on before and after their attendance on the course. Researchers in the social sciences in particular have recognized the value of quasi-experimental research, admittedly it is not *scientific* in the true meaning of the experimental method but at least it can 'approximate the logic of the true experiment' (Gill and Johnson 2002).

One of the recent and most interesting, and many would argue, useful approaches to quasi-experimental research in management and organizations, is the so-called *action research* approach, which has been introduced earlier and which we shall now consider in more detail.

9.4 Action research

Like experimental research in general, action research in fact, is more a strategy or approach to research rather than a specific methodology. Within a strategy or approach of action research the researcher may use a wide variety of methodologies including, for example, observational research, questioning and surveys and even laboratory experimentation. Although considered a variant of the quasi-experimental research approach, in some ways perhaps action research can be considered as different and important enough in its own right to represent a separate branch of methodology. We need not concern ourselves though with these arguments regarding where it is placed in the gamut of research methodologies, but we certainly need to consider what action research is, how it is used and its relevance and value to organizational research in general and the process of executive development and consultancy research in particular. So what is action research?

Unfortunately, virtually every protagonist of, or writer on, action research seems to have their own perspective on precisely what action research is and what it entails (Schon 1995; Alvesson and Wilmott 1996; Dickens and Watkin 1999; McNiff 2000). However, thankfully, there are some broad measures of general agreement regarding the nature and purpose of action research. Based on these, here is what is felt to be a good interpretation of the meaning and purpose of action research.

Action research involves practical hands-on field research in an organization where the researcher has the objective of solving practical, real-world problems in the organization.

> (An) approach to design (that) involves a planned intervention by a researcher, or more often a consultant, into some naturally occurring events. The effects of that intervention are then monitored and evaluated with the aim of discerning whether or not that action has produced the expected consequences, in other words, the researcher acts upon his, or her, beliefs or theories.
>
> ... action researchers intend not only to contribute to existing knowledge but also to help resolve some of the practical concerns of the people, or clients who are trying to deal with a problematic situation.
>
> *Source*: Gill and Johnson (1997) p. 59.

We can immediately see from this explanation how relevant action research is in the context of consultancy-based research in an organization. In fact, action research essentially is a consultancy or rather at least an approach to conducting consultancy. In one of the earliest and most significant discussions of action research, Lewin (1946) although not proposing any comprehensive definition of the term, described action research as being essentially 'problem centred research' which in turn involved some kind of action and research on the effects of that action in the organization. But what does action research entail and what are the characteristics of action research?

- *Problem centred*: As already outlined, action research centres on investigating and addressing practical issues and problems in organizations with a view to trying to address these.
- *Participation*: In action research the researcher actively participates in the organization and in addressing the problems identified. The researcher is active rather than passive. The researcher also participates in implementing proposed solutions to problems and in turn assessing the outcomes and effectiveness, and so on, of any actions taken.
- *Cyclical*: Related to the above, action research involves a feedback loop in which changes are implemented and then evaluated with a view to further research and change processes.

- *Co-operation/partnerships*: Where research is conducted for a client, as in many consultancy projects of course, both consultant and client co-operate as partners in the research itself, implementing proposals and taking further action.
- *Professional development*: Action research is also aimed at helping individuals develop as better managers. In other words, unlike much academic research, which focuses almost exclusively on the development of theoretical and scientific knowledge, action research is also aimed at developing the individual through implementing and evaluating action programmes in organizations.

The development of action research in some ways stemmed from an awareness of the limitations of most traditional academic approaches to research and particularly where this was based on using the more traditional and classical experimental methods of research when it came to researching social phenomena including, of course, organizations and management. In a sense then, action research evolved from a feeling of dissatisfaction with the artificiality of laboratory-type research which was examined earlier. Action researchers felt that the disadvantages of less control and *unscientific methodologies* that to some extent are inherent in action research, were offset by much more problem-centred real-world approaches to research and problems in organizations. Action research, then, is virtually akin to conventional managerial consultancy approaches rather than the more academic research approaches associated with the social scientist. Having said this, action research has more often than not been used by academics in their research into organizations and management. Where action research is used for academic purposes in this way, there can be issues with regard to, for example, who owns the research, and related to this, the use and publication of the research findings. There are also issues related to the extent to which the research should only focus on solutions to organizational and management problems as opposed to the development of knowledge in its own right. Again, we need not concern ourselves with these issues here. More relevant issues with regard to this text concerning action research relate to the following:

- *Consultancy or academic research*: This issue with regard to action research concerns the fact that action research, being centred on real organizational problems, and implementing actions in an attempt to resolve these, very much fits the consultancy mode of approach. On the other hand, action research is also used in the context of developing knowledge and theories about organizations and their functioning. In this case, although addressing practical organizational problems is still the focus, the main aim of the researcher is to develop broader theoretical knowledge. In fact, these two aims or objectives for action research are not mutually exclusive, nor need they necessarily conflict. Some of the most useful additions to our theories of management and organizations have stemmed from consultancy-type problem-centred action research. So long as both researcher and client agree upon the objectives and remit for the action research at the start, then this should pose no problems.

- *Who chooses the problem to be addressed*: Related to the issue of consultancy versus academic research is the issue of who decides which organizational issues or problems are to be addressed. In much consultancy research, at the entry stage, or the start of the consultancy process, it is the client that presents problems and defines goals. In action research, however, it may be that the researcher presents the problem. For example, an organizational researcher might be interested in exploring the area of *the effect of internal marketing on an organization* and elects to use an action-based research methodology to explore this. Here then the researcher takes the *problem* to the client. Again, this apparent dilemma between who chooses the problem to be addressed can best be resolved where irrespective of who presents the problem in the first instance, both client and consultant mutually agree upon the goals for the research and how these will be approached.

- *Who owns the problem*: Yet again, there is an issue that stems from action research as an academic exercise versus action research as a consultancy exercise. This issue is concerned with the extent to which action research results and findings are made available to the wider organizational and academic community. In a conventional consultancy exercise, any findings including prescriptions for action normally *belong* to the client organization, as for example, any suggestions for improvement as a result of action research findings would not be expected to be made available outside of the organization. Because, however, action research is often undertaken by academics, albeit in a consultancy-type mode, very often the idea is to make any important findings about an organizational issue or problem revealed through the action research available to the wider academic community, often in published form. Again, the solution to this dilemma is for researcher and client to agree upon at the outset who owns the problem and the extent to which results and findings can be made available or published on a wider basis.

There is no doubt that in management research, action research is a particularly valuable and useful tool where the research is organizational/problem-based and where the researcher, to a great extent, approaches this as a consultant. Moreover, the very nature of action research allows both organization and researcher to implement actions and observe the results of these interventions at first hand. Ideas, theories and techniques can be actioned in response to an identified problem and the effects monitored and evaluated. In some ways, then, action research is akin to *real-life* experimentation.

Activity 9.3. Identify a hypothetical organizational issue or problem that might usefully be addressed through an action research approach.

What would be, in your view, the advantages of using an action-based research approach to your identified problem or issue?

9.5 Concluding comments

In this chapter we have investigated the experimental approach to collecting primary data and conducting research in organizations. We have considered the nature and purpose of experimental research designs and the problems of the application of these in the social sciences and in management/consultancy research in particular. We have seen that although there are problems in applying this approach, in fact experimental research can, and does, have a major potential role to play. Because of the difficulties, however, in applying true experimental research design in organizations, researchers often use quasi-experimental research designs for data collection in this area. When it comes to consultancy-type research, and particularly where the consultancy exercise is related to the process of executive and manager development, action research has several advantages as a methodology.

 ## 9.6 References

Alveson, M. and Wilmott, H. (1996) *Making Sense of Management,* London: Sage.

Babbie, E. (2001) *The Practice of Social Research,* 9th edn, Belmont, CA: Wadsworth/Thomson.

Bechhofer, F. and Paterson, L. (2000) *Principles of Research Design in the Social Sciences,* London: Routledge.

Black, T. R. (1999) *Doing Quantitative Research in the Sociall Sciences: An Integrated Approach To Research Design, Measurement and Statistics,* London: Sage.

Bryman, A. (1989) *Research Methods and Organisation Studies,* London: Routledge.

Campbell, D. T. (1969) 'Reforms as experiments', *American Pschycologist,* 24, 409–29.

Denscombe, M. (1998) *The Good Research Guide,* Buckingham: Open University Press.

Dickens, L. and Watkins, K. (1999) 'Action research: rethinking Lewin', *Management Learning,* 30(2): pp. 127–40.

Gill, J. and Johnson, P. (1997) *Research Methods for Managers,* 2nd edn, London: Paul Chapman.

Gill, J. and Johnson, P. (2002) *Research Methods for Managers,* 3rd edn, London: Sage, p. 66.

Graziano, A. M. and Raulin, M. L. (2004) *Research Methods: A Process of Inquiry,* 5th edn, Boston: Pearson Group.

Hakim, C. (2000) *Research Design,* London: Routledge.

Kerlinger, F. N. (1992) *Foundations of Behavioural Research,* 3rd edn, Fort Worth, TX: Harcourt Brace.

Lewin, K. (1946) 'Action research and minority problems', *Journal of Social Issues,* 2(4) pp. 34–46.

McBurney, D. H. and White, T. L. (2004) *Research Methods,* 6th edn, Belmont, CA: Wadsworth/Thomphson.

McNiff, J. (2000) *Action Research in Organizations,* London: Routledge.

Parson, R. and Tille, N. (2004) 'Go forth and experiment', in C. Seale (ed.) *Social Research Methods: A Reader,* London: Routledge.

Schon, D. (1995) @Knowing-in-action: the new scholarship requires a new epistomology', *Change,* November–December.

Wysocki, D. K. (2004) *Readings in Social Research Methods*, 2nd edn, Belmont, CA: Wadsworth/Thompson.

9.7 Glossary

alternative hypothesis	Presented as a contrast to the null hypothesis. If the evidence rejects the validity of the null hypothesis, the alternative hypothesis is accepted.
chi-squared test	A statistical test which compares recorded or observed data with that which would have been expected in order to measure the degree of association between dependent and independent variables.
control group	The group, including individuals, units, departments, and other such, which is not subjected to experimental variables and change and therefore serves as a reference point with regard to any observed changes and their possible causes in the experimental group.
dependent variables	Those variables which change only as a result of changes to the independent variables.
experimental group	The group, including individuals, units, departments, and other such, which is subjected to experimental variables and change by the researcher.
***ex post facto* research**	A quasi-experimental research method based on observing cause and effect and then working backwards from the effect to try and establish the cause.
hypothesis	A set of assumptions provisionally accepted as a basis of reasoning, experiment or investigation.
independent variables	Those variables which are responsible for changes in other variables.
null hypothesis	an underlying assumption made about a population, the validity of which is the subject of a statistical test.
operationalize	The process whereby the dependent and independent variables to be researched are defined and specified in a way that allows both dependent and independent variables to be observed and measured and allows for the variation and manipulation of the independent variables.
quasi-experiments	Techniques of research aimed at analysing causal relationships between independent and dependent variables but where full experimental control is not present.

10

Data Collection: Asking Questions

Learning Outcomes

By the end of this chapter you will:

- understand the importance and value of using questioning as a means of collecting data,
- know the advantages and disadvantages of questioning as a means of data collection,
- understand the range and types of approaches to using questioning,
- understand the major considerations in planning and designing interviews in an organization,
- appreciate the importance and value of questionnaires as a means of data collection,
- understand the links between questionnaires, surveys and sampling techniques.

Introduction

In this chapter we shall be considering what is probably one of the most obvious ways of collecting data in organizations, especially where this data involves collecting data from, or about, people – namely, asking questions. After all, if you want to know, say, how someone feels about some aspect of an organization's functioning or what problems they encounter, or perhaps what they feel

---

I am grateful to Richard Charlesworth and Peter Morley for permission to *use* their materials on 'Questionnaire Design'.

might be done about something, it makes sense to simply ask them. Asking questions, then, is one of the most direct ways of collecting data and is potentially at least, one of the simplest. However, as we shall see, in fact asking questions can also involve complex techniques and processes especially when it comes to asking questions through the use of, say, questionnaires or when using sampling surveys. In addition, even the apparently simplest questioning exercises involve and require considerable skills and planning on the part of the questioner. We shall be examining these skills and planning elements in addition to considering the range of approaches and techniques for asking questions as a way of collecting data, ranging from highly unstructured open-ended approaches involving what are essentially conversations to the highly structured forms of questioning used in survey-type approaches using questionnaires.

10.1   Questioning as a means of data collection

As already mentioned, we can see that if we often are in a management research consultancy exercise, concerned to elicit the opinions, ideas, and feelings of people, it makes a lot of sense to ask them directly. After all, what could be easier than asking individuals about the problems or issues we are researching in an organization. As already mentioned, and as we shall see, collecting data through questioning involves a wide range of possible approaches and techniques, some of them technically complex and all of them encompassing a range of high-level skills and knowledge on the part of the researcher. In fact many advise that designing questionnaires in particular is much more difficult than one might suppose (Bell 1999; Oppenheimer 2000). We shall see that there are many limitations and problems, to collecting data through questioning techniques, but as you would expect, with a set of data collection techniques that are so widely used by researchers in the social sciences, there are also distinct advantages to using questioning in general as a method of producing data. Some of the main advantages of questioning as a set of techniques include the following:

Advantages of questioning

- *Depth and complexity of data*: Questioning, and especially techniques such as face-to-face interviews, is a particularly useful way of collecting data which has the potential at least for substantial depth and detail, and where the data encompasses complex issues.
- *Flexibility*: Questioning can allow for much greater flexibility on the part of he researcher. The researcher can, depending on the techniques of questioning being used, adapt the line of questioning to suit the circumstances. Admittedly not all questioning techniques are highly flexible and the use of standardized questionnaires in particular does not offer this advantage. In general, questioning is the most flexible approach of all the research methods available.
- *Simplicity*: Admittedly, not all questioning techniques are simple, but many are and may involve, for example, no more than the researcher having to make

contact with the respondent and engaging the respondent in conversation. In contrast to, for example, some laboratory-type experimentation, questioning is essentially simple in concept.

- *Feedback/validity*: Face to face questioning techniques in particular allow the researcher to provide feedback to respondents immediately upon collecting the data. This, in turn, enables the researcher to check the validity and relevance of data as it is collected.
- *Personal/motivating*: Many of the approaches to collecting data through questioning involve the researcher in personal contact with the respondents. The skilled questioner can, through the establishment of trust and openness, quickly build a personal rapport with respondents enabling data which would be impossible to elicit through any other method. Simply being asked questions about their opinions, views, and so on, may, if the researcher has the requisite interpersonal skills, actually provide a rewarding and motivating experience for the informant. Most people like to be asked, and like to talk.
- *Large numbers/wide coverage*: The use of questionnaires and survey techniques as a way of administering questions can enable the researcher to question potentially large numbers of respondents and achieve, if required, a wide coverage. Related to this, effectively planned sampling can, in combination with potentially large numbers, add to the validity and reliability of data.
- *Speed*: Compared to some other methods of data collection, in particular for example, experimentation, questioning can be designed and implemented relatively quickly, being particularly useful therefore, where the researcher has a short implementation horizon and/or where circumstances dictate speed of data collection.

These, then, are some of the major advantages of questioning as a means of data collection. As you would expect, of course there are also some potential disadvantages as well.

Disadvantages of questioning

- *Respondent bias/reaction*: With face-to-face questioning in particular there is a potential disadvantage that respondents may react to the fact that they are being questioned and/or to the questioner himself. In particular there can be problems of fear or mistrust when people are asked, for example, about how they perform a task, or how they feel about senior management, and so on. This in turn can lead to the respondent providing, consciously or not, inaccurate data.
- *Data collection and analysis*: Although some techniques of questioning such as formal questionnaires allow relatively straightforward data collection and analysis processes, some questioning techniques such as unstructured interviews produce data that is both difficult to record and difficult to subsequently analyse. Attempts to resolve problems of data collection through the use of, say, tape recorders, video cameras and other such methods (i.e. some of the observational tools described earlier), can affect and/or inhibit respondents.

- *Fear/antagonism*: Although the skills of an experienced questioner can reduce this problem, as we saw earlier, there is always the potential for questioning by someone either inside, and particularly, outside of the organization to give rise to fear and consequently antagonism. Admittedly, as we have suggested, questioning can be a rewarding experience for respondents but it can also be daunting.
- *Lack of control/unreliability*: Although we saw that questioning can, through feedback and probing on the part of the questioner, lead to greater reliability, often questioning techniques are used in situations and contexts where it is difficult to achieve consistency across different situations. For example, an interview schedule may go very well with one individual but not with another.
- *Some questioning devices are limited*: Questionnaires in particular are limited in the sorts of data that can be collected. They are, for example, less effective for exploratory type research (Saunders et al. 2003) and where the information required is of a more qualitative or open-ended nature (Robson 2002).

The range and scope of questioning techniques

There is an extremely wide range of different types of approaches to using questioning techniques to collect data. Taxonomies of questioning techniques distinguish the different types of techniques and approaches using a number of dimensions. For example, we have techniques classified with regard to how structured the questioning process is. Another dimension used to distinguish between different techniques distinguishes between how the questions are administered, for example personal/face-to-face techniques of questioning versus questions asked through, say, a postal questionnaire or perhaps a telephone interview (Fink and Kosecoff 1998, Sapsford 1999). Some of the key dimensions that can be used to differentiate and distinguish between different questioning techniques and approaches for data collection are shown in Figure 10.1 which illustrates the alternative extremes for each dimension.

With so many dimensions which can be combined in different ways, we can see that there is a plethora of different approaches to, and techniques of, questioning ranging from, for example, the highly informal and unstructured

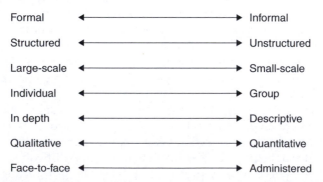

Figure 10.1 Questioning approaches and techniques: dimensions and differences

open-ended technique of *conversation* questioning, through to large scale administered questionnaires highly formalized and structured and using large samples. We cannot hope to consider all of these techniques of and approaches to
questioning in this chapter, so subsequent discussion will introduce you to the
main types of questioning techniques concentrating on the main categories of
techniques available to the management researcher/consultant. In doing so, I
shall include in our discussion the topics of questionnaire design and survey
methods. It is to these techniques that we now turn our attention, beginning
first with the category of techniques labelled 'Interviews'.

Activity 10.1. List three hypothetical organizational issues/problems for which
interviewing might be a useful and appropriate method of data collection.

10.2   Interviews

Interviews are a major category of techniques for collecting data through questioning and are acknowledged as being some of the most effective ways of collecting data in the social sciences (Healey and Rawlinson 1994; Easterby-Smith
et al. 2002). As we shall see, the range of possible approaches to planning and
conducting interviews encompasses the full range of dimensions shown in
Figure 10.1. Among the major techniques and approaches to interviewing are
the following.

Conversations and story telling

Perhaps at first glance this might seem to be a surprising technique to include
in a discussion of primary research methods. It is in fact an approach to collecting data which often proves extremely fruitful in the context of organizational and management research.

Essentially in this approach the researcher/consultant begins to gather data
through the process of joining in or in some circumstances simply listening in
to conversation and general gossip and story telling in an organization (Wilkins
1983; Yiannis 1998). Perhaps not surprisingly then, this interviewing technique
is felt to be particularly appropriate in ethnographic research (Foddy 1993;
Morton Williams 1993; Arksey and Knight 1999). Data gleaned in this way has
characteristics that often cannot be achieved in any other way. For example,
data revealed in day-to-day conversations and gossip in an organization may
be much more open and honest than where, for example, the researcher specifically questions respondents about an issue. Obviously, to gain data in this way
means that the researcher must be able to at least listen in to, or better still, par-
ticipate in conversation with informants. It is possible to listen in on conversations in a covert way even perhaps recording such conversation, but this raises
all sorts of ethical and even legal issues, and for the most part, is to be avoided.

On the other hand, listening into conversations as a non-participant observer,
where the researcher reveals their presence and objectives, but does not take

part, can inhibit the sorts of information that might be gleaned in this way. Ideally, conversational approaches work best where the researcher is involved in some sort of ethnographic research, as outlined earlier and where the researcher, therefore, is accepted and treated as a normal member of the group. At first glance, we might be tempted to discount this approach as questioning conversations and story telling seem a little too unscientific and unstructured to be valuable, but we should not neglect this potentially powerful approach to organizational research. In any event, the researcher can often introduce structure into a 'normal' conversational situation perhaps initiating conversation about areas and topics of interest and/or skilfully steering the conversation to explore issues that the researcher is concerned to explore.

Individual semi-structured interviews

Here, the questioning centres around the researcher taking a respondent through predetermined issues and topics, but not in a rigid manner or necessarily in a rigid order. The difference between this type of questioning technique and conversations is, of course, the fact that the topics and issues to be covered are largely determined in advance as are the individuals whom the researcher intends to interview. Normally, interviews of this type will not involve the use of a pre-prepared interview schedule and certainly rarely will a questionnaire be used. The semi-structured individual interview is designed to be focused in terms of topics covered and yet flexible in that it is possible and often desirable to steer questions into areas that appear promising from the point of view of providing rich data and/or additional insights. A second major difference between this approach to interviewing and the conversational/story telling approach is that respondents will, of course, be aware that they are being interviewed and questioned, a fact that needs to be taken account of, in both the design and the interpretation of questions and answers.

Depth interviews

This is where a respondent is interviewed in some detail and often for a protracted period in order for the researcher to explore topics, issues and responses in some depth (Walker 1985). There will often be less structure than in the semi-structured interview with the questioning reflecting the responses given by the informant. Depth interviews are of course widely used in psychological research and examination. A number of techniques are available for use during depth interviews including, for example, critical incident analysis, fantasy exploration, and projective techniques (Strauss and Corbin 1990; Symon and Cassell 1998).

Group interviews

Although conversational questioning often takes place in a group setting, other approaches to interviewing outlined so far in this chapter are primarily individual interviews. Sometimes, however, the researcher may wish to interview several informants together. Group interviews are used where the interaction between the members of the group, that is, the group dynamics, leads to data which otherwise might not be made available. For example, often the responses of one group member will spark an idea or perhaps even a rebuttal on the part of another group member. Group interviews have several advantages over individual interviews, in particular with respect to this generation of richer data and the possible revelation of consensus views. Conducting group interviews, however, requires considerable skills on the part of the interviewer and an awareness of some of the potential pitfalls of interviewing in groups. For example, in most groups there is always one person who will try to dominate the conversation. Often, however, it is the quiet ones in the group who have the most valuable things to say. Another problem with group interviews is that certain views or ideas may not be expressed because they are felt to be unacceptable in some way to the norms of the group. The skilful interviewer can, with experience, overcome these problems and disadvantages and use the dynamics of the group situation to generate extremely rich data.

Focus groups

In some areas of management research the focus group has become the most widely used form of interview technique. The term *focus group* has superseded the old term used to describe this kind of research which was *group discussion*. Marketeers in particular lean heavily on the techniques of focus group interviews in their market research and other activities. In fact, focus groups are a variation, if you like, of a particular type of group interview, the difference being that the focus group interviewing approach uses certain techniques and stratagems to elicit data. Briefly, focus groups operate in the following way:

Focus groups normally consist of between six and ten participants. A trained researcher or *moderator* as they are often termed, steers the group to discuss predetermined areas or aspects that the researcher is interested in exploring. This is where the term 'focus' comes from in that the interviewer will focus the discussion between members of the group into these areas. This focusing usually takes the form of a prompt or some sort of stimulus introduced by the moderator that is relevant to the researcher's interest. For example, the moderator might ask the group to consider *attitudes* towards female managers in the organization. The moderator will then encourage the group to interact in discussing the issues surrounding the prompt or trigger with a view to trying to establish overall group feelings, any consensus, and so on.

Focus groups are particularly useful for exploring attitudes, perceptions and feelings about a topic and like group interviews in general, may reveal data and insights that individual interviews would not (Denscombe 1998; Marshall and Rossman 1999).

These, then, are the most widely used interviewing techniques. They are not mutually exclusive either between each other or with other data collection methods and techniques. Indeed, interviewing is often used in conjunction with other approaches to collecting data. Either as preliminary research before, for example, setting up experimentation or perhaps to help support or refute data collected by other means. Remember, this is what was referred to in Chapter 6 as the process of 'triangulation' using several data collection techniques. You may be surprised that I have not included the use of questionnaires in our discussion of interview techniques. Certainly, questionnaires can be and are used to conduct interviews, but the general view is that they are more properly a technique of *questioning* in their own rights. With this in mind we shall shortly consider questionnaires as a method of data collection in more detail, but to conclude our discussion of interviews as questioning devices we need to consider some of the considerations and issues in the planning, conducting and interpretation of interviews.

Planning and conducting interviews

The precise steps in planning and conducting interviews will vary according to, for example, the type of interview being conducted including the sorts of data being collected, the circumstances of the interview, whether or not the interviewer is from inside the organization or is external to it, and so on. However, there are a number of key steps and considerations in planning and conducting interviews that are common to virtually all interview methods of collecting data. These are as follows:

- *Determine data objectives and topics for discussion*: As with all data collection preferably the researcher should have a clear idea about what data is required and what, therefore, ideally should be collected. Obviously with unstructured interviews sometimes the interview itself determines the direction for data requirements, but even in unstructured interviews it is a good idea to at least think about what topics are going to be discussed.
- *Identifying and approaching interviewees*: Interviewees may be selected using a number of approaches, again depending on the circumstances. Sometimes, albeit rarely, interviewees will be identified and selected using sampling methods such as random sampling. More often than not, however, the researcher must determine who is likely to have the data required and/or can shed light on the issue being explored; who is likely to volunteer this data most readily, and who might be approached for information.
- *Permission*: In some circumstances permission to approach and interview respondents will be required. Obviously, it is important to secure any needed permissions in advance. It is important to note that simply obtaining permission may not mean that respondents will automatically comply and/or be willing to disclose information to an interviewer.
- *Arranging interviews*: Assuming permission has been granted and respondents have indicated that they are willing to be interviewed, the interviewer can then make the necessary arrangements. This will involve determining the time and venue for the interview and may, in some circumstances, include an indication to the respondent of the topics to be covered. Obviously in the case of conversational and unstructured interviews, some of these considerations may not apply.

• *Conducting the interviews*: Again, depending on the type of interview, the circumstances, and so on, a variety of approaches can be taken to actually conducting the interviews. However, in general terms it is important to quickly put the respondent(s) at ease and to establish a rapport between interviewer and interviewee. Any equipment being used to record or take notes of the interview should be kept as discreet as possible so as not to put the interviewee off. In most circumstances it is preferable, and certainly more ethical, to reveal to respondents how the interview data is being recorded.

Interviewing involves several key skills that can often only be gained through experience. Interviewers not only need to be skilled at questioning but in particular need to be good at listening. Good interviewers use the techniques of interviewing including using silence, probing answers, using prompts to explore responses further, and in the case of group interviews, ensuring that all respondents get a chance to have their say.

Activity 10.2. Which of the interviewing approaches/techniques might be appropriate as a means of collecting data in the following situations:

(a) A pilot research study to explore fears and worries of employees with regard to a possible future merger.
(b) A research study to establish how individuals feel in an organization about the amount of training they are being given.
(c) Attitudes of a functional work group, for example, marketing, towards other functions in the organization.
(d) Possible new approaches in an organization to improved communication and motivation.

10.3 Questionnaires, surveys and samples

Our discussion of questioning as an approach to primary data collection would not be complete without a discussion of the use of questionnaires and the related approaches to data collection of surveys and sampling. In the remaining part of this chapter we shall consider the approaches to using questionnaires to collect data and the associated use of surveys in research that often use samples.

Questionnaires

Questionnaires are among one of the most widely used and valuable means of data collection. Having said this, the range and types of questionnaires that can be used, their design, uses and implementation can vary enormously, both from the point of view, for example, of the structure of the questionnaire, how it is administered, and methods of analysis and interpretation. For example, on the one hand, we have questionnaires that comprise a series of questions centred on topics or areas of interest that serve to prompt the interviewer about the areas to be covered and discussed with the respondent during an interview. On the other hand, we have highly formalized and structured questionnaires comprising predetermined closed questions which are administered not face-to- face with the respondent but through, for example, some sort of telephone interview, or even completed by respondents in their own time – the question-naire having been distributed to selected respondents through some mechanism.

With all the possible variants on, and considerations in, questionnaire design, this mechanism for data collection through questioning can be a highly com-plex activity requiring skills and techniques that quite honestly require spe-cialist training and knowledge. In some areas of research in fact, questionnaire design is best left to experts. However, most researchers and consultants will at some stage be in a situation where using a questionnaire will be the most appropriate method of collecting data. For this reason it is important that the researcher should have at least a basic knowledge of the issues in questionnaire design, encompassing areas such as: types of questions; question styles and for-mats; approaches to administering questionnaires; and the general principles of good practice in questionnaire design.

The following represent some of the key aspects of questionnaire design and implementation, and here the researcher must consider the following:

- the range and scope of questions to be included,
- question types, for example, open or closed,
- content of individual questions,
- question structure,
- question wording,
- question order.

With regard to implementing and administering the questionnaire, the researcher must further consider the following:

- method of administering the questionnaire, for example, face to face versus non personal,
- methods of distributing/returning questionnaires, for example, telephone, mail, computer-based
- methods of recording responses.

These are just the basic considerations in questionnaire design and implemen-tation. In addition, we have issues such as, for example, pre-testing or piloting questionnaires, methods of dealing with non-responses, and where appropri-ate sometimes the training and management of interviewers or fieldworkers being used to administer questionnaires.

Again, as with all methods of data collection, the precise issues and problems together with what will constitute effective questionnaire design and imple-mentation will vary according to the circumstances. The researcher must first of all ensure that the questionnaire is an appropriate and useful method of col-lecting data. The researcher must also be clear about what kind of information is being sought, why and how it will be interpreted and analysed. When administering questionnaires on a face-to-face basis, the skills and techniques of questioning referred to earlier in this chapter will come into play.

As you will appreciate then, with such a wide range of factors to consider in the design and administration of questionnaires, and as already mentioned, this is often an area best left to experts if serious commercial conclusions are to be addressed. However, in the case of the typical postgraduate student who has to devise a questionnaire and then administer it, then it might be a case of do-it-yourself. There are, in fact, a number of excellent texts in this area, especially in the specific subject of marketing research. We can, however, address the main issues in questionnaire design in the next section.

Questionnaire design based on material provided by Richard Charlesworth and Peter Morley (2000)

A questionnaire is a series of questions designed to provide accurate information from every member of the sample. To help achieve this, the questionnaire should be clear and unbiased, easy to understand and should maintain the respondent's interest, and motivation.

To design a questionnaire we need to have a clear idea of our overall objectives, the information we want to secure, and how we intend to summarize the results. It is important to write a draft of the questionnaire and then try this out as a pilot on a few people before committing ourselves to the main survey.

In brief the questionnaire should:

- be as short as possible;
- have a logical structure (a clear focus and evolution from topic to topic. It is a good idea to start off with factual and background information, then move on to explore the main areas of interest);
- have questions which are simple wherever possible (e.g. avoid jargon, over-complex language or question structure);
- avoid ambiguous questions (e.g. linked questions in the same statement);
- avoid leading questions (questions which anticipate a particular response);
- use a specific choice of answers where possible.

Question types

Surveys tend to focus on three main areas of information: factual information, behavioural patterns and opinions. These are explored through questions which fall broadly into two categories:

- *Closed (or pre-coded) questions*: These are the most common type of question. They are good for routine questions with limited or structured answers and can be easily summarized and analysed. They are typically easy and quick to answer; but they may only 'scratch the surface' or be superficial.

They depend on anticipated responses; the pilot study is likely to be useful to gauge the breadth of responses and can sometimes be used to give a coded focus to what might originally have been open-ended (see below).

- *Open questions*: These are more suitable for open-ended and flexible enquiries, particularly in an interview context. Such responses are likely to give deeper insights. They often reveal a richness of information (they 'dig deeper' than closed questions), but may therefore be difficult to easily summarize and analyse. They are particularly good for identifying the unexpected and are therefore valuable in exploratory contexts; but can be time-consuming to answer.
- *Pre-coded questions*: Most surveys concentrate on pre-coded questions because the results are in a format which can easily be collated and analysed. Often pre-coded questions contain an open component to take account of responses which had not been anticipated. It is a good idea to put a small number of open questions in a survey. They give the respondent the opportunity to cover relevant issues not on the questionnaire and encourage a positive attitude – the respondent is allowed their say, not merely forced to reply in a pre-packaged format. Studies which concentrate on open questions fall in to the category of *qualitative research* (whereas a pre-coded focus leads to *quantitative research*), and the data is more difficult to collate and analyse. Often the interviewer will use a tape recorder in order to capture everything that the respondent says.

Gallup (1947) has classified five levels of depth which can be built into opinion questioning:

Awareness: Is the respondent aware of an issue; have they given it any thought?

Open/free answer: An unstructured approach is used to indicate the direction of the respondent's thinking; what are the respondent's general feelings on the issue?

Specific issues: Often requires a yes/no answer; what are the respondent's answers to specific proposals/parts of the issue?

Reasons why: Often put in an open format; help to describe opinion; why does the respondent think thus?

Intensity: Measures strength of feeling; how strongly are these views held by the respondent?

Types of data

It is also important to see the links between the type of question, or more specifically the type of answer required, and how all the responses can later be analysed. Data can be classified into three main hierarchical categories:

Nominal data (or categorical) is used to describe *labels* (or categories) such as male/female, occupation.

Ordinal data can be ordered, sequenced or ranked; questions based on a rating scale, such as a Likert scale (see 'Question styles and formats', below), might ask respondents to score 'level of satisfaction' on a 1 to 5 scale where 1 represents very dissatisfied and 5 represents very satisfied and so on.

Cardinal data however has order, sequence and units of measurement; for instance the number of visits to a doctor's surgery, length of service. Some authors like to split down cardinal data into interval data (which has no fixed zero) and ratio data (which has an absolute zero). For instance, temperature is measured on an interval scale (0°C and 0°F are different temperatures; there is no fixed zero); whereas age is measured on a ratio scale (an age of 0 implies an absence of age; accordingly somebody aged 42 is twice as old as someone aged 21 because they are both measured from the absolute zero).

The important thing to note here is that different data types have to be analysed in different ways; and different types of question lead to different types of data. Questions which lead to nominal data can be summarized using counts/tables, proportions, percentages, bar and pie charts. These measures can also be used for interval data, but a *higher level* of analysis stems from measures based on sequence or ranking such as the median. Such measures can be used for cardinal data, but it is most powerfully analysed using the mean and standard deviation. These issues are further developed later.

Note: Some market research texts permit the use of the mean and standard deviation for Likert-type data. For instance, a mean score might be used to give some overall sense of satisfaction. Technically this is incorrect because although the data is ordered, it is not interval data and has no (consistent) unit of measurement. Where the mean (and standard deviation) have been calculated in this way, we should apply a clear 'health warning' and interpret with care!

Question styles and formats

There is a wide range of styles and formats, and the same question can often be presented in a variety of different, but equally acceptable ways. The response to a question might be to tick a box, fill in a number, or to circle an answer or number.

Opinion questions often make a statement and invite the respondent to rate his/her level of agreement, usually by ticking a box or circling a coded reply which is measured on a *verbal scale*, known as a Likert scale. For instance the scale may use terms such as:

| strongly agree | agree | neither agree nor disagree | disagree | strongly disagree |

Similar variations could include replacing the word 'agree' with 'aware', or 'satisfied'.

Worcester and Burns (1975) point out that such scales are among the most used and misused types of scale. The difficulty is that although they are easy questions for researchers to construct, and for respondents to answer, it is not necessarily easy for the researcher to understand how they were comprehended by the respondent. The problem is one of constructing a balanced scale, which rests on the potential ambiguities of language and the nuances of interpretation. Furthermore, such difficulties are exacerbated by differences of perception between cultures and countries. Worcester and Burns recommend the use of adverbs to reinforce the 'moderate' positions. So an improved version of the above scale would be:

| strongly agree | slightly agree | neither agree nor disagree | slightly disagree | strongly disagree |

Instead of 'slightly' we might use 'quite' or 'fairly', with suitable modifications elsewhere in the wording (e.g. 'satisfied' replacing 'aware'). The example above employs a 5-point Likert scale. Sometimes researchers like to use an even-numbered scale (for instance 4-point) which forces the respondent towards an overall positive, or negative view.

As well as language, the researcher should not discount the importance of presentation and layout. This should be clear and uncluttered; and full use should be made of word processing to supply both text and symbols such as boxes, and ticks. Mayer and Piper (1982) have noted the importance of layout in which even a repositioned dividing line between sections of a question was found to reduce response errors.

Examples of question type, style and format

The following examples, taken from a range of questionnaires, illustrate a variety of question type, style and format.

Some closed (or pre-coded) questions:

Are you: Male   Female   *(please ring)*
                or we may use....

Are you   male   or female   *(please tick ✓)*
                or we may use...

How old are you?   ....years   *(please enter figure)*
                or we may use...

How old are you?   <15 ☐   *(please tick ✓)*
                        15–19 ☐
                        20–29 ☐
                        30–39 ☐
                        40–49 ☐
                        50–59 ☐
                        >60 ☐

Does your organization have a Website?   Yes Unsure No

□   □   □   *(please tick ✓)*

What is your organization's main business activity:
(please ring number)

1. Wholesale/retail
2. Hotels/restaurants/hospitality
3. Transport/distribution
4. Financial services
5. Real estate
6. Manufacturing
7. Power supply
8. Education/training
9. Construction
10. Other – please state

Please show the extent to which you agree with the following statement:

'I am fully satisfied with ...'   *(please ring number below)*

strongly agree	slightly agree	neither agree nor disagree	slightly disagree	strongly disagree
1	2	3	4	5

'I use public transport to travel to my place of work'   *(please tick ✓)*

always	usually	sometimes*	rarely	never
□	□	□	□	□

(Note with this format, it may be difficult defining a 'sensible' middle category)

Please rank in order of importance why you chose this University for your MBA
(1 – most important, ... 6 – least important)

Factor:	Importance
MBA course programme/design	□
Discussion with tutor at student recruitment fair	□
Recommended by a colleague/friend	□
Living in London	□
Nothing else to do with my spare time	□
Photos of the staff in the brochure	□

Other variations would include a list as above, (but generally with more alternatives) where the respondent is asked to tick those factors (say up to 3) which were important in the decision to take their MBA at this university.

Some Open Questions:

Please list the range of different types of organization with which you have first-hand experience (e.g. work experience, membership of clubs/societies, voluntary work).

. . . .

. . . .

. . . .

Please list 3 good points and 3 bad points about your experience to date as a student at this university:

Good	Bad
1	1
2	2
3	3

Please complete the following sentence:

'If there was one thing I could change about induction week at this university'

In what respects was your prior experience in management helpful before taking your MBA?

Do you have any further comments to make on (this topic)?

If you have any other comments that you would like to make please use the space below:

. . . .

. . . .

. . . .

Thank you for taking the time to complete this questionnaire; please return it (in the enclosed pre paid envelope/via the internal mail).

Data collection methods and questionnaire design

We need to take account of our data collection method in the design of the questionnaire. Although the questionnaires used could be very similar from a structural point of view, a questionnaire which is to be completed independently by the respondent needs to be worded in such a way as to encourage a response. For instance there should be a covering letter explaining what the survey is all about, how the results will be used, and whether or not replies are anonymous (often preferable). The route through the questionnaire needs to be clear – how should questions be answered (for instance, tick, ring, underline, giving a number, letter); whether 'if then' consequences are clear. Most important with the postal questionnaire is the role of the pilot study. The postal questionnaire must be tried and tested, and be foolproof.

Postal surveys have the advantage of not requiring time-consuming interviews, but do require other resources such as prepaid reply envelopes. They permit the respondent the opportunity for a more reflective and considered contribution, so will be useful in detailed studies; but they are also likely to suffer from higher levels of non-response which may need to be followed up in a further exercise. Note, to simply ignore non-response may introduce bias into the results.

With the development of communications technology, survey researchers are beginning to use faxed and e-mailed questionnaires as alternatives to the postal questionnaire. Potentially they offer much the same benefits as postal studies allied to a more efficient communication medium, but the anonymity of the respondent may be more difficult to ensure. Fax surveys can be comparable to postal surveys, and in some circumstances, can yield faster response rates and at a reduced administrative cost. However Tse et al. (1995) found less encouraging results for e-mail surveys. They found e-mail resulted in inferior response rates compared to postal surveys; however response speed (perhaps surprisingly) and response quality were similar for the two modes of survey. It is likely that these results were influenced by the extent to which the respondents were familiar and comfortable with the use of e-mail itself; for instance many e-mail users still read their mail infrequently, and the study highlighted a number of transmission errors when sending and receiving e-mail.

Clearly the use of electronic media depends on the permeation of suitable and compatible technology throughout the population to be sampled, allied to appropriate user skills on the part of the respondents. An e-mail survey would not currently be appropriate for a consumer research survey; but may be feasible for an in-house survey of employees in an organization which had a well-established IT culture.

Questionnaire design – some reminders of good practice

Be clear about objectives; does the questionnaire meet management objectives (if appropriate)? What information are we seeking from respondents:

- [ ] general background/contextual, specific; details about the respondents,
- [ ] their opinions, motives, expectations, awareness of issues (for instance, advertising, codes of practice),
- [ ] past/future behaviour (e.g. purchasing of products).

Think through the overall questionnaire design:

- [ ] what are the design implications of using interviews (one or more inter-viewers?); a postal or electronic approach,
- [ ] introduction/purpose/how will results be used/anonymity – gain the good-will of respondent,
- [ ] be user-friendly: stimulate the interest of the respondent; be careful about wording sensitive question areas,
- [ ] be aware of the question sequence/flow – take an overview,
- [ ] it is often sensible to use a funnel (broad → specific areas; easy → hard questions),
- [ ] be aware of the length of the questionnaire,
- [ ] check the questionnaire spelling and instructions to respondents.

Be aware of potential biases due to question wording:

- [ ] 'do you hold the commonly accepted view that ...',
- [ ] be aware of implicit assumptions on your part,
- [ ] use simple language, avoid jargon,
- [ ] avoid ambiguity,
- [ ] avoid multiple questions (e.g. two questions in one).

Try to use a mix of question styles – this helps to maintain the respondent's interest/focus; but don't over complicate.

Be aware of the analysis implications of your questions.

Conduct a pilot study – test your questionnaire; get feedback on the questionnaire design and wording from pilot study respondents and other relevant parties.

10.4   Surveys

Collecting data through questioning is the main method used in what is known as survey research. Some consider survey research as constituting a research methodology in its own right and lying possibly somewhere between the ethno-graphical research methodology and true experimental research. Survey research is essentially an approach to data collection that involves collecting data from large numbers of respondents. This is the main distinguishing fea-ture of survey research compared to many other types of research design that are primarily concerned with small numbers. However, having said this, sur-veys can take all sorts of forms encompassing, for example, full-scale censuses using highly structured questionnaires and essentially looking for descriptive data, to, on the other hand, relatively small-scale surveys exploring relation-ships between variables through structured questioning and essentially look-ing for analytical data. More often than not, although not exclusively, surveys, of whatever form and purpose often use questionnaires as the main vehicle for collecting data, hence the reason for including them in this chapter.

Surveys may be used to investigate any organizational issue or problem, either inside or outside of the organization, or both. Most people associate surveys in the context of organizations, with the area of marketing and marketing research. Indeed it is true that this is a major application of survey techniques in business with surveys being used to investigate marketing issues such as,: customer satisfaction, pricing policies, responses to new products, and so on. However, surveys can be just as valuable and relevant to, collecting data say, on internal human resources problem or perhaps opinions on the introduction of new or proposed working agreements/contracts/procedures, relocation plans, and so on.

Sample surveys

Social and business surveys vary greatly in size and application. Some surveys involve undertaking commissioned research, for example, encompassing a national coverage of respondents, whereas others involve relatively small surveys encompassing, say, a company's immediate customers or workforce. Depending on both the scope and the purpose of the survey, together with considerations regarding issues such as time, cost, and accuracy, surveys also vary with regard to the extent to which the survey encompasses the whole population – that is the whole population with regard to the particular area of study – or alternatively will be based on a sample of respondents from the total population. Like questionnaires, sampling, although not exclusive to survey work is also strongly linked to surveys. With survey techniques in particular, the researcher will need to understand the principles of, and approaches to, sampling.

Samples and populations based on material provided by Richard Charlesworth and Peter Morley (2000)

Business analysis often involves investigating information contained in samples. A *sample* is part of a *population* (or universe). It is generally chosen so that it reflects the characteristics of the population, so that by careful analysis we can learn about the wider population. For instance, in order to gauge employee satisfaction in a large organization, we could explore the views of a representative group of staff (the sample) and thereby build up a picture of the views of the full workforce (the population). Note the term 'population' does not necessarily imply a human population; for instance, in a quality control context it could refer to the output of a manufacturing process. The use of samples in business analysis is often driven by resource constraints or pragmatic considerations. However, providing the sample is selected and analysed appropriately, we can be confident about the outcomes.

As with questionnaire design, this too is a specialist area and once again I am grateful to Richard Charlesworth and Peter Morley for the material covering the basic principles of samples and populations.

It is very important to distinguish between one particular sample and the population as a whole. A good example of this is that of opinion polls. Research organizations such as MORI & GALLUP generally ask about 1,000 people, spread across the UK, who they would vote for if there were a general election tomorrow. They obviously assume that these 1,000 people are representative of the entire voting population of about 32 million. To carry out a very accurate opinion poll, they should really ask everyone, but interviewing 32,000,000 people is not only very time-consuming and costly, but also pretty impractical because people change their minds.

One main problem affecting all polls and surveys is the need to:

(a) ask enough people to make the results representative;
(b) ask few enough people for it to be cheap and practical.

The relationship between a sample survey, or poll, and the population needs to be carefully controlled in order to ensure meaningful results. Control is exercised through the way in which the sample is chosen, the conduct of the *interview*, and how the results are processed and summarized.

The distinction between sample and population is therefore at the heart of statistical practice. This distinction is typically further reinforced by notation in many textbooks. Greek letters are often used to describe population characteristics (known as *population parameters*) – for instance: μ the mean, σ the standard deviation, π the proportion and Roman letters to describe the sample equivalents (known as *sample statistics*) – $\bar{x}$ the mean, s the standard deviation, p the proportion. You don't need to worry too much about the notation, but it is important that you realize whether you are dealing with sample or population information.

Surveys in business

Surveys are used extensively in business to inform managers and help them in their decision-making.

Market research undertaken by an organization may be used to investigate a wide range of issues including: customer satisfaction with services or products, pricing policies, facilities, quality, effectiveness of promotions and advertising. A lot of market research aims to find out more about the customer (for instance by banks and building societies); this helps the organization profile their clients and target goods and services. Similarly the demand for new services or products can be assessed. An organization's human resource department may wish to investigate staff morale, or opinions on the introduction of new or proposed working agreements/contracts/procedures, relocation plans and so on

Business surveys vary greatly in size and application. For instance MORI and similar organizations undertake commissioned research; many organizations have marketing departments which conduct survey consumer research; and surveys may be internal or external to the organization. Business surveys can therefore be equally relevant and effective in nationwide campaigns as in internal reviews. Research carried out by voluntary organizations, charities or small businesses use the same skills and techniques as multinational, commissioned studies.

Selecting the sample

When conducting a survey, we need to make sure that the sample is sufficiently large and representative of the population because our confidence in the results rests largely on these two factors. The size of the sample links to notions of uncertainty. Here we concentrate on the process of selection.

The principle of sampling is one we quite confidently put into practice when cooking. We taste a small spoonful of a soup (say) from a casserole to check whether more seasoning needs to be added (or whether too much has already been added). Moreover we are assured that this spoonful (the sample) is representative of the whole casserole of soup (the population) because we remembered to fully stir the contents before tasting. We do not need to eat up the contents of the full casserole to know whether the flavour is to our satisfaction.

Business and social surveys function in much the same way. The key factor is to ensure that the sample is representative of the population from which it was drawn. Many research exercises use a *quota sample* in which you choose respondents to match predetermined categories. For example, we may want a representative number of men and women of all age groups so we choose interviewees to fit in with the specified demographic patterns. This approach is the one favoured by organizations such as Gallup who ensure that their sample covers the correct demographic mix to ensure representativeness in relation to the subject of the enquiry.

From a statistical point of view, the best sample is one which is truly random because this enables us to accurately quantify and control uncertainty. A *random sample* is one in which every member of the population has an equal chance of being selected. Ideally we need to have a numbered list of the population (known as a sampling frame – for instance, a staff or customer record system). Sample members are then chosen by generating random numbers from a computer (most spreadsheets have this facility), or by using a table of random numbers.

For instance, suppose we wish to interview a sample of 50 out of the 582 employees of an organization, about a proposed incentives scheme. We could number the employees 001 to 582 then use random numbers to select the 50 participants. Taking an arbitrary starting point on the table, we could look down *three consecutive columns of digits* noting the first 50 to lie between 001 and 582. So, if we decide to start in the top left hand corner of the table shown below, we would include in our sample employee number 386; the next number in the sequence, 601 falls outside of our required range of 001 to 582 and does not represent an employee, so we move on to the next number, employee number 251 who is included, and so on. Thus the first few employees to be selected in the sample will be numbers 386, 251, 345, 233, 153 and so on. This process is illustrated in Figure 10.1.

386	87	73160	23725	13803	66458	19539
601	46	24972	38717	91227	30305	06912
251	69	43064	18722	98880	50342	65596
752	21	59742	90981	91557	21348	71695
345	61	81615	86790	78094	35602	72719
233	06	27094	96449	63921	67671	49174
970	30	28913	50194	54538	27808	60684
738	75	23452	37074	83196	34998	61779
153	52	19384	14435	08631	93859	92831
826	80	54380	47410	59758	02076	34330
526	34	35063	83703	21419	29557	89314
321	92	95964	67436	89696	71422	91845
935	30	97474	52422	97541	35562	68734
058	47	82600	26350	04264	38701	71412
498	13	54351	91082	80185	69439	20544
975	44	25966	85838	70576	59454	84518

Figure 10.1   Extract from table of random number

When we reach the bottom of the table we can start again at the top using the next three columns of digits, and so on until we have our sample membership. Note that the table consists of random digits which we group together to make into larger numbers; the display presents the digits in blocks of 5 rows and 5 columns purely for convenience of use. The starting point is entirely arbitrary, we could start somewhere in the middle if we wish; also we might have chosen to work across the rows of the table, rather than down the columns.

We can apply the same principles to selecting representative sub groups. Suppose in the example above, we wanted to get employee representation from each of the organization's four departments, we could use random numbers to select the sample so that it reflected the relative sizes of the four departments. This is known as *stratified random sampling*.

If a numbered list doesn't exist, a pseudo random sample may be chosen. For instance we may choose to interview every tenth person arriving at a supermarket on a given morning. If the time and day is likely to have some bearing on the response of the interviewees we may choose to conduct similar interviews on different days and/or at different times in order to cover a representative cross section of shoppers.

It is important to recall the distinction between a sample and a population. This distinction is fundamental to statistical theory and research practice in general. Typically we summarise information generated by the sample (for instance, mean income, % who prefer a salary plus commission method of remuneration etc) in order to make inferences about the whole population. Although there may be situations where we actually collect information from everyone in the total population (e.g. a survey of all staff in a small organization), it is often still appropriate to see this as a sample, because it does not cover past and future population members (staff turnover) or any changes of opinion (say) of the population.

The media, politicians and businesses all tend to miss this point. For instance, an advertising campaign may claim: "8 out of 10 owners say their cats prefer Whiskas"; but how big a sample of cat owners are we talking about? Asking only 100 or even 500 cat owners is still quite a limited sample. One would also need to check whether the sample was in any way biased (e.g. containing a larger proportion of elderly people, or people on high incomes than is representative for Whiskas customers and/or cat owners) and whether the survey method itself was free from bias. We will avoid the question of *how* people know whether their cat prefers one type of cat food over another!

When people claim that statistics lie, they are usually questioning the relevance of the statistics. Remember, most descriptive statistics used in business and management are measures of a sample and should only be applied to the population or used for making generalizations with the utmost care.

▮ 10.5 Concluding comments

There is no doubt that a major tool for collecting primary data is that of questioning. Questioning seeks to elicit data from respondents by asking them for this data in some way. Questioning is widely used in social and management research. Questioning techniques and approaches range from the highly unstructured but nevertheless potentially valuable informal techniques such as conversation and gossip through to highly structured questionnaires administered to large numbers of respondents.

Questioning involves many skills and techniques with which the researcher/consultant must be familiar if they are to get the best out of this approach. Not only are technical skills required for say, questionnaire design or sampling, but also interpersonal skills are crucial when it comes to conducting personal interviews in particular.

The researcher must determine the extent to which questioning is a cost effective and valid approach to generating the data required and must understand the principles and methodologies associated with the specific techniques of questioning selected.

10.6   References

Arksey, H. and Knight, P. (1999) *Interviewing for Social Scientist*, London: Sage.

Bell, J. (1999) *Doing your Research Project*, 3rd edn, Buckingham: Open University Press.

Charlesworth, R. and Morley, P. (2000) *Managing Information: Module Learning Guide*, London: University of North London Business School.

Denscombe, M. (1998) *The Good Research Guide*, Buckingham: Open University Press.

Easterby-Smith, M. Thorpe, R. and Lowe, A. (2002) *Management Research: An Introduction* 2nd edn, London: Sage.

Fink, A. and Kosecoff, J. (1998) *How to Conduct Surveys*, Sage: London.

Foddy, W.(1993) *Constructing Questions for Interviews and Questionnaires: Theory and Practice in Social Research*, Cambridge: Cambridge University Press.

Gallup, G. (1947) 'Qualitative measurement of public opinion. The quintamensional plan of question design', *Public Opinion Quarterly*, Fall, American Institute of Public Opinion.

Healey, M.J. and Rawlinson, M.B. (1994) 'Interviewing techniques in business and management research', in Wass, V.J. and Wells, P.E. (eds), *Principles and Practice in Business and Management Research*.

Marshall, C. and Rossman, G.B. (1999) *Designing Qualitiative Research*, 3rd edn, Thousand Oaks, CA: Sage.

Mayer, C. S. and Piper, C. (1982) 'A note on the importance of layout in self-administered questionnaires', *Journal of Marketing Research*, Vol XIX, August.

Morton-Williams, J. (1993) *Interviewer Approaches*, Aldershot, UK: Dartmouth.

Oppenheimer, A. N. (2000) *Questionnaire Design, Interviewing and Attitude Measurement*, London: Continuum International, Aldershot, UK: Dartmouth, pp. 123–46.

Robson, C. (2002) *Real World Research*, 2nd edn, Oxford: Blackwell.

Sapsford, R. (1999) *Survey Research*, Sage: London.

Saunders, M., Lewis, P. and Thornhill, A. (2003) Research Methods for Business Students, 3rd Edn, Harlow: Pearson Education.

Strauss, A. and Corbin, J. (1990) *Basics of Qualitative Research: Grounded Theory Procedures and Techniques*, London: Sage.

Symon, G. and Cassell, C. (1998) *Qualitative Analysis and Methods in Organizational Research*, London : Sage.

Tse, A.C.B., Tse, K.C., Yin, C.H., Ting, C.B., Yi, K.W., Yee, K.P. and Hong, W.C. (1995) 'Comparing two methods of sending out questionnaires: email versus mail', *Journal of the Market Research Society*, 37 (4).

Walker, R. (ed.) (1985) *Applied Qualitative Research*, Aldershot: Gower.

Wilkins, A.L. (1983) 'Organizational stories as symbols which control the organization', in L.R. Pondy, P.J. Frost, G. Morgan and T.C. Tandridge (eds), *Organizational Symbolism*, Greenwich, CT: JAI Press.

Worcester, R.M. and Burns, T.R. (1975) 'A statistical examination of the relative precision of verbal scales', *Journal of the Market Research Society*, 17 (3)

Yiannis, G. (1998) 'The use of stories' in Symon, G. and Cassell, C. (eds), *Qualitative Methods and Organizational Analysis in Organizational Research*, London: Sage, pp. 135–60

 ## 10.6   Glossary

cardinal data	Has order, sequence and measurement, for example, number of employees, age, height, length of service and so on.

moderator	The person who takes responsibility for administering and operating focus group discussions.
nominal data	Is used to describe 'labels' (or categories) such as male/female, occupation and so on; also known as categorical data.
ordinal data	Can be ordered, sequenced or ranked.
population	The full set of items or people under investigation
population parameter	Summary measures used to describe a population usually denoted by Greek letters, for example, μ to denote the mean.
quota sample	A sample selected so that its most important demographic characteristics match those of the population of interest.
random sample	A sample in which every member of the population has an equal chance of being selected.
sample	A part (or a subset) of a population.
sample statistic	Summary measures used to describe a sample usually denoted by Roman letters, for example, S to denote the standard deviation.
stratified random sample	A sample which treats each segment of the population as separate for sampling purposes.

11
Analysing Data

Learning outcomes

By the end of this chapter you will:

- understand the role and importance of analysis in turning data into information,
- understand the elements of effective data analysis,
- understand the differences and interrelationships between the analysis of qualitative and quantitative data,
- understand the meaning and nature of content and grounded data analysis techniques,
- Understand the meaning and potential application of semiotics.

Introduction

Earlier we discussed the distinction between data and information. Most researchers and virtually all managers are ultimately interested in information rather than data. Information derives from the process of subjecting data to analysis. It is this process of turning data into information through analysis that is considered in this chapter.

In assessing the process of analysing data in this chapter, we shall be less concerned with the detailing of individual techniques of analysis and more with the overall approach to this process, and in particular some of the major differences between analysing qualitative and quantitative data. Without effective analysis both researcher and manager potentially face being overwhelmed with a mass of data which does not really mean much, and certainly cannot be used to address organizational and managerial problems and issues.

We shall be primarily concerned with examining the importance of analysis and the types of analysis related to different types of data in this chapter. Detailed ways of summarizing and presenting data and techniques of analysing data including some of the more frequently used statistical and mathematical techniques are not covered in this book as this dimension is not within its remit, but there are many excellent texts on these aspects (Wisniewski 1997; Burns 2000; Greenfield, 2002; Graziano and Raulin 2004).

 ## 11.1   Analysis: nature and roles

As already mentioned, analysing data is the process of turning data into information. Information, remember, is data which is in a form which can be used for explanation, or more specifically in the context of this book, for decision making. Four key roles for analysis in this respect involve the processes of *distillation, classification, identification* and *communication*.

Distillation

Most research/consultancy exercises often result in huge amounts of data. Neither the researcher nor the client wants to be faced with a mass of data with the ensuing need to sift through it and try and establish what it all means. A key purpose of analysis, therefore, is to distil potentially large amounts of data into forms that are more readily managed and absorbed, and also discard data that is not appropriate in the context of the research project. At its simplest, this distillation will take the form of summarizing data using, for example, tables, diagrams, or may alternatively, and in addition, summarize and distil data numerically through measures such as average dispersion, standard deviation, and so on. Failure to distil data effectively is one of the most frequent reasons for failures to understand and implement research findings.

Classification

Related to the above, data analysis should also help to classify data. This involves the grouping of data into categories that allow the researcher and manager to quickly see what factors are involved and potentially what the data means. Classifying data helps to encourage the development of order from chaos.

Identification

Much data analysis is concerned with establishing causes and/or relationships between factors. Data analysis enables these relationships, and particularly causal relationships to be identified (Krzanowski 1988)

Communication

The final purpose for analysis involves the important aspect of communicating research findings. It is very difficult to communicate raw data, either to managers in an organization, or to other researchers in a field of enquiry. The processes of distillation, classification and identification referred to above ultimately allow the researcher to communicate research findings and their meanings to other people.

Blaxter et al. (2001) identifies four related terms that he puts at the heart of the purpose and process of analysis. These terms are: *concepts, theories, explanations* and *understanding*. The meaning of Blaxter's terms is explained below:

- *Concepts:* Analysis is often aimed at developing concepts regarding how we think about particular subjects or issues.
- *Theories:* Analysis may also seek to explain something. In particular, it seeks to explain the nature of cause and effect.
- *Explanations:* This form of analysis seeks to make things intelligible explaining why things are the way they are.
- *Understanding:* A development of explanations, this aspect of analysis seeks to develop and underpin knowledge about the meaning of a subject area, issues, or the research problem under consideration.

We can see that the process of analysis performs several functions, and where effective, produces several possible outcomes. Although the precise purpose of the analysis may differ, all analysis is ultimately about explaining and understanding which in turn may stem from the development of concepts and theories (Kuhn 1970; Babbie 2001).

In the context of management consultancy research, to some extent concepts and theories play a secondary role in the process of analysis. In this type of research, understanding and explanations are much more important in as much as these lead directly to possible solutions to management issues and problems, together with proposals for their implementation. Again, I would stress within the context of consultancy research, that we are much more concerned with turning data into information, and moreover, the information should enable us to plan courses of action to resolve organizational and management problems, which in turn may lead to more effective organizational performance. In some ways, both manager and researcher are less concerned with the subtleties and technicalities of data analysis and how this is performed, and more with the output of this analysis with particular regard to what it means for management and organizational practice and performance. Having said this, how data is analysed and interpreted, and in particular how effectively these processes are performed is crucial to developing recommendations and action programmes. (Seale and Kelly 1998; de Vaus 2002; Thomas 2004) Put simply, ineffective data analysis can lead to a number of potentially disastrous outcomes with regard to tackling organizational and management problems. Just some of the possible results of ineffective or inappropriate data analysis methods and techniques include the following:

- Key cause and effect relationships may be missed entirely,
- Management may not be provided with a sufficient understanding of the nature of the management problem/issue being researched,

- Key data, which may have been expensive to collect may not be sufficiently explored and assessed,
- *Sophisticated*/complex data analysis techniques may begin to take precedence over understanding

Ultimately, ineffective or inappropriate data analysis may lead to key information being missed or misunderstood, and as a result, can sometimes lead to inappropriate courses of action. In the Hawthorne Studies example cited in earlier chapters, initially, a misunderstanding of what the observed results or data was telling the researchers led them to miss the observation that a major issue/problem affecting productivity in the organization where the research was being conducted was group processes and effects. As a result, the management of the company initially took the wrong steps to improving productivity by concentrating on the physical environment rather than the more important element of effective workgroup design and management.

Ineffective or inappropriate data analysis methods can lead to a waste of part of expensive data collection. Even worse, it can lead to a misunderstanding of the issues and problems being researched, leading in turn to inappropriate courses of action. Effective data analysis, supported by the selection of appropriate data analysis methods is essential. However, it can be questioned what constitutes effective data analysis and what methods are available for this purpose? In analysing this question we can usefully distinguish between the purpose(s) of data analysis in any given research exercise, and between the two major categories of data types, namely quantitative and qualitative. Together, the purpose(s) of data analysis and the two categories of data enable researchers to identify the range of applicable techniques of data analysis that might be utilized.

11.2   The purpose of analysis

Although we have seen that overall, analysis is the process of turning data into information that in turn can serve to develop concepts, theories, explanations or understanding, we can develop this notion of the purpose of data further, which in turn we can use to identify and ultimately select the most applicable techniques of data analysis. The assumption here, of course, is that the purpose of analysis is a major determinant of the technique(s) of data analysis selected. Sharp and Howard (1996) make this assumption in relating the purpose of the analysis to examples of applicable techniques. In so doing, they provide an extremely useful taxonomy for analysis purposes, linking the different categories of purpose to techniques. This is shown in Table 11.1.

You should note that although this framework provides a useful link between the purpose of research and the aims and techniques of analysis that relate to the purpose, it does not purport to show every category of purpose nor every available technique. However, the notion that purpose and techniques are linked, the latter deriving essentially from the former, is correct. The researcher

Table 11.1   Common tasks of analysis and techniques applicable to them

Purpose	Aim of analysis	Applicable techniques
Description	{ Concept formulation { Classification	{ Content Analysis { Factor analysis Cluster analysis
Construction of measurement scales	{ Multiattribute scale construction	{ Unidimensional scaling Multidimensional scaling
Generation of empirical relationships	{ Pattern recon { Deprivation of empirical laws	{ Correlation methods { Graphical techniques
Explanation and prediction	{ Policy analysis { Theory Generation	{ Loglinear analysis Experimental design model Regression model Path Analysis

Source: Sharp J.A. and K Howard (1996) p. 108.

must, therefore, decide what the purpose of the analysis is defining, specific aims or outcomes. These aims or outcomes should link to the objectives of the research or consultancy project decided at the initial planning stages of the research/consultancy brief. As was noted in Chapter 5, in planning the consultancy and research process, methods of data analysis interpretation and diagnosis should be decided at the planning stage of the project, and in turn should stem from the agreed upon research/consultancy objectives. In some ways, therefore, the methods of data analysis, like the data collection methods, are predetermined and certainly constrained by the research plan. Put another way, the researcher should not collect the data first and then decide how to best analyse it. Rather, the researcher should determine from the research objectives and other considerations such as time, resources, and so on, the type of data required, the methods of data collection and the methods of data analysis. These should all be part of a consistent and totally planned process. In fact, the methods of data analysis may, to some extent, shape the earlier stages of data collection, and even the determination of research objectives, rather than always being the other way around. For example, lack of access to sophisticated techniques and tools of analysis that may require, extensive computer analysis may suggest a particular research design and method of data collection. Having said this, today's professional researcher/consultant should be skilled in the full range of data analysis techniques and therefore this should be less of a constraint or influencing factor on the research plan.

11.3   Quantitative versus qualitative data analysis

The second major influence on the nature of the data analysis step, and the selection of the most relevant and effective techniques of analysis, relates to what has been described as being the two major categories or types of data collected as part of a research exercise, namely, quantitative versus qualitative data. You will recall that we have discussed the distinction between these two major categories of data types at several points in earlier chapters. In Chapter 5 in particular, it was suggested that both methods of data collection and methods of data analysis would in part be determined by whether or not the researcher was interested in qualitative or quantitative data. This distinction between the two major categories of data is particularly important when it comes to the data collection and analysis steps of the research. It is certainly true that some techniques of data analysis are specifically designed and are only, therefore, applicable to quantitative data, whereas other techniques have been specifically designed for and are only applicable to data that is qualitative in nature. We shall examine these two categories of data and some of the techniques applicable to each shortly. However, we need to remember that often the distinction between qualitative and quantitative data is blurred. Some qualitative data can often be translated into, and analysed using some of the quantitative techniques, whereas some quantitative data often needs to be analysed further using qualitative techniques. The point that is being made here is that as Cronbach (1975) points out, quantitative as opposed to qualitative is not a dichotomy, and the researcher may often combine both quantitative and qualitative analysis of the same data so as to develop a richer understanding of a phenomenon or issue through the data collected, while at the same time being able to use a combination of techniques to check data for aspects such as representativeness, reliability and validity. Bearing this in mind, outlined below are some of the tools and techniques of data analysis for each category of quantitative and qualitative data.

Analysing quantitative data

Perhaps it seems obvious, but only data that is amenable to quantitative analysis can be analysed using quantitative tools and techniques. Again, then, the research design and particularly the type of data collected together with the methods used in this collection, will determine not only whether quantitative techniques can be used, but often will determine the specific quantitative technique to be used. Yet again, we can see that data analysis techniques should be planned at an early stage of the research process and not simply selected as an afterthought. For example, nominal data is simply no more than counting things or observations, and then placing them into a category. For example, we might count the number of university graduates employed in the organization's workforce.

This type of data does not afford much opportunity for any sort of statistical analysis, and therefore severely restricts the type of quantitative tools of analysis that can be used. On the other hand, ratio data allows the researcher to compare and contrast phenomena Descriptive statistics and measurements. This type of data is amenable to much more sophisticated tools of mathematical and quantitative analysis. Of course, there are all sorts of other types of quantitative data besides these two categories, but I am simply illustrating here the fact that the type of quantitative data and how it was collected/measured, will affect which tools of quantitative analysis can be applied. Quantitative analysis therefore may be at a number of levels according to how the data was collected, the type of data, the amount of data and sampling methods, if any. In addition, the selection of appropriate and effective qualitative analysis tools will also be determined by:

- the degree of accuracy, or more specifically, validity and reliability required,
- the time and resources available,
- the needs of the client, and so on.

Together, this wide range of factors affecting the choice of appropriate and effective techniques of quantitative analysis partly explains the fact that there are literally dozens of different specific techniques of quantitative analysis. It is not necessary to detail every possible technique of quantitative analysis from which the researcher may potentially select, but it is useful to describe in broad terms the major categories or levels of quantitative analysis available to the consultant/researcher.

Blaxter et al. (2001) suggest the following major categories or levels of quantitative analysis ranging from the most basic and simple through to the most complex and sophisticated. These different categories or levels are shown in Table 11.2

The simplest level of quantitative analysis, descriptive statistics, is limited to, at most, the analysis of frequencies, average and ranges, as shown. Even at this level, the type of data collected will affect what analyses can be performed. For example, if the data is nominal or ordinal, descriptive statistics will relate to proportions, percentages and ratios whereas for interval or ratio data, mean, medium and mode (i.e. measures of central tendency) can be analysed.

Table 11.2 Levels of quantitative analysis

Levels of quantitative analysis	Types of data
Descriptive statistics	Variable frequencies; averages; ranges
Inferential statistics	Assessing the significance of data and results
Simple interrelationships	Cross-tabulation or correlation between two variables
Multivariate analysis	Studying the linkages between more than two variables

Source: L Blaxter et al. (2001) p. 216.

At the next level, inferential statistics can be used to analyse the significance of data and results using statistical techniques such as, Chi-square, the Students' t-test or other more powerful tools of inferential statistics. Again, this category of quantitative analysis tools and the specific methods of analysis selected within this category will in large measure be determined by the type of data, and how this was collected.

With simple interrelationships and levels of quantitative analysis we are moving towards linking variables and therefore establishing causality. At this level the interrelationships between only two variables is being assessed. The tools and techniques for assessing statistical associations between two variables come into play here. At the fourth level of quantitative analysis, multivariate analysis, the tools of quantitative analysis, are intended to assess the linkages between several variables. This level represents the most complex level of quantitative analysis and the most sophisticated and powerful techniques including, for example, multiple regression, cluster analysis, factor analysis and so on.

With such a wide range of possible quantitative tools and techniques of analysis to choose from, again, it is stressed that it is important not only to select appropriate methods for the type of data collected, but also techniques which fulfil the purpose of the research/consultancy exercise with regard to the information required, and in particular, the needs of the client organization as specified in the research brief. Quantitative analysis of data offers several advantages over qualitative analysis. In particular, quantitative analysis potentially offers the advantage of increased objectivity in interpreting data, measures of validity and reliability and can be used to analyse large volumes of data that in turn can be succinctly presented in a way which is readily communicable to others (Byrne, 2002). On the other hand, there is a danger of assuming that all quantitative data is invariably scientific and objective. In fact, there is always a degree, and sometimes a surprising degree, of subjectivity in interpreting quantitative data. There is also a danger of using complex and sophisticated quantitative methods of analysis for their own sake, rather than from the perspective of how useful they are in achieving the purposes of the research and particularly the provision of useful information for management. Finally, quantitative analysis can lead to the problem of data or even information overload for both researcher and client. Even the most sophisticated quantitative analysis must ultimately be interpreted in terms of what it means for the research problem and in the case of consultancy research, for the client organization.

Qualitative analysis

Qualitative analysis involves the analysis of data that is not amenable to numerical measurement. This is not to say that all qualitative data cannot be translated into data that is amendable to quantitative techniques. For example, the measurement of attitudes, essentially a qualitative dimension, can be translated into numerical attitudinal scales that can then be analysed using quantitative techniques. Again, we can see that the distinction between quantitative and qualitative data is not always clear-cut. However, some qualitative data simply cannot be subjected to numerical measurement and analysis, even if the researcher should wish to do so. In many social science research projects, it is qualitative data which is sought and attempts to turn the data into numbers so as to quantify it, even where this is possible, might detract from its potential richness. This potential conflict between the desire to quantify, and the inherent richness of unquantified qualitative data, has led to two broad alternative ways of analysing qualitative data. The first of these ways is referred to as *content analysis* and the second as *grounded theory*.

Content analysis

This has long been used as an approach to analysing qualitative data (Miles and Huberman 1984; Cassell and Symon, 1994). The precise application of this technique will vary according to the nature of the research project and the objectives of the researcher. Essentially, the researcher decides in advance what is being looked for and measured through the qualitative research, and then develops frameworks of classifications for assessing the content of the data with regard to these measures. For example, if the researcher is interested in examining the role of money as a motivator in the workforce, and has then conducted a series of personal interviews with a sample of respondents in the organization about this aspect, the content of the interviews can then be examined and, say, the number of times the word 'money' is mentioned by the interviewee noted. Another example might be, say, where observation has been used to generate the data the researcher might note the number of times a particular event or action takes place. We can see, then, that content analysis is an attempt to quantify qualitative data by noting, for example, frequencies of events, words, actions and so on. A key aspect of content analysis, therefore, is deciding on what is to be measured or noted. It could be, for example, as already indicated, looking for specific words or particular events. Deciding on what is to be measured is sometimes known as *unitising* the data. This is because the researcher needs to decide which units will be used for the analysis. Obviously, which units are appropriate depends again on the precise nature of the research and the research objectives. Decisions about the units to be analysed are part of the research design process and should be determined before the data is collected. The researcher can use existing theories, client needs, or simply hunch and intuition to determine the units to be measured in the first place. However, the units and categories can be refined and amended during the research so that if the initial units and categories are not appropriate, further research can refine and improve them.

Once the data has been analysed and the units categorized and measured, the researcher can then seek to identify themes and relationships between the observed frequency, for example, of the units. From these, the researcher can then develop explanations and conclusions with regard to what the observed categories and frequencies might mean. Content analysis, then, is essentially an objective/deductive approach and more nearly accords to the conventional *scientific* method for testing hypotheses.

Grounded theory

This theory was first suggested by Glaser and Strauss (1967) who introduced the idea that the methods and approaches to analysing much qualitative data will vary according to the nature and purpose of each research project and the predilections of the individual researcher. Put another way, Glaser and Strauss were arguing against a standardization of analysis methods for qualitative data. As they saw it, the large amounts of non-standard data produced by qualitative methods renders a predetermined external structure to analysing the data unsuitable. In grounded theory, therefore, the researcher takes the qualitative data and attempts to identify key themes, patterns and categories from the data itself. Obviously, the researcher will inevitably have preconceptions and certainly personal values when it comes to looking for and explaining patterns and categories in data. Essentially, the concepts and categories derived from the empirical data itself, and to the extent that it is possible, the researcher who uses the principles of grounded theory should assess the data with an open mind. Grounded theory, therefore, does not set out to test, for example, an hypothesis, or even with a preconceived set of ideas that shape the research process and the methods of data collection. Any theories or explanations developed by the researcher are instead derived from or *grounded* (hence the term for this approach) in empirical reality. Grounded theory, and the approach to the analysis of qualitative data which it gives rise to represents, therefore, essentially an inductive approach to research based on a much more holistic view. There is no doubt that grounded theory is particularly appropriate to the analysis of much of the type of qualitative data that is often generated in organizational research and partly for this reason we have seen a significant growth in this approach to data collection and analysis in recent years (Goulding 2002). It does, however, require the researcher to accept that the data itself will determine the outcomes and findings of the research irrespective, very often, of what the researcher would hope or wish to find. Adopting this attitude and approach to analysing data can sometimes be very difficult for the management consultant researcher to achieve. However, grounded theory, and the analysis approaches which it gives rise to, can be extremely valuable, particularly where the researcher is not certain about the nature of the research problem and the information required when assessing and resolving this criterion. The researcher must also accept that the individual nature of grounded theory and analysis techniques means that it is not an effective approach to producing or proving general theories, but rather offers explanations which are relevant to a particular set of circumstances and situations. Given that the management consultant researcher is more concerned with producing results and recommendations for a particular organization or problem rather than the production of grand theories, in some ways grounded theory and analysis techniques are extremely useful and relevant to consultancy-type research. We can also see that grounded analysis would be particularly appropriate to some of the methodologies of data collection outlined in earlier chapters and in particular observational and action research. It is probably fair to say, however, that compared to quantitative data analysis, the techniques of qualitative data analysis are still in their infancy.

Qualitative analysis – some key issues

The following quote from Miles and Huberman (1994) well illustrates the situation with regard to qualitative techniques of analysis.

> The most serious and central difficulty in the use of qualitative data is that methods of analysis are not well formulated. For quantitative data, there are clear conventions the researcher can use. But the analyst, faced with a bank of qualitative data has very few guidelines for protection against self-delusion, let alone the presentation of unreliable or invalid conclusions to scientific or policy-making audiences. How can we be sure that an 'earthy', 'undeniable', 'serendipitous' finding is not, in fact, wrong. (p. 2.)

In addition to highlighting the relative infancy, and some may say, crudity, of techniques of qualitative data analysis compared to quantitative data analysis, Miles highlights the central issue which this comparative infancy of qualitative data analysis techniques gives rise to, namely the issue of trying to ensure that the results through the interpretation of qualitative data are reliable and valid. We have seen in Chapter 3 that the whole process of developing knowledge and understanding through research centres on the development of theories which are both reliable and valid. Both deductive and inductive research methods centre on reliability and validity of data collection and analysis. As Miles points out, without these twin pillars of theory development and scientific research then, the researcher can never be truly sure, and certainly will find it difficult to convince others that his or her research findings are correct.

Much qualitative data analysis, it has to be admitted, does stem from the often subjective and individual interpretations of the researcher. Put another way, with much qualitative data two researchers could put entirely different interpretations on a set of data depending on their perspectives, experiences, agendas, predispositions and so on. Because of this, in the past, researchers wishing to develop knowledge and understanding, and particularly when trying to develop theories, have sought to avoid collecting and using qualitative data, or alternatively have sought to develop techniques for transforming essentially qualitative data into a quantitative form through, for example, scaling techniques, and so on. However, as already mentioned, in the study of management and organizations, it has increasingly been recognized that much of the data collected in the process of a research or management consultancy exercise will be, by its very nature, qualitative rather than quantitative. In addition, and related to this, it is increasingly appreciated that such qualitative data, far from being 'inferior' to its quantitative counterpart is in fact often the most powerful and useful data. If anything these days, the use of qualitative techniques of data collection and the need to analyse qualitative data, probably predominate in management research and consultancy exercises. As a result, there has been a growing interest in it accompanied by the development of better and more powerful techniques for analysing qualitative data. As we shall see, most of these developments in qualitative data analysis centre on techniques for improving the reliability and validity of qualitative data analysis techniques. In other words, researchers have attempted to move towards techniques of analysis which fit the *scientific* model of theory development and analysis with an emphasis on codifying and classifying data, removing subjective interpretations, and developing data which is amenable to statistical analysis and verification. We have to be careful here, in as much as in trying to impose a more rigid scientific approach to the analysis of qualitative data, we may in fact, by attempting to impose a system of order and consistency, which does not fit the natural data collected, detract from the essential nature of qualitative data and its potential value in providing 'earthy', 'undeniable', and 'serendipitous' findings which, although they cannot be proved 'right' (in a scientific sense) offer major insights into organizational and management issues. In other words, we should not let a desire for more *objective* and *scientific* techniques of analysis panic us into imposing an artificial framework of rigour onto qualitative analysis, thereby detracting from the essential nature and inherent advantages of qualitative data analysis. Churchill (1999) captures this caveat well in referring to the analysis of focus group data.

> One has to remember that the results (of focus group analysis) are not representative of what would be found in the general population, and us are not projectable ... The unstructured nature of the responses, makes coding, tabulation, and analysis difficult. Focus groups should *not* be used therefore to develop head counts of the proportion of people who feel a particular way, focus groups are better for *generating* ideas and insights than for systematically examining them. (p. 113.)

To reiterate, the very strength of qualitative data stems from its open-ended and often subjective nature, particularly when it comes to analysis. However, as already mentioned, the growth in qualitative techniques of data collection allied to a desire to develop more systematic and *scientific* techniques of analysis for such data has led to attempts to develop less subjective approaches to analysing quantitative data. It is now accepted that it is possible and potentially advantageous to try and develop more systematic techniques of analysis along the lines of the processes conventionally used in analysing quantitative data. Gradually then, analysers of qualitative data are moving away from simply presenting their interpretations of thousands of words of field notes collected using qualitative techniques in ways in which the researcher simply informs us of the patterns drawn from this enormous amount of data without telling us how, or allowing other researchers to replicate the analysis of the data. Similarly, researchers are now recognizing that analysis of qualitative data which enables the validity of findings to be assessed by others is indeed possible and often desirable. As already discussed, the main theoretical approaches to qualitative data analysis which embody this relatively new acceptance of the possibility and desirability of more systematic/scientific analysis of qualitative data are those of content analysis and grounded theory. More recently however, the desire to develop more analytical methods of qualitative analysis have led to a welter of individual techniques for analysing qualitative data embodying more systematic and analytical frameworks. These include for example: cognitive mapping, pattern coding, cause and effect diagrams, case ordered effects matrices, scatter plots and perhaps one of the most interesting techniques of qualitative analysis to be developed, namely the technique of semiotics. Because of its relevance and potential usefulness to management research in organizations, we shall now consider semiotics as a technique in more detail.

11.4 Semiotics

There are many ways of analysing qualitative data that have already been discussed, but in this section we are going to focus on one of these in more detail namely – semiotics or semiology, the names are interchangeable. This is an essentially interpretive methodology based upon linguistic theory. Language is a means of communication between people sharing a common culture, or at least with sufficient commonality to enable communication to take place. This cultural commonality can be in terms of a societal culture or a business culture. In communication language provides not merely a representation of objects and events that the communicator of information has in mind but also a representation of the desires, intentions and goals of the communicator. These are either consciously embedded into the communication according to the communicator's intentions or unconsciously embedded despite the communicator's intentions. As such these intentions are subject to analysis and interpretation.

In order for communication to take place, it is necessary for the language used to have some formal structure to ensure common understanding, and this is the function of syntax and grammar, as well as of the meaning ascribed to individual words. In speech, as opposed to written language, this formal structure of language is simpler and the rules are often broken, with meaning being partly given by contextual information as well as speech content. Thus it is possible for a conversation to be understood by all parties to it that would be meaningless if written down and shown to a third party because the vital contextual and implied content of the communication is missing. Such shorthand can, however, be considered to be nothing more than a special case of the elaborated code used by technical experts in the language. Halliday (1978) argues that the format of this code both determines social structure and is determined by such social structure, and that the use of language socializes the child into the adult.

I am grateful to David Crowther, London Metropolitan University, for providing the material on Semiotics.

Linguistic studies have shown that language is used to identify social class (Klein 1965; Labov 1966; Hewitt 1989) but that language also defines identity much more narrowly in terms of the social group to which one belongs. This view has been identified by Le Page (1968) who states:

> Each individual creates the systems for his verbal behaviour so that they shall resemble those of the group or groups with which from time to time he may wish to be identified. (p. 194.)

Thus this view suggests that language acts like a membership card and assumes that language usage and behaviour is adopted to gain membership. However, a contrary argument from feminist discourse suggests that language is used as a source of power and dominance, and is used in this manner by the dominant group in order to exclude others. Thus, Lakoff (1975) considers language in the context of power and dominance, stating:

> The language of the favoured group, the group that holds the power, along with its non-linguistic behaviour, is generally adopted by the other group, not vice versa. (p. 136)

The origins of semiotics

Semiotics has been defined simply as 'the study of signs' (Guiraud 1975). However, this description must be viewed as being overly simplistic. In fact, semiotics can be considered to be the study of the creation of the symbolic and its subsequent signification. Thus Saussure (1966) defines semiology as 'a science which studies the life of signs within society'. Semiology can, therefore, be considered to be a study of communication and more specifically the study of communication acts or events, a study of the message itself and its relationship with the recipient of that message. According to semiotic theory, communication is determined by the interrelationship between the message itself and the recipient of that message. This inevitably places a heavy burden upon the recipient of the message in extracting meaning from that message, but it also places a heavy burden upon the writer of the message. Thus, rather than being irrelevant to the message, the writer of the message is in fact central to the message itself as she must endeavour to ensure that the meaning wished to be imparted is actually the one which is extracted by the recipient rather than any alternative meaning.

In spoken communication this is a relatively simple process, as the speaker knows something about the hearer, has a general understanding of the context in which the communication is being made, and receives feedback which enables the message to be modified during its transmission. When the message is transmitted in written form, either as text or as pictures, however, the situation is very different as there is no framing context for the message, or rather a different framing context for each reader, and no relationship between the writer and the reader other than the message itself. The message itself therefore becomes the sole form of mediation between the writer and the reader and thereby assumes the dominant role in the communication. This message becomes the totality of the communication act, and the communication event becomes the relationship between the message and the reader of the message. Semiology is the study of both the communication act and the communication event.

Postmodern analysis of society and its organs provides a mechanism for the semiotic analysis of external reporting. In this context, Baudrillard (1988) claims that there is a need to break with all forms of enlightened conceptual critiques and that truth in the postmodern era is obsolete, while Fish (1985) claims that truth and belief are synonymous for all practical purposes. In terms of any analysis of data, this would suggest that the meaning of any such data becomes whatever it is interpreted to mean and this interpretation will depend upon the perspective of the person performing that interpretation, and the purpose for which that interpretation is undertaken. This need for interpretation naturally places a heavy emphasis upon the interpretative ability of the receiver of the reported information as well as presupposing that this receiver understands the language of the culture being analysed sufficiently well to be able to extract meaning from this information. It also provides an opportunity for those under-taking the analysis to structure the information reported in such a manner as to facilitate their desired manner of interpretation.

This kind of semiotic analysis is based upon the premise that such interac-tions take place upon a stage, labelled the semiotic stage (see Crowther, 2002), and that the data can be considered to be the script which determines the inter-actions between the participants. Every script needs an author and, in the con-text of this analysis, the author can be considered to be the originator of the data, with you, as the person analysing the data, acting in an editorial capacity.

In a conventional view of such a script, time is considered in a linear manner so that the authors produce the script that is then presented to the audience. The audience, that is the readers of the script, in this linear depiction have no involve-ment in the script but are merely passive recipients. This can be depicted as Figure 11.1, with a linear movement of the text from the authors to the audience. In this conventional view there is, therefore, no communication event but merely a script passed from one person to another. At the same time as the script is passed the burden of interpretation of the meaning of the script is also passed and this burden falls entirely upon the recipient to make of the script what he will

A semiotic analysis takes a very different view and removes the linear con-straint assumed within a traditional view of temporality. Here the communi-cation event is viewed as an interaction between the audience and the script and as an interaction between the authors and the audience using the script as a mediating mechanism. These interactions take place upon what is defined as the semiotic stage, which encompasses the communication event. This stage can be depicted thus:

Traversing the semiotic stage

According to Saussure (1966), language consists simply of a system of differ-ences and this led to his identification of the binary opposite of *langue* and

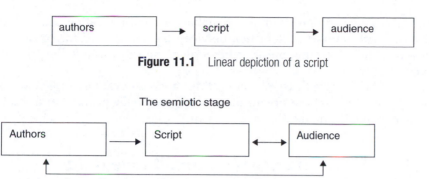

Figure 11.1   Linear depiction of a script

The semiotic stage

Figure 11.2   The semiotic stage

parole, which were considered by Barthes (1967) as being synonymous with language and speech. This notion of binary opposition, however, was extended by Hjelmslev (1963) into a binary opposition of scheme and usage. This notion of binary opposition provides a mechanism for meaning construction, through categorization, in the semiotic exploration of a text. This binary opposition provides a structure to the text and, according to Greimas (1990), the construction of a text as an integral structure is tantamount to the recognition of its constituent pairs of binary opposites. Furthermore, Greimas and Rastier (1968) argue that what is important is not the binary opposites themselves, but rather the meaning already existing within them. Berger (1982) supports this notion of binary opposition as a means of discovering meaning within a text and claims that the reading of a text semiotically implies an understanding of the binary opposites embedded within them, while Baudrillard (1988) regards the notion of binarism as an essential and sacred part of the text. The examination of binary opposites, therefore, provides a mechanism for traversing the semiotic stage and examining the communication event surrounding the text and its actors.

The importance of semiotics as a tool for analysis of corporate reporting is based upon the argument of Derrida (1978) that the meaning of any message is entirely in the interpretation of that message and that, once the message has been transferred into a permanent context, (in the case of corporate reporting on to the paper on which the message is produced and reproduced) then the author becomes irrelevant to the message. Thus for Derrida, interpretation by the reader of the message is paramount. This argument has been modified by Lacan (1977) who argues that, as human beings, every person is inextricably intertwined in the message and its meaning, and by this means the author is partially reintegrated into the communication event. Thus for Lacan the message itself is dominant and the author and the reader of the message enact out a dialogue through the message conveyed in the text. Semiology provides a tool for the exploration of the message itself in the context of the relationship between the author of the message and the reader of that message, with the author seeking to shape the communication event in such a way that the reader makes the interpretation which the author wishes to convey. However/the communication event differs from speech in that the communication takes place at a distance with no direct interaction between the author and the reader of that message. Thus the communication takes place entirely through the printed message.

Semiotics, then, represents an interesting and innovative approach to analysing qualitative data in organizational research. However, what are the key steps in analysing qualitative data overall?

11.5   Steps in analysing qualitative data

The selection of individual techniques of qualitative data analysis obviously depends on a wide number of factors including, for example, the type of qualitative data, the objectives of the research/analysis, data availability, costs and resources, and so on. Irrespective of the qualitative data analysis technique being used, however, all of the techniques designed to produce more systematic and analytical approaches to analysing qualitative data centre on an understanding of the key steps and common features of analytical methods of data analysis which has already been mentioned are inherent in most of the quantitative analytical methods.

The three key steps in analysing any form of qualitative data, and common therefore to any of the techniques of qualitative data analysis, examples of which are referred to above, comprise of the following as explained by Miles and Huberman (op. cit. 1994):

Data reduction

This is the first step in analysing qualitative data. This is the process of selecting, focusing, simplifying, abstracting and transforming qualitative data by identifying and organizing the data into clear patterns. For example, if the qualitative data has stemmed from a series of focus groups or depth interviews resulting in a set of transcripts and notes or possibly tape recordings, then the researcher should first sift the data reducing it into patterns which best summarize the data and enable preliminary findings to begin to be determined.

Obviously, the very process of selecting and identifying chunks of data into patterns, inevitably means that the researcher's own often subjective viewpoints and ideas serve to shape and determine the data reduction process. One might argue, therefore, that at this stage the process is still entirely subjective and unscientific. However, so long as the reasons for, and thinking behind, the data reduction process are made clear by the researcher, then the validity and reliability or otherwise of this first stage of analysing qualitative data can at least be assessed and evaluated by others. In our example of focus group data, then, accompanying the data reduction process would be an explanation of how this process was performed and the reasons for selecting and identifying patterns in the data.

Data display

This second stage in analysing qualitative data involves the presentation of the qualitative data in ways which enable others to assess, interpret and evaluate the interpretations and conclusions drawn by the researcher. In the past, much qualitative data has been displayed in the form of, say, extended text based on field notes involving interviews, and so on. Often extended text is impossible for someone else to understand and analyse what the data means and the interpretations which have been drawn from it. Recognizing this, qualitative researchers have moved towards developing ways of presenting condensed data in ways in which others can understand and evaluate. Again, the emphasis is on increasing validity and reliability. A wide number of techniques are now used to display data including, for example, matrices, graphs, charts and networks. In our example of focus groups, again, having reduced what is often a large amount of data, by looking for common threads or trends in response patterns, the researcher may then look for similar patterns between different focus groups. These similar patterns can then be cut apart and matched between the groups displaying the data in folders containing relevant material by subject matter.

Conclusion drawing and verification

This third element in developing more systematic techniques of analysing qualitative data comprises drawing definitive conclusions from the data. Conclusions in fact begin to emerge the very latest at the stage of data reduction, but in fact may emerge much earlier in the research process in as much as the sorts of data collected and the reasons for this may stem from initial ideas or 'early conclusions' of what the data may reveal. Final conclusions, however, will evolve from the complete analysis of the qualitative data after data reduction and data display. Throughout the process of analysis, initial and often tentative conclusions should begin to firm up and be verified as the analysis proceeds. Verification obviously involves comparing initial ideas and thoughts with the data and hence may involve simply a process of second thoughts as the data is analysed through to further research to replicate observed patterns in the data. The process of how conclusions were drawn and verified again should be open for others to evaluate, again lending validity and reliability to the data and findings. Continuing our example of focus group analysis, then, conclusion drawing and verification would involve checking the data against initial ideas or theories, possibly verified by more detailed examination of the data, possibly discussions with colleagues and clients about the meaning of the data and interpretations placed on it, and finally possibly further focus group interviews to replicate findings and conclusions drawn from the initial research.

In concluding this note on qualitative data analysis, we have seen that accompanying the growth of qualitative research, there has been a trend towards trying to develop more structured and analytical methods of qualitative data analysis along the lines, and for the same reasons, of the techniques used for quantitative data. Researchers are trying to move towards increasing the reliability and validity of qualitative data analysis thereby adding to its credence and acceptability. Certainly, there are advantages to moving from entirely subjective and often unsystematic interpretations of qualitative data or from the non-interpretive presentation of such data in order to avoid criticisms of subjectivity by simply presenting a mass of raw data without analysis and interpretation by systematically condensing, displaying, and conclusion drawing and verification. However, it is important to stress again that there are dangers in trying to shoehorn qualitative data analysis into a framework which was always intended for quantitative data.

11.6   Issues in and approaches to analysing qualitative data

Combining data analysis methods

We have seen that with some techniques of analysis the distinction between qualitative and quantitative methods begins to blur. It has also been suggested that both of these categories of data analysis can be, and often are, used together in a particular research project. In fact, sometimes it is essential to combine several types of analysis to analyse and make sense of data. The use of multiple, but independent measures is referred to as *triangulation* which has been discussed before. Using several different methodologies and techniques of analysis therefore, can give much more accurate and insightful findings than where only one method of data collection and analysis has been used. Virtually every technique of data collection and analysis has some weakness and therefore using several methods of data collection and analysis can help offset these weaknesses.

Making data analysis user/client friendly

Remember, in this book we have been primarily concerned with applied type business research, including consultancy research, that is, research that centres on helping to solve client problems. The client here, of course, will be for example an organization or rather a manager or management team within an organization. It can also be an academic supervisor, but this person is equally looking for an objectively presented set of findings. It is important, therefore, that the methods of data analysis are presented and explained to a client in a way that is user-friendly. In particular, it is important not to try to *impress* the client by using overly complex and technical language. Sometimes the techniques of data analysis will be complex and technical and may be difficult for a non-specialist to understand. The consultant researcher, therefore, should ensure that data analysis techniques are explained as clearly as possible. In addition, the results of the data analysis should be made available in a clear, concise and again, user-friendly format. Sometimes the client may not be interested at all in how the data was analysed, but only in what it means in terms of actions and recommendations. We shall consider this aspect or outcome of data analysis in Chapter 12.

11.7 Concluding comments

In this chapter we have examined the nature and purpose of data analysis in the research process. In doing so, we have concentrated on outlining the importance of effective data analysis and its role in turning data into information. We have seen that the techniques of data analysis differ according to the nature of the data itself, with a major distinction between the categories of qualitative and quantitative data. We have also seen that the purpose of the analysis is a key factor in the technique(s) of analysis selected. Quantitative techniques of data analysis range from the relatively simple and straightforward production of descriptive statistics, through inferential statistics and simple interrelationships to the most complex levels and techniques involving multivariant analysis. With regard to qualitative techniques, we have distinguished between content and grounded techniques of analysis; examined the key steps in analysing qualitative data; and introduced the intriguing techniques of semiotics for analysing interactions and processes in organizations. Finally we have highlighted the fact that data analysis and its presentation need to be user-friendly in meeting the needs and requirements of the client.

11.8 References

Babbie, M. (2001) *The Practice of Social Research*, 9th edn. Belmont, CA:Wadsworth/ Thomson Learning.

Barthes, R. (1967) *Elements of Semiology*, trans. Lavers, A. and Smith, C. New York, Noonday Press.

Baudrillard, J. (1988) in M. Poster, (ed.), *Jean Baudrillard*, Selected Writings, Cambridge: Polity Press.

Berger, A. A. (1982) *Media Analysis Techniques*, Newbury Park, CA: Sage.

Blaxter, L. Hughes, C. and Tight, M. (2001) *How to Research*, 2nd edn, Buckingham: England.

Burns, R. L. (2000) *Introduction to Research Methods* London: Sage.

Byrne, D. (2002) *Interpreting Qualitative Data*, London: Sage.

Cassell, C. and Symon, G. (eds) (1994) *Qualitative Methods in Organizational Research: A Practical Guide*, London: Sage.

Churchill, G. A. (1999) *Marketing Research: Methodological Foundations, 7th edn*, The Dryden Press.

Cronbach, L. J. (1975) 'Beyond the two disciplines of scientific psychology', *American Psychologist*, 30, pp. 116–26.

Crowther, D. (2002) *A Social Critique of Corporate Reporting*, Aldershot: Ashgates.

de Vaus, D. A. (2002) *Analysing Social Science Data:50 Key Problems in Data Analysis*, London: Sage.

Derrida, J. (1978) *Writing and Difference*, trans. Bass, A., London: Routledge & Kegan Paul.

Dunn, A. D. and McConway, K. J. (1995) *Elements of Statistics*, Wokingham:

Fish, S.(1985) *Is there a text in this class?*, in Mitchell, W. T. J. (ed), *Against Theory*, Chicago: University of Chicago Press.

Glaser, B. and Strauss, A. (1967) *The Discovery of Grounded Theory*, Chicago: Aldine.

Goulding, C. (2002) *Grounded Theory : A Practical Guide for Management, Business and Market Researchers*, London: Sage.

Graziano, A. M. and Raulin, M. L. (2004) *Research Methods : A Process of Enquiry*, Boston: Pearson Education Group.

Greenfield, T. (2002) *Research Methods for Postgraduates*, 2nd. Edn, London: Arnold

Greimas, A. J. (1990) *The Social Sciences: A Semiotic View*, Minneapolis, University of Minneapolis Press.

Greimas, A. J. and Rastier, F. (1968) *The Interaction of Semiotic Constraints*, Yale French Studies, 41, pp. 86–105.

Guiraud, P. (1975) *Semiology*, London: Routledge & Kegan Paul.

Halliday, M. A. K. (1978) *Language as Social Semiotic*, London: Edward Arnold.

Hewitt, J. (1989) 'White adolescent creole users and the politics of friendship', *Journal of Multicultural and Multilingual Education*, 3 (3) pp. 340–57.

Hjelmslev, L. (1963) *Prolegomena to a Theory of language*, trans. Whitfield, F.J., Madison: University of Wisconsin Press.

Khun,T. (1970) *The Structure of Scientific Revolutions*, Chicago: University of Chicago Press.

Klein, J. (1965) *Samples from English Cultures*, London, Routledge & Kegan Paul.

Krzanowski, W. (1988) *Principles of Multivariate Analysis*, Oxford:Clarendon Press.

Labov, W. (1966) 'The linguistic stratification or' in New York City department stores', in W. Labov (ed.) *Sociolinguistic Patterns*, Philadelphia: Pennsylvania University Press.

Lacan, J. (1977) *Ecrits: A Selection*, trans. Sheridan, A., London: Tavistock.

Lakoff, R. (1975) *Language and Woman's Place*, Cambridge: Harper & Row.

Le Page, R. (1968) 'Problems of description in multilingual communities', *Transactions of the Philological Society*, pp. 189–212

Miles, M. B. and Huberman, A. M. (1984) *Qualitative Data Analysis: A Sourcebook of New Methods*, Beverley Hills, CA:Sage.

Miles, M. B. and Huberman, A. M. (1994) *Qualitative Data Analysis: A Sourcebook of New Methods*, 2nd edn, London: Sage

Saussure, F. de (1966) *Course in General Linguistics*, trans. Baskin, W., New York: McGraw-Hill.

Seale, C. and Kelly, M.(1998) 'Coding and analysing data', in C. Seale (ed.) (2004) *Social Research Methods: A Reader*, London: Routledge.

Sharp, J. A. and Howard, K. (1996) *The Management of a Student Research Project*, Aldershot, England: Gower, p. 108.

Thomas, A. B. (2004) *Research Skills for Management Students*, London: Routledge.

Wisniewski, M. (1997) *Quantitative Methods for Decision Makers*, 2nd. Edn, London:Financial Times Management.

11.9 Glossary

content analysis	An approach to analysing qualitative data based on trying to quantify qualitative data by, for example, counting 'frequency' and so on.

grounded theory   An approach to analysing qualitative data based on identifying and interpreting themes and patterns contained in the data.

triangulation   A term borrowed from navigation and surveying where multiple reference points are taken to check an object's location. In the context of data collection and analysis the term indicates that a number of different and independent methods of data collection and analysis have been combined.

unitising   Determining the objects of measurement in content analysis.

12

Actioning Research

Learning outcomes

After completing this chapter you will be able to:

- discuss the issues in diagnosing and interpreting research data and findings with a view to making recommendations and making decisions about courses of action;
- appreciate the issues in implementing courses of action and the consultant/ client roles in this process;
- understand the importance of evaluation and follow-up in consultancy research and the issues in the process of disengagement.

Introduction

In this final chapter we are going to be looking at what has been referred to as actioning research. For academic research that leads to the award of a business qualification, actioning research is less critical, as the major criterion is to obtain the qualification. However, much academic research of this nature is sponsored by an organization (often an employer) and this makes the research akin to a consultancy project. Unlike pure academic research, business consultancy-type research is normally undertaken to resolve, or at least address, a practical organizational problem or issue with a view usually to improving organizational effectiveness and efficiency.

As we saw in Chapter 5, the research process does not end in data analysis and findings and the production of a learned paper, perhaps to be presented at an academic conference or published in the appropriate journals as it might be with academic research. Rather, the findings from the analysis of the data in a management consultancy research project are but a prelude to the most important activities in this type of research, namely, diagnosing what the data means, making recommendations for actions and taking decisions about these and finally implementing recommendations, together with any necessary follow up actions and controls. In addition, and again unlike purely academic research projects, with a consultancy research project there are issues surrounding the process of disengaging from the client. Remember, in earlier chapters of this text we discussed the importance of and the issues arising from working with clients when it comes to conducting consultancy as opposed to academic research. We saw that it was crucial to take a client-centred approach to issues such as the design of the research project, the selection of the problems and issues to be addressed and so on. However, we also saw that when it comes to actually conducting the research and in particular the methods of data collection and analysis, consultancy research does not differ much from academic research.

Having completed collection and analysis of data, it is important for the business consultant researcher to return once again to a client-centred perspective. When it comes to actioning research, the consultant, whether internal or external to the organization, must work extremely closely with the client if the final stages of a consultancy research project are to be effective.

12.1   Interpreting and diagnosing research findings, making recommendations and taking decisions

Once the research project, issues and problems to be addressed, agreement about the consultancy/research brief and the research plan have been identified with the client, the consultant/researcher will usually have direct responsibility for the next two stages of data collection and data analysis. However, data collection and analysis serve only to provide the information that will ultimately allow organizational problems and issues to be addressed through decision making and implemented courses of action. Once the data has been analyzed, therefore, we must move to interpret and diagnose the data specifically with a view to making recommendations and decisions as to courses of action. So what then is the importance and nature of these elements of the business consultancy research project; how should they be approached; and what are the responsibilities and roles of consultant and client?

Looking first at responsibilities for interpreting and diagnosing data, and for making recommendations, one might be tempted to feel that the consultant responsible for the research should also always be responsible for these steps. After all, is not this why most organizations employ a consultant? Certainly, since most consultancy type research is about taking courses of action so as to address organizational problems and issues, many feel that the onus should be on the consultant to diagnose and interpret the data and recommend clear courses of action. In fact, in the past, most consultancy projects have indeed ended with the consultant making a set of recommendations based on his/her diagnosis and interpretation of the findings from the consultancy research. Both client and consultant can agree at the outset that a set of recommendations to the client is the main objective of the consultancy project and is therefore the consultant's primary responsibility with the consultant's obligations effectively having been discharged at this point. In this situation it is the client's responsibility to decide whether or not and how to implement these recommendations. Increasingly, however, it has been recognized that the effectiveness of a consultancy research project is heightened where, both client and consultant work together to make sense of the research findings, interpreting and diagnosing these and agreeing together upon what courses of action to take and how to implement these (Bellman 2001; Schaffer 2002). In other words, increasingly the consultant stays with the project through and even beyond the implementation stage working with the client to implement and sometimes evaluate proposed courses of action. This represents a much more client-centred approach, but moreover offers the following advantages compared to the consultant's responsibilities ending at the recommendations stage:

- Diagnosing and interpreting the research findings helps to clarify the data and ensure that the right problems and issues have been identified.
- Related to the above, the client may be able to provide additional insights into what the research findings mean and what underpins, or may be causing identified problems.
- Interpreting and diagnosing research findings with the client is likely to lead to the client accepting ownership of, and commitment to, any courses of action which stem from this process.

The advantages that have been cited require that there be close and continuing collaboration and discussion between consultant and client. Research findings should be fed back as early as possible to the client, and indeed this may serve to help shape and inform any required changes in ongoing methods of data collection and analysis. In turn there must be a high degree of trust and openness between client and consultant (Cohen and Bradford 1991; Maistor et al, 2001; Schwarz 2002). For example, the consultant should be able to discuss organizational problems and issues with the client without the client becoming defensive or guarded. In addition, where there is to be joint interpretation and diagnosis, leading to either joint or even client generated recommendations then this must be discussed and agreed at the outset in the research brief and plan.

In interpreting and diagnosing research findings then, ideally the consultant and client should work together towards generating recommendations and solutions. The increasingly accepted role of the consultant is to work together with clients to help the clients themselves to identify the key issues and problems, and then to help them to decide on courses of action for improvement. This is in line with most thinking and practice with regard to organizational interventions and organizational development (French and Bell 1978; Huse and Cummings 1985; Mohrman et al. 1989; Schein 1998). The idea is that clients will be much more motivated and committed to any courses of action if they feel that they themselves have had a major part in deciding them. Working with the client and preferably including any parties who may be ultimately affected by any proposed courses of action and/or be associated with a problem and its causes, the research findings should be used as a framework for asking questions to help the client assess the problem, define it, and generate possible solutions. The consultant, however, may usefully apply the frameworks and techniques of problem solving in this process following the stages shown below.

- Initial statement of problems/issues,
- Exploration of problem to identify possible causes: redefinition of problem,
- Generation of alternative solutions,
- Evaluation of options,
- Suggested courses of action.

Many have shown that techniques of decision making and creativity such as decision trees and techniques of creativity such as for example brainstorming are useful at the this stage of the consultancy process (Haefele 1962; Bazerman 1984; Bartol and Martin 1998). Again, it should be stressed that the most important aspect of this stage is that the emphasis should be on the consultant helping the client to identify their own issues, options and solutions so as to increase the clients feeling of ownership and commitment. In a very real sense the role of the consultant at this stage is that of helping the client change their behaviour, or helping them to learn (Nutt 1986; Fisher 1995). At this stage, sometimes it is useful for the consultant to use theories or models with clients which the consultant feels are useful in understanding and interpreting research findings and their implications. For example, if the research findings suggest to the consultant that a major underpinning factor in an identified problem of labour turnover is job design, then the consultant in helping the client interpret the research findings may introduce relevant models and theories of job design and motivation. Cockman, et al. (1999) strongly believe that theories and models are best introduced when the client is presented with the data analysis and research findings. They suggest that presenting theories and models at this stage means that the models are much easier for the client to understand and see the relevance of and so can be more useful in helping the client address problems, isolate issues and develop solutions. The final outcome of this stage is for the client, with the guidance and help of the consultant, to make decisions between alternatives with regard to proposed solutions.

12.2 Designing the implementation and action plans

Once the alternatives have been identified and assessed and decisions made, then again the consultant should work together with the client to design detailed implementation and action plans.

The plan should contain, in detail, all the actions that need to be accomplished to implement the client's decisions. It should encompass for example, timings, budgets, training and other programmes. It should include clear and specific objectives and standards of performance and ways in which performance and progress will be measured and evaluated. Again the extent to which the consultant will be involved in designing these detailed plans will vary from project to project and in particular will be determined again through prior agreement regarding the consultant's remit as expressed in the research brief and plan. Yet again, there should be extensive discussion and communication between client and consultant regarding any proposals and detailed action plans together with allocated responsibilities. Planning techniques such as critical path analysis, and techniques of change management have been shown to be effective at this stage (Lewin 1951; Strebel 1994, Kanter 1983; Haveman 1992).

Activity 12.1. As a result of a consultancy exercise it has been determined that an organization's sales force needs better training. The training manager in the organization has been instructed to run a training programme. What tasks and activities might the training manager need to complete in planning for these proposed training programmes.

12.3   Implementation and follow up

'Plans are nothing unless they degenerate into action'.

(Drucker 1973)

Unfortunately, and perhaps somewhat perversely, often consultancy plans are never translated into action. This may seem strange, given that presumably an organization has commissioned and in some way paid for the consultancy research project. However, the fact is that many consultants' reports are never acted upon or at least are only implemented in part. Obviously, failure to implement negates and undermines the central purpose of most consultancy projects that result in improving organizational performance. We need to understand, therefore, why clients often fail to implement consultancy findings and what can be done by the consultant and client to improve this process.

Cockman et al. (op. cit. pp. 162–8) suggest that four key factors are important in successful implementation of courses of action namely: 'Ownership', 'Leadership', 'Capability', and 'Organisation'. But what do Cockman et al. mean by these in the context of successful implementation?

- *Ownership*: In fact the importance of ownership has been referred to several times already in this chapter. Remember, it was suggested that the more the client can be made responsible for recommendations and actions stemming from the consultancy research, the more likely they are to be committed and motivated to implementing these. In addition, the implementation of consultancy research recommendations often involves change in the organization. As we all know, there is a tendency for individuals to resist change as it often makes us feel uncomfortable, insecure or fearful and even angry. Ownership through involvement in the plans for change and their implementation can help reduce resistance to change. Not only should the client and specifically the commissioning manager(s) for the consultancy be closely involved in plans for change, but those people affected by any proposed changes should also be involved as far as possible and appropriate, not only in implementing the changes, but also again, as far as possible, in determining what these are. Of course, there will be times when the manager has to impose change on other people, but again ideally the whole client system should be involved and hence have a feeling of ownership in problem diagnosis and decision making. At the very least people affected by proposed changes should be informed about the changes and the rationale behind them.

- *Leadership*: Cockman's second factor in implementing action plans and changes, again in part, stems from ownership of the proposed changes by those charged with responsibility for implementing these. In particular, senior management should lead by example in implementing action plans and demonstrate commitment and enthusiasm to their achievement. Quite simply, if senior management are not committed then other people are unlikely to be.

- *Capability*: Perhaps a rather obvious factor, but both management and organization must have the necessary skills, knowledge and resources to implement proposed courses of action. Where these are not present, or at least not present to a sufficient degree, then part of the action programmes may include plans for acquiring/improving capabilities including, for example, proposals for training programmes, recruitment, or commitment of financial and other corporate resources.

- *Organization*: Organizational procedures and structures will need to be in place in order to implement action plans. Indeed, in some cases the recommendations will encompass proposals for ensuring that these are in place. Procedures may relate to, for example, methods of reporting, assigning budgets, evaluation and control systems, and so on. Structure may relate to, for example, issues of how activities are grouped together ensuring effective teamwork and structures for communication.

These, then, are Cockman's four key requirements for effective implementation. You may be wondering however, what, if any, role the consultant plays in this implementation stage other than making suggestions or recommendations. It may appear that we are suggesting that the consultant plays little or no role in the actual process of implementing plans and actions. Certainly, as has been suggested, both ownership and leadership are likely to be more effective where the implementation is in the hands of the client. In addition, encouraging the client to be responsible affords learning and development opportunities for the client team and reduces the danger of the client being or becoming over-dependent on the consultant. Sometimes, however, the consultant will be expected, and/or have to play a more active role in implementation where, for example, the client simply has not the required skills and where these cannot be acquired quickly enough. Overall though, wherever possible the consultant should try to act more as a supporter/facilitator for implementing proposed action plans.

12.4 Control and evaluation: disengagement

The final stages of the business consultancy research process involve assessing or evaluating the effectiveness of any actions or changes in the organization undertaken on the basis of the consultancy research recommendations and disengaging from the client/project. Control and evaluation is essential for any programmes involving scarce resources. Certainly, the client will be evaluating the extent to which any time, money and other resources invested with the consultancy research project and the actions taken as a result of these have been effective. Again, unlike purely academic research, the research process does not end with the publication of a paper or even with a set of recommendations. Not only will the client be evaluating the success or otherwise of the project and learning from this, but the consultant researcher too should also learn from every consultancy project through a process of evaluation. It is important, therefore, and is part of the consultancy research plan, to establish in advance what control mechanisms and measures will be used to evaluate the effectiveness of the consultancy research.

Normally, such controls will relate to the nature of the problem being addressed, the performance outcomes agreed upon with the client, and the extent to which results in the problem can be measured and evaluated. The appropriate point to consider evaluation, then, is at the beginning of the research consultancy. However, it is only when consultancy recommendations have been implemented that both client and consultant are in a position to determine how effective the research and project have been. Again, continuing our theme of client-centred consultancy research, although as we have already stated, the consultant must evaluate his or her own efforts and approaches with a view to further learning and improvement, the thrust of the evaluation process should be based on the client's evaluation and views. For this reason it is an essential part of the consultancy research process for the consultant to seek information and feedback from the client as to their views regarding the project. At the very least, discussions should take place between client and consultant with a view to making this evaluation. In many consultancy research projects questionnaires can be used to obtain feedback from clients. The evaluation of the project should encompass not only the effectiveness of any recommendations and actions based on these, but also the overall effectiveness of the consultancy process from beginning to end. In this respect, the consultant should be considering and evaluating how effective each stage of the consultancy project was. Cockman et al. (op. cit. pp. 182–5) include the following areas in a proposed checklist for evaluating a client-centred consulting assignment.

- gaining entry,
- the contract and problem diagnosis,
- the contract and relationship with clients,
- strategies and technologies,
- collecting data,

- interpreting the data, making the decisions and planning,
- implementation.

We can see that evaluation involves every stage of the consultancy research process, and that this involves evaluation by both client and consultant with regard to effectiveness and efficiency. In some ways, however, we can assess the real effectiveness of a consultancy project by the extent to which the consultant is able to leave the clients to continue managing themselves with respect to the problem areas or issues addressed by the consultancy research once the work of the consultant has finished. In other words, the outcome of a successful consultancy project is where a problem has been effectively resolved for the client and the client can be left to deal with this, and perhaps any further problems without the continuing help of the consultant. Where the consultant is able to leave the client in this way is often referred to as the point of *disengagement*. Effective planning and procedures for disengagement is an essential part of professional consultancy.

Clearly the timing and nature of disengagement will vary enormously between different consultancy research projects. For example, in some cases the nature of the consultancy project will involve a long period of follow-up where, for example, the consultant is still involved in monitoring and evaluating any changes made in the organization and perhaps even making further recommendations. In other circumstances the consultancy project will terminate as soon as the consultant's report has been presented. Both consultant and client must determine when it is appropriate to disengage and the most effective process of disengagement. Again, both timing and circumstances of disengagement, together with the procedures to be followed and the responsibilities and duties of both parties should be discussed and agreed upon early in the consulting relationship. In this way both consultant and client will know when and how the project is to be ended and on what terms. Unless this is done, sometimes client or consultant may be tempted to abort the consultancy process and disengage at an inappropriate time. For example, the client may begin to think about disengagement where, the consultant is uncovering information which the client manager may not welcome about his or her own role and responsibilities with regard to an organizational problem. Similarly, the consultant may begin to think about disengagement when the project begins to look particularly difficult or things aren't going quite as smoothly as was envisaged. Disengagement may not be the final end of the project, as there may be agreements with regard to follow-up actions or further evaluations by the consultant, for example. Disengagement may involve deciding who is to take over any tasks that the consultant has been performing and may involve, therefore, provisions for staff training or even new personnel, for example. Cockman, et al. (op. cit. p. 227) suggests the following checklist for successful disengagement:

- Is there a clear contract about when and how disengagement will take place?
- Is everyone clear about the plan for disengagement?

- Has the original contract been fulfilled?
- Is there a plan for ensuring how the client system will become and remain self-sustaining?
- Is there a contract for any further support that might be required by the client?
- Are you satisfied that the reasons for disengagement are legitimate and not simply a way of avoiding difficult issues for you or for the client?
- Has your relationship with the client developed to the point where you can leave the door open for further work as and when needed in the future?
- How will the learning from the project be recorded, documented and made available to others?
- Is there an opportunity for both you and the client to give one another feed-back on how the project was managed?
- How will the endpoint be formally acknowledged and celebrated by every-one involved?

We can see, then, that the consultancy research project ends as it should start, as has been stressed throughout the text, with a professional, planned and above all client-centred approach.

12.5 Concluding comments

In this chapter we have looked at the final stages of the consultancy research project. We have seen that a key part of this final stage is the actioning of research, encompassing diagnosing the research findings, making recommen-dations, and taking decisions. Throughout this process it is important for con-sultant and client to continue to work closely together and ideally the consultant should work towards encouraging and guiding the client to make decisions between alternative courses of action themselves. Clearly, most consultancy projects are aimed at generating some sort of action with regard to solving organizational problems and/or improving organizational effectiveness. It is, therefore, vital that consultancy proposals are implemented and followed up. Once again, client commitment and acceptance of responsibility for this process are crucial. We identified Cockman et al.'s four factors as being important in successful implementation, namely ownership, leadership, capability and organization. Once actioned, consultancy research recommendations should be controlled and evaluated not only with respect to their effectiveness with regard to the organizational issue or problem which was addressed by the con-sultancy research, but also, by the consultant with regard to each step and stage of the consultancy research project. The final stage of the consultancy research project involves the process of disengagement. Both client and con-sultant should agree upon and plan at the outset how this is to be addressed and it should be just as carefully planned as the preceding stages of the consultancy research process.

12.6 References

Bartol, K. M. and Martin, D. C. (1998) *Management*, 3rd edn, Irwin/McGraw-Hill.
Bazerman, M. H. (1984) *Judgement in Managerial Decision Making*, New York, Wiley.
Bellman, G. M. (2001) *Getting Things Done When You Are Not In Charge*, 2nd edn, Berret-Koehler.
Cockman, P., Evans, B. and Reynolds, P. (1999) *Consulting for Real People*, 2nd edn, Berkshire, England: McGraw-Hill.
Cohen, A. A. R. and Bradford, D. L. (1991) *Influence Without Authority*, New York: Wiley.
Drucker P. F. (1973) Management: Tasks, responsibilities, practices, New York, Harper & Row.
Fisher, A. B. (1995) 'Making change stick', *Fortune*, April 17, 1995, pp. 121–8.
French, W. L. and Bell, C. H. (Jr) (1978) *Organization Development: Behavioural Interventions for Organisational Improvement*, Englewood Cliffs, N.J: Prentice-Hall.
Haefele, J. W. (1962) *Creativity and Innovation*, New York, Reinhold.
Haveman, H. A. (1992) 'Between a rock and a hard place: organisational change and performance under conditions of fundamental environmental transformation', *Administrative Science Quarterly*, 37, pp. 48–75.
Huse, E. F. and Cummings, T. G. (1985) *Organisation Development and Change*, 3rd edn, St Paul, Minn: West.
Kanter, R. M. (1983) *The Change Masters*, New York, Simon & Shuster.
Lewin, K. (1951) *Field Theory in Social Science*, New York, Harper and Rowe.
Maistor, D. H., Green, C. H. and Galford, R. M. (2001) *The Trusted Adviser*, Free Press.
Mohrman, A. M. (Jr), Mohrman, S. A., Ledford, G. E. (Jr), Cummings, T. G., Lawlor, E. E. III. (1989) *Large-Scale Organisational Change*, San Francisco, Jossey-Bass.
Nutt, P. C. (1986) 'Tactics of implementation', *Academy of Management Journal*, 29, pp. 230–61.
Schaffer, R. M. (2002) *High Impact Consulting: How Clients and Consultants Can Work Together to Achieve Extraordinary Results*, San Francisco: Jossey-Bass.
Schein, E. H. (1998) *Process Consultation Revisited: Building The Helping Relationship*, Prentice-Hall.
Schwarz, R. (2002) *The Skilled Facilitator*, San Francisco: Jossey-Bass.
Strebel, P. (1994) 'Choosing the right change path', *California Management Review*, 36, pp. 29–35.
Tisdall, P. (1983) *Agents of Change: The Development and Practice of Management Consultancy*, Trafalgar Square Publishing.

12.7 Glossary

disengagement. That point in a consultancy project when the consultant withdraws from the client system and leaves the internal managers to continue managing on their own.

Appendix I
Activity Solutions

Note: Solutions shown in this section are only for those activities which require further discussion or illustration in the form of worked examples.

Solution 3.1. The concepts in the hypothesis which will need *operationalizing* are the concepts of *job satisfaction* and *managerial level*. These abstract concepts must be translated and defined in a way which enables them to be accurately measured.

Among the problems and issues in achieving the operationalization of these terms are, for example, the fact that what constitutes job satisfaction may differ from one situation and from one researcher to another. We also need measures of job satisfaction which allow us to assess the degree of job satisfaction. Similarly, in operationalizing the notion of managerial level, how do we in fact measure or define different managerial levels. Is it for example by salary, responsibility or simply the place in the organizational chart, and so on.

We can see that operationalizing abstract concepts in order to test out hypotheses or theories is by no means easy.

Solution 3.3. To Gill and Johnson's stages in the research sequence we would add the following when it comes to applied management research and particularly consultancy research.

- Conclusions and recommendations,
- Implementation proposals,
- Control and evaluation.

Admittedly, conclusions and recommendations could form part of the presentation element of Gill and Johnson's framework but it is felt that in the context of applied management research, they are so important as to merit a separate mention. Similarly, and particularly where the research is of a consultancy type, then it would be expected and required for the process to include implementation proposals. Finally, most applied management research, and again particularly consultancy research which is usually aimed at some sort of managerial action would normally include control and evaluation as part of the sequence.

Solution 3.4. Examples of cultural issues which might affect the process of conducting management research would include:

- different cultural attitudes among employees towards being questioned,
- differences in availability of data in different cultures,
- differences in ethical issues and values in different cultures.

Solution 4.1. Using internal employees for organizational consultancy type activities and projects is in fact quite common. Some organizations utilize special project teams which are formed for the purpose of conducting a consultancy-type project, especially where a team is to be used. Where individuals are liberated from their normal duties to act on a consultancy basis in the organization they may be given sabbatical-type leave from their normal functions. Finally, some organizations utilize matrix type structures to conduct consultancy projects using internal staff.

Solution 4.2. Obviously approaches to reducing or at least minimizing resentment, fear and antagonism towards a consultant/consultancy team depends on the circumstances and in particular on the reasons for the resentment, fear or antagonism. In general terms, however, these problems can be reduced where:

- employees affected by the consultancy process or outcomes are kept fully informed,
- management makes an effort to reassure employees that wherever possible their interests will be protected,
- the culture in the organization is one of openness and trust.

Solution 4.3. An example where the task oriented approach to consultancy might be most appropriate would be, where the problem is of a technical/functional nature, for example, the design of a new management information system.

The process orientation approach would be more suitable, for example, where the organization is concerned to improve its approach to creative problem-solving.

Solution 4.4. Below are listed some of the factors that might affect the choice of an appropriate consultancy approach.

- The objectives of the consultancy process,
- The nature of the contract agreed between client and consultant,
- Personal limitations and inclinations of the consultant,
- Personal limitations and inclinations of the client,

- Norms and standards of the client's system,
- Budgetary and other resource constraints,
- Organizational culture and systems,
- Time available/speed of decision making required, and so on.

Solution 4.5. Remembering that many factors will affect the choice of an appropriate consultancy style the following represent what are probably the most appropriate styles for each situation based on the information given.

(a)   Prescriptive style,
(b)   Catalytic style,
(c)   Confrontational style,
(d)   Acceptant style.

Solution 4.6.
Advantages – examples:

- can establish client system more readily;
- familiar with organizational systems, procedures and culture;
- may be familiar with background to problem;
- familiar with potential internal data sources: internal secondary information;
- may find it easier to gain access to different parts of the organization;
- can be involved with implementation and follow-up;
- may be feared/resented less than outside consultant.

   Disadvantages – examples:

- may be resented or feared due to internal conflicts/hostilities, and so on;
- may find it more difficult to be objective;
- consultant may be part of the problem;
- organizational status or grade of consultant may be a barrier/problem;
- concern for future career prospects may interfere;
- concern for personal relationships/image may interfere;
- may have access to confidential/sensitive information which cannot be revealed.

   NB: It is important to stress that these are potential rather than certain advantages/disadvantages. Both consultant and client, however, need to consider the extent to which either disadvantages or advantages will exist when considering conducting management consultancy using an internal consultant.

Solution 5.1. Because of this it is vital that the consultant plans and manages this initial contact/meeting stage as carefully as possible. What the consultant should be aiming to achieve through this initial contact and meeting as quickly and as fully as possible are the following between the consultant and client.

- openness and trust,
- good communication,
- removal of any organizational or personal barriers between consultant and client.

Solution 5.2. Obviously we are only speculating here, but using Revans' three questions for our hypothetical marketing consultant, the following might be part of this consultant's real client or real-client system.

- *Who knows?* Persons or parties who could potentially provide information or shed light on this particular consultancy problem might include, for example: The sales force, the advertising and marketing manager, the advertising agency, distributors and customers.
- *Who cares?* Persons or parties who might have occasion to care about the consultancy problem and its potential solution would include the above parties plus possibly the accountancy function and the shareholders.
- *Who can?* Who can do something about the solution to the problem might again include, now, all of the above plus the main Board.

Solution 5.3. In our experience of organizations just some of the possible needs and values which a management consultant might bring to the work situation and which might affect how, or even if they conducted a management consultancy project for a client would include the following:

- Need for financial gain in relation to need for job satisfaction.
- Values with regard to treatment of employees.
- Values with regard to disclosure of information.
- Values with regard to ethical issues in business.

Solution 6.1. There are probably many areas or aspects of the company's operation which the consultant might need data on for this problem, but examples of four areas where data might be required/useful would include:

- How does the organization currently motivate its managers?
- What are the signs, signals and effects of poor motivation in the organization?
- To what extent and in what ways are managers unhappy with current approaches to motivation?
- How might the organization increase motivation amongst its managers?

Solution 6.2. The main reasons why secondary data is usually collected and assessed before collecting any primary data are:

- cost: secondary data is usually cheaper to collect and analyse than primary data;
- time: secondary data can usually be collected more quickly than primary data;
- availability: perhaps an obvious one, this, but secondary data already exists.

Solution 6.3. Certainly, the notion that only quantitative data is *scientific* can be dismissed. Admittedly, qualitative data cannot be analysed and interpreted in the same sort of mathematical and statistical ways that quantitative data can. This, in turn, has implications for, for example, research which is designed to support or refute specific hypotheses. In particular, qualitative data often means that we cannot use the statistical techniques of data analysis which involve tests of uncertainty, estimation and so on, through the application of probability. This is not the same, however as saying that qualitative data is inherently unscientific. It is not, and can be collected at least in a scientific manner. The truth is that most research and consultancy projects involve a combination very often of both qualitative and quantitative research and data.

Solution 7.1. Obviously the examples you have identified will be specific to your own particular set of circumstances. Here are one or two ideas of examples of the ways in which secondary data could be used in a consultancy project in an organization.

- Secondary data could help frame the objectives for the consultancy project. So, for example, data on customer complaints held by the sales and marketing part of the organization could point the way to a useful consultancy project in this area.
- Continuing the same example, secondary data might indicate that poor product quality is a major element of customer complaints and that this variable needs to be investigated further.

Solution 7.2. Jankowicz's framework, remember, is based on considering the issues of 'What to look for', 'Where to look', and 'How to look'. In broad terms for our hypothetical consultancy problem, these questions will help shape the secondary data collection process. In terms of what to look for, we should be looking for secondary data which will shed light on new product development systems and processes, both inside and outside of the organization. In terms of where to look, the researcher will be able to establish which published external secondary sources might provide useful data. Any syndicated sources and possibly online/CD Rom computerized databases. Finally, with regard to how to look, the researcher will clearly need to know how effective or otherwise the company is in terms of its new product development, what the problems (if any) are, and what constitutes best practice.

Solution 7.3. Again, obviously the ways in which each of these aspects of data management could help improve secondary data depends on the circumstances in your chosen organization. Here are some experiences of the author with regard to these aspects.

Data mining: Investigation of a company's database indicated that levels of average spend by the company's customers was strongly associated with the type of neighbourhood which customers lived in. This data was analysed further to provide a very effective geodemographic basis for segmenting and targeting high spend customers.

Data warehousing: The quality control department of an organization were not aware of some severe and particular quality problems which were causing the company to lose customers because this data was held only in the sales department of the organization. Pooling of this information enabled the company to take the necessary steps to resolve the problem.

Database cleaning: The marketing department of a company contacted all those customers who had not renewed their subscriptions to the company's services that year. Five per cent of these customers were dead.

Solution 8.1. Obviously you will have your own list of organizational research areas for which observational research techniques might be particularly suited. Given the characteristics and advantages of observation here are our four examples of research problems for which observation is particularly well suited.

- intra group communication,
- leadership patterns and style,
- inter group conflict,
- informal versus formal authority and communication.

Solution 8.2.
(a) Circumstances which would favour a totally artificial setting for observational research would be those where it was important to control the variables being observed. At the extreme, the most contrived settings for observational research are where the observations are carried out in a *laboratory setting*.
(b) Unrevealed observation would be used where knowledge that they were being observed might affect the behaviour of the participants and where the researcher wishes to avoid this possibility.
(c) Complete participation as an approach to observational research would be appropriate to a situation where the observer wishes to gain data and insights into behaviour and processes, which can best be observed through the observer becoming an unrevealed participant in the processes being observed.

Solution 8.3. Reasons and situations for not piloting observational research methods would include the following:

- where it is vital to ensure that a proposed observational research exercise is not signalled to those to be observed,
- where the time frame for the observational research does not permit,
- where the event(s)/individuals and others being observed can only be observed at a particular and unique point in time.

Solution 8.4. Although it can be disadvantageous for an observer to *go native* there are also potential advantages as well including:

- the observer may obtain insights which would otherwise not be possible,
- where it is important for the observer to remain unrevealed *going native* may help,

- the observer may encounter much more openness and trust in terms of relationships with those being observed.

Solution 9.1. The first part of this activity requires you to select a hypothetical organizational issue or problem which could usefully be explored and researched using an experimental approach.

In fact, most organizational issues or problems can be explored using this approach provided that Denscombe's three criteria or key factors in the process of effective experimentation can be achieved, namely 'controls', 'identifying causal factors', and 'observation and measurement'.

For the second part of this activity you were required to consider how the first of the key factors above, that is, control could be achieved in your selected hypothetical problem. Obviously, the issues and problems of achieving control will depend on the problem/issue selected but you should have considered the various ways in which control can be introduced into the design of experimental research, namely one or a combination of: eliminating factors; holding factors constant; the use of 'balancing groups'; sampling/large numbers; the use of control groups.

Solution 9.2. This one is not an easy activity. As with Activity 9.1 how you fared with this one depends on the problem or issue you selected. You should, however, have been able to couch the problem or issue in the form of a hypothesis which could be tested through an appeal to the facts. This in turn requires that you understand and be able to identify the distinction between independent and dependent variables in your proposed hypothesis. Finally, operationalizing your variables essentially requires you to consider how the variables will be observed and measured and precisely therefore what they mean.

Solution 9.3. In fact this is not a trick question. Actually there is no organizational issue or problem that could not, in essence, be addressed through action research. However, action research is particularly suited to consultancy-type research where there are real organizational problems to which the organization or client is seeking a solution.

Solution 10.1. In fact, there are very few organizational issues or problems for which interviews of some kind would not be appropriate. However, interviews are a particularly useful approach to collecting data where, for example, in-depth data is required, the topic or problem is sensitive or where perhaps large numbers of people need to be asked.

Solution 10.2. For each of our hypothetical research situations, a range and combination of interviewing approaches/techniques could be used. I have selected one of the approaches for each situation which would be almost certainly appropriate and useful.

(a) Conversation/story telling,
(b) Individual unstructured interviews,
(c) Group interviews,
(d) Focus group interviews.

Solution 12.1. The precise details, steps and activities will no doubt vary according to the particular situation and organization but the following represent some of the key considerations and activities when planning to run these training programmes.

- complete a training needs analysis through interviews with sales persons,
- formulate objectives and targets for the training programme,
- formulate the structure of the training programme,
- decide training methods,
- design and produce training materials,
- identify participants, locations, timings,
- arrange budgets,
- inform participants,
- establish methods and procedures for evaluation and control of training.

Appendix II

Bibliography

Alveson, M. and Wilmott, H. (1996) *Making Sense of Management*, London: Sage.

Arksey, H. and Knight, P. (1999) *Interviewing for Social Scientist*, London: Sage.

Babbie, E. (2001) *The Practice of Social Research*, 9th edn, Belmont, CA: Wadsworth/ Thomson.

Bales, R. F. (1950) *Interaction Process Analysis: A Method for the Study of Small Groups*, Cambridge, MA: Addison-Wesley.

Barthes, R. (1967) *Elements of Semiology*, trans. Lavers, A. and Smith, C., New York, Noonday Press.

Bartol, K. M. and Martin, D. C. (1998) *Management*, 3rd edn, Boston, Mass: Irwin/McGraw Hill.

Baudrillard, J. (1988) in M. Poster, (ed.) *Jean Baudrillard, Selected Writings*, Cambridge: Polity Press.

Bazerman, M. H. (1984) *Judgement in Managerial Decision Making*, New York: Wiley.

Bechhofer, F. and Paterson, L. (2000) *Principles of Research Design in the Social Sciences*, London: Routledge.

Becker, H. S. (1998) *Tricks of the Trade: How To Think About Your Research While You're Doing It*, Chicago: University of Chicago Press.

Bell, J. (1999) *Doing your Research Project*, 3rd edn, Buckingham: Open University Press.

Bellman, G. M. (2001) *Getting Things Done When You Are Not In Charge*, 2nd edn, San Francisco, CA: Berret-Koehler.

Belman, G. M., (2001) *The Consultants Calling: Bringing Who You Are to What You Do*, San Francisco, CA, Jossey-Bass/Pfeiffer.

Benyon, H. (1973) *Working for Ford*, Harmondsworth: Penguin.

Berger, A. A. (1982) *Media Analysis Techniques*, Newbury Park, CA: Sage.

Bhaskar, R. (1989) *Reclaiming Reality: A Critical Introduction to Contemporary Philosophy*, London, Verso Press.

Biech, E. (1998) *The Business of Consulting: The Basics and Beyond*, Jossey-Bass, Pfeiffer, San Francisco, CA.

Biswas, S. and Twitchell, D. (1999) *Management Consultancy: A Complete Guide to the Industry*, London, John Wiley.

Black, T. R. (1999) *Doing Quantitative Research in the Social Sciences: An Integrated Approach to Research Design, Measurement and Statistics*, London: Sage.

Blake, R. R. and Mouton, J. S. (1983) *Consultation: A Handbook for Individual and Organisation Development*, Wokingham: Addison-Wesley.

Blaxter, L., Hughes, C. and Tight, M. (2001) *How to Research*, 2nd edn, Buckingham: Open University Press, p. 65.

Block, P. (1999) *Flawless Consulting: A Guide to Getting Your Expertise Used*, 2nd edn, San Francisco, CA, Jossey-Bass/Pfeiffer.

Bryman, A. (1989) *Research Methods and Organisation Studies*, London: Routledge.

Burns, R. B. (2000) *Introduction to Research Methods*, 4th edn, London: Sage.

Burrell, G. and Morgan, G. (1979) *Sociological Paradigms and Organisational Analysis*, London: Heinemann.

Byrne, D. (2002) *Interpreting Qualitative Data*, London: Sage.

Campbell, D. T. (1969) 'Reforms as experiments' *American Pschycologist*, 24, pp. 409–29.

Cassell, C. and Symon, G. (eds) (1994) *Qualitative Methods in Organisational Research: A Practical Guide*, London: Sage.

Charlesworth, R. and Morley, P. (2000) *Managing Information: Module Learning Guide*, London: University of North London Business School.

Churchill, G. A. (2001) *Marketing Research: Methodological Foundations*, 8th edn, San Francisco, CA, South-Western College Publishing.

Clark, T. (1995) *Managing Consultants: Consultancy as the Management of Impressions*, Buckingham: Open University Press.

Cockman, P., Evans, B. and Reynolds, P. (1992) *Client-Centred Consulting*, Maidenhead: McGraw Hill.

Cohen, A. A. R. and Bradford, D. L. (1991) *Influence Without Authority*, Indianopolis, Indiana Wiley.

Cook, T. and Campbell, D. T. 'Popper and falsificationalism' in *Social Research Methods: A Reader*, C. Seale (ed) (2004) London: Routledge.

Cope, M. (2000) *The Seven Cs of Consulting: Your Complete Blueprint For Any Consultancy Assignment*, Harlow Essex: Financial Times/Prentice Hall.

Cronbach, L. J. (1975) 'Beyond the two disciplines of scientific psychology', *American Psychologist*, 30, pp. 116–26.

Crowther, D. (2002) *A Social Critique of Corporate Reporting* Aldershot: Ashgates.

Czerniawska, F. (2003) *The Intelligent Client: Managing your Management Consultant*, London, Trafalgar Square Books.

Dale, A. Arber, S. and Proctor, M. (1998) *Doing Secondary Analysis*, London: Unwin Hyman.

de Vaus, D. A. (2002) *Analysing Social Science Data: 50 Key Problems in Data Analysis*, London:Sage.

Delbridge, R. and Kirkpatrick, I. (1994) 'Theory and practice of participant observation', in P. Wass, and P. Wells, (eds), *Principles and Practice in Business and Management Research*, Aldershot: Dartmouth, pp. 35–62.

Denscombe, M. (1998) *The Good Research Guide*, Buckingham: Open University Press.

Derrida, J. (1978) *Writing and Difference*, trans. Bass, A., London: Routledge & Kegan Paul.

Dickens, L. and Watkins, K. (1999) 'Action research: rethinking Lewin', *Management Learning*, 30(2) pp. 127–40.

Daly F., Hand, J., Jones, M. C., Lunn A. D. and McConway K. J. (1995) *Elements of Statistics*, London: FT/Prentice-Hall.

Drucker P. F. (1973) Management: Tasks, responsibilities, Practices, New York, Harper & Row.

Easterby Smith, M., Thorpe, R. and Lowe, A. (2002) *Management Research: An Introduction*, London, Sage.

Feyerabend, P. (2004) 'Against method' in C Seale (ed.), *Social Research Methods: A Reader*, London: Routledge.

Fink, A. and Kosecoff, J. (1998) *How to Conduct Surveys*, London: Sage.

Fish, S. (1985) *Is there a text in this class?* in W. T. J. Mitchell, (ed.) *Against Theory* Chicago, University of Chicago Press.

Fisher, A. B. (1995) 'Making change stick', *Fortune* April 17, pp. 121–8.

Foddy, W. (1993) *Constructing Questions for Interviews and Questionnaires: Theory and Practice in Social Research*, Cambridge: Cambridge University Press.

Freedman, R. (2000) *The IT Consultant: A Commonsense Framework for Managing the Client Relationship*, San Francisco, CA, Jossey-Bass/Pfeiffer.

French, W. L. and Bell, C. H. (Jr) (1978) *Organisation Development: Behavioural Interventions for Organisational Improvement*, Englewood Cliffs, N.J: Prentice Hall.

Gallup, G. (1947) 'Qualitative measurement of public opinion. The quintamensional plan of question design', *Public Opinion Quarterly*, American Institute of Public Opinion, Fall.

Ghosh, B. N. and Chopra, P. K. (2003) *A Dictionary of Research Methods*, Leeds (UK): Wisdom House Publications.

Gibb, S. (2002) *Learning and Development Processes, Practices and Perspectives at Work*, Hampshire, Palgrave Macmillan.

Gilbert, N. (ed) (1993) *Researching Social Life*, London: Sage.

Gill, J. and Johnson, P. (1997) *Research Methods for Managers,* 2nd edn, London: Paul Chapman Publishing.

Gill, J. and Johnson, P. (2002) *Research Methods for Managers,* 3rd Edn, London: Sage.

Gill, J. and Johnson, P. (1997) *Research Methods for Managers,* 2nd edn, London: Paul Chapman.

Glaser, B. and Strauss, A. (1967) *The Discovery of Grounded Theory*, Chicago: Aldine.

Goulding, C. (2002) *Grounded Theory: A Practical Guide for Management, Business and Market Researchers*, London: Sage.

Gouldner, A. W. (1954) *Patterns of Industrial Bureaucracy*, New York: Free Press.

Graziano, A. M. and Rawlin, M. L. (2004) *Research Methods: A Process of Enquiry*, 5th edn, Harlow: Pearson Education Group.

Greenfield, T. (2002) *Research Methods for Postgraduates*, 2nd edn, London: Arnold.

Greenwood, R. G. and Wrege, C. D. (1986) 'The Hawthorne Studies', in D. A. Wren, and J. A. Pearce (eds), *Papers Dedicated to the Development of Modern Management*, Academy of Management, pp. 24–35.

Greimas, A. J. (1990) *The Social Sciences: A Semiotic View*, Minneapolis: University of Minneapolis Press.

Greimas, A. J. and Rastier, F. (1968), 'The interaction of semiotic constraints', *Yale French Studies*, 41, pp. 86–105.

Guiraud, P. (1975) *Semiology*, London, Routledge & Kegan Paul.

Gummesson, E. (2002) *Qualitative Methods in Management Research*, London, Sage.

Haefele, J. W. (1962) *Creativity and Innovation*, New York, Reinhold.

Hakim, C. (1982) *Secondary Analysis in Social Research*, London: Allen and Unwin.

Hakim, C. (2000) *Research Design: Successful Designs for Social and Economic Research*, 2nd edn, New York: Routledge.

Hakim, C. (2000) *Research Design* London: Routledge.

Halliday, M. A. K. (1978) *Language as Social Semiotic*, London: Edward Arnold.

Harrison, R. (2002) *Learning and Development*, London, Chartered Institute of Personnel and Development.

Haveman, H. A. (1992) 'Between a rock and a hard place: organisational change and performance under conditions of fundamental environmental transformation', *Administrative Science Quarterly*, 37, pp. 48–75.

Healey, M. J. and Rawlinson, M. B. (1993) 'Interviewing Business Owners & Managers: A review of Methods & Techniques, Geoforum 24(3), 1993, 339–55.

Hewitt, J. (1989) White adolescent creole users and the politics of friendship, *Journal of Multicultural and Multilingual Education*, 3 (3), pp. 340–57.

Hjelmslev, L. (1963) *Prolegomena to a Theory of language*, trans. Whitfield, F. J., Madison, University of Wisconsin Press.

Howard, K. and Sharp, J. A. (1983) *The Management of a Student Research Project*, Aldershot: Gower.

Huse, E. F. and Cummings, T. G. (1985) *Organisation Development and Change*, 3rd edn, St Paul, Minn. – West Publishing.

Jankowicz, A. D. (1991) *Business Research Projects for Students*, London: Chapman & Hall.

Kanter, R. M. (1983) *The Change Masters*, New York: Simon & Shuster.

Kemmis, S. and Grundy, S. 'Educational Action Research in Australia' AARE Annual Conference, November 1981, Adelaide.

Kerlinger, F. N. (1992) *Foundations of Behavioural Research*, 3rd edn, Fort Worth, TX: Harcourt Brace.

Kervin, J. B. (1999), *Methods for Business Research*, 2nd edn, New York: Harper Collins.

Khun, T. (1970) *The Structure of Scientific Revolutions*. Chicago: University of Chicago Press.

Klein, J. (1965) *Samples from English Cultures*, London, Routledge & Kegan Paul.

Krzanowski, W. (1988) *Principles of Multivariate Analysis*, Oxford: Clarendon Press.

Kubar, M. (1996) *Management Consulting: A Guide to the Profession*, 3rd edn, International Labour Office.

Labov, W. (1966) 'The linguistic stratification of "r" in New York City department stores', in W. Labov (ed.) *Sociolinguistic Patterns*, Philadelphia, Pennsylvania University Press.

Lacan, J. (1977) *Ecrits: a selection;* trans. Sheridan, A., London, Tavistock.

Lakoff, R. (1975) *Language and Woman's Place*, Cambridge: Harper & Row.

Lancaster, G. A., Massingham, L. and Ashford, R. (2001) *Marketing Fundamentals*, Oxford: Butterworth Heinemann.

Le Page, R. (1968) 'Problems of description in multilingual communities', in *Transactions of the Philological Society*, pp. 189–212, Oxford: Blackwell.

Lee, K. (2003) *Consulting into the Future: Key Skills*, Trafalgar Square.

Lewin, K. (1946) 'Action research and minority problems', *Journal of Social Issues*, 2, (4) pp. 34–46.

Lewin, K. (1951) *Field Theory in Social Science*, New York, Harper and Row.

Lewin, K, (1991) 'Group decision and social change' in T. Newcomb and F. Hartley, eds, *Readings in Social Psychology*, New York: Holt.

Lippitt, G. and Lippitt, R. (1978) *The Consulting Process in Action*, California: University Associates.

Lupton, T. (1963) *On the Shop Floor*, Oxford: Pergamon.

Maistor, D. H., Green, C. H. and Galford, R. M. (2001) *The Trusted Adviser*, New York, Free Press.

Malhotra, N. K. (1993) *Marketing Research an Applied Orientation*, New Jersey: Prentice Hall.

Marchington, M. and Wilkinson, A. (2002) *People Management and Development*, London, Chartered Institute of Personnel.

Margulies, N. and Raia, A. (1972) *Organisation Development: Values, Processes and Technology*, Maidenhead: McGraw Hill.

Markam, C. (1997) *Practical Management Consultancy*, London, The Institute of Chartered Accountants.

Marshall, C. and Rossman, G. B. (1999) *Designing Qualitiative Research*, 3rd edn, Thousand Oaks, CA: Sage.

Mayer, C. S. and Piper, C. (1982) 'A note on the importance of layout in self-administered questionnaires', *Journal of Marketing Research*, Vol XIX, August.

McBurney, D. H. and White T. L. (2004) *Research Methods*, 6th edn, Belmont, CA: Wadsworth/Thomson Learning.

McNiff, J. (2000) *Action Research in Organisations*, London: Routledge.

Miles, M. B. and Huberman, A. M. (1984) *Qualitative Data Analysis: A Sourcebook of New Methods*, 2nd edn. Thousand Oaks, CA: Sage Publications.

Miles, M. B. and Huberman, A. M. (1994) *Qualitative Data Analysis – a source-book of new methods*, 2nd edn, London, Sage.

Mintzberg, H. (1980) *The Nature of Managerial Work*, New York: Harper and Row.

Mohrman, A. M. (Jr), Mohrman, S. A., Ledford, G. E. (Jr), Cummings, T. G., Lawlor, E. E. III, (1989) *Large-Scale Organisational Change*, San Francisco, Jossey-Bass.

Morgan, P, (2002) *Managing Yourself*, Harlow: Pearson.

Morton-Williams, J. (1993) *Interviewer Approaches*, Aldershot, UK: Dartmouth.

Mullins, L. (2002) *Management and Organisational Behaviour*, 6th edn, Harlow, Financial Times-Prentice Hall.

Nutt, P. C. (1986) 'Tactics of implementation', *Academy of Management Journal*, 29, pp. 230–261.

Oakley, A. (1999) 'People's way of knowing: gender and methodology', in S. Hood, B. Mayall and S. Oliver, (eds), *Critical Issues in Social Research: Power and Prejudice*, Buckingham: Open University Press, pp. 154–77.

Oppenheimer, A. N. (2000) *Questionnaire Design, Interviewing and Attitude Measurement*, London: Continuum International, Aldershot, UK: Dartmouth.

Orna, E. and Stevens, G. (1995) *Managing Information for Research*, Buckingham: Open University Press.

Parson, R. and Tille, N. (2004) 'Go forth and experiment', in C. Seale, (ed) *Social Research Methods: A Reader* London: Routledge.

Pedler, M., Burgoyne, J. and Boydell, T. (2001) *A Manager's Guide to Self Development*, Maidenhead: McGraw-Hill.

Phillips, E. M. and Pugh, D. S. (1994) *How to get a PhD: A Handbook for Project*. Aldershot: Gower.

Pinault, L. and Pollan, S. M. (2000) *Consulting Demons: Inside the Unscrupulous World of Global Corporate Consulting*, NY, Harper Collins.

Popper, K. R. (1967) *Conjectures and Refutations*, London: Routledge.

Rasiel, E. M. (1999) *The McKinsey Way*, NY, McGraw-Hill.

Revans, R. W. (1980) *Action Learning – New Techniques for Managers*, London: Kogan Page.

Revans, R. W. (1971) *Developing Effective Managers*, London: Longman.

Robson, C. (2002) *Real World Research*, 2nd edn, Oxford: Blackwell.

Rosen, M. (1991) 'Breakfast at Spiro's dramaturgy and dominance', in P. Frost, L. Moore, M. Louis, C. Lundberg, and J. Martin, (eds), *Reframing Organisational Culture*, Newbury Park, CA: Sage, pp. 77–89.

Roy, D. (1952) 'Quota restriction and goldbricking in a machine shop', *American Journal of Sociology* 57, pp. 427–42.

Sadler, P. (2001) *Management Consultancy*, London: Kogan Page.

Salacuse, J. W. (2000) *The Wise Adviser: What Every Professional Should Know About Consulting and Counselling*, Westport: Praeger.

Sapsford, R. (1999) *Survey Research*, London: Sage.

Saunders, M., Lewis, P. and Thornhill, A. (2003) *Research Methods for Business Students*, 3rd edn, Harlow: Pearson Education.

Saussure, F. de (1966) *Course in General Linguistics*, trans. Baskin, W., New York: McGraw-Hill.

Sayer, A (2000) *Realism and Social Science* London: Sage Publications.

Schaffer, R. M. (2002) *High Impact Consulting: How Clients and Consultants Can Work Together to Achieve Extraordinary Results*, San Francisco: Jossey-Bass.

Schein, E. H. (1998) *Process Consultation Revisited: Building The Helping Relationship*, Prentice Hall.

Schon, D. (1995) 'Knowing-in-action: the new scholarship requires a new epistomology' *Change*, November–December.

Schwarz, R. (2002) *The Skilled Facilitator*, San Francisco: Jossey-Bass.

Scott, B. (2000) *Consulting on the Inside*, American Society for Training and Development.

Seale, C. and Kelly, M. (1998) 'Coding and Analysing Data' in C. Seale (ed.) (2004) *Social Research Methods: A Reader*, London: Routledge.

Sharp, J. A. and Howard, K. (1996) *The Management of a Student Research Project*, Aldershot, England: Gower.

Stewart, D. W. (1984) *Secondary Research: Information Sources and Methods*, Beverley Hills: Sage, pp. 23–33.

Stewart, D. W. and Kamins, M. A. (1993) *Secondary Research: Information Sources and Methods*, 2nd edn, Newbury Park, CA: Sage.

Stewart, J. (1995) *Employee Development Practice* Harlow: FT Prentice Hall.

Strauss, A. and Corbin, J. (1990) *Basics of Qualitative Research: Grounded Theory Procedures and Techniques*, London: Sage.

Strebel, P. (1994) 'Choosing the right change path', *California Management Review*, 36, pp. 29–35.

Symon, G. and Cassell, C. (eds) (1998) *Qualitative Analysis and Methods in Organisational Research*, London: Sage Publications, pp. 135–60.

The Social Research Association's Ethical Guidelines (2002): http://www.thesra.org.uk/ index2.htm

Thomas, A. B. (2004) *Research Skills for Management Students*, London: Routledge.

Tisdall, P. (1983) *Agents of Change: The Development and Practice of Management Consultancy*, North Pontret, Vermont, Trafalgar Square Publishing.

Tse, A. C. B., Tse, K. C., Yin, C. H., Ting, C. B., Yi, K. W., Yee, K. P. and Hong, W. C. (1995) 'Comparing two methods of sending out questionnaires: e-mail versus mail: Toward of the Marketing, Research Society Vol. 37, No. 4.

Van Der Velde, M., Jansen, P. and Anderson, N. (2004) *Guide to Management Research Methods*, Oxford: Blackwell Publishing.

Walker, R. (ed) (1985) *Applied Qualitative Research*, Aldershot: Gower.

Walker, R. (1985) *Doing Research: A Handbook for Teachers*, London: Methuen.

Weiss, A. (2001) *The Ultimate Consultant: Powerful Techniques for the Successful Practitioner*, San Francisco, CA: Jossey-Bass/Pfeiffer.

Weiss, A. (2002) *How to Establish a Unique Brand in the Consulting Profession: Powerful Techniques for the Successful Practitioner*, San Francisco, CA: Jossey-Bass/Pfeiffer.

Wickham, P. A. (2004) *Management Consulting: Delivering an Effective Project*, 2nd edn, NY: Prentice Hall.

Wilkins, A. L. (1983) 'Organisational stories as symbols which control the organization', in L. R. Pondy, L. R. Frost, P. J. G. Morgan, and T. C. Tandridge, (eds), *Organizational Symbolism*. Greenwich, CT: JAI Press.

Wilson, J. (1999) *Consultancy*, London: Hodder & Stoughton.

Wisniewski, M. (1997) *Quantitative methods for Decision Makers*, 2nd edn, London: Financial Times Management.

Worcester, R. M. and Burns, T. R. (1975) 'A statistical examination of the relative precision of verbal scales', *Journal of the Market Research Society*, 17 (3).

Wysocki, D. K. (ed) (2004) *Readings in Social Research Methods*, 2nd edn, Belmont CA: Wadsworth/Thomson Learning.

Yiannis, G. (1998) 'The use of stories', in Symon G, & Cassell C., *Qualitative methods and Organisational Analysis in Organizational Research*, A Practical Guide – London: Sage Publications.

Appendix III
Internet Gateways, Research and Databases, Search Engines and Directories for Social Science Researchers

The following represent some of the key current sites for social science researchers. Please note that this is only a small selection, but it does include some of the major ones.

 Internet gateways

The Social Science Information Gateway (SOSIG): http://www.sosig.ac.uk
The National Information Systems and Services (NISS) Gateway: http://www.niss.ac.uk

Research, research reports, bibliographic databases

Economic and Social Research Council (ESRC): http://www.esrc.ac.uk
UK Office for National Statistics: http://www.statistics.gov.uk/
British Library site: http://www.bl.uk/

 Directories

http://www.dir.yahoo.com/Social-Science/
http://www.ipl.org/ref/

Appendix IV
Amalgamated Glossary

action research
A set of research methodologies based on monitoring and evaluating the effects of the actions of a planned intervention by the researcher.

alternative hypothesis
Presented as a contrast to the null hypothesis. If the evidence rejects the validity of the null hypothesis, the alternative hypothesis is accepted.

applied research
Research that is directed towards a practical aim or objective and is concerned with working out the solution to a specific problem.

bibliographic databases
Databases which contain references to summaries or abstracts of published materials in journals, magazines, newspapers, market and technical reports and government documents.

Boolean operators
A system of syntax which can be used to refine searches on the web.

cardinal data
Has order, sequence and measurement, for example, number of employees, age, height, length of service and so on.

chi-squared test
A statistical test which compares recorded or observed data with that which would have been expected in order to measure the degree of association between dependent and independent variables.

client system
All those persons or groups who might provide information, care about, or be affected by the proposed solutions with regard to a consultancy project.

consultancy
An approach that is based on the consultant acting as problem sensor, technical expert and facilitator for the client, employed to make specific and concrete recommendations to the client. The

	consultant also raises questions for the client to reflect upon and essentially is responsible for proposing solutions.
content analysis	An approach to analysing qualitative data based on trying to quantify qualitative data by, for example, counting 'frequency,' and other such.
contract	A term used by consultants to denote that point where both client and consultant have agreed to proceed with a consultancy project and where there is an understanding what the consultancy project is to be about and what it will encompass.
control group	The group, including individuals, units, departments, and so on, which is not subjected to experimental variables and change and therefore serves as a reference point with regard to any observed changes and their possible causes in the experimental group.
data mining	The process of analysing and manipulating data to provide insights into a company's operations.
data warehousing	Systems for ensuring that data from different parts of the organization are collected and analysed in a central database within the company.
data	Data is comprised of the raw unprocessed details and facts pertaining to the issue or problem being explored.
database cleaning	Procedures whereby a database is regularly checked and maintained to ensure that data is up to date and accurate.
database	An organized store of data in an organization.
deductive research	Research aimed at testing theories and hypotheses through empirical observation.
dependent variables	Those variables that change only as a result of changes to the independent variables.
directory databases	Databases containing information on individuals, organizations or services.
disengagement	That point in a consultancy project when the consultant withdraws from the client system and leaves internal managers to continue managing on their own.
epistemology	A philosophical approach to theory building that investigates the nature, grounds, limits and validity of human knowledge.
ethnography	A set of research methodologies based on the researcher using primarily naturalist modes of enquiry such as participant observation.
***ex post facto* research**	A quasi-experimental research method based on observing cause and effect and then working backwards from the effect to try and establish the cause.

experimental group	The group, including individuals, units, departments, and other such, that is subjected to experimental variables and change by the researcher.
external secondary data	Data which already exists but which has been produced by sources external to the organization.
falsificationism	That school of philosophy of science which suggests that scientists must attempt to refute rather than verify their theories.
full text databases	Databases which contain the complete text of the source documents in the database.
gaining entry	The term used by many consultants to refer to the initial contact/meeting stage between consultant and client.
generalisability	The extent to which the patterns and results observed in a research project can be applied to other situations outside of the specific research study.
grounded theory	An approach to analysing qualitative data based on identifying and interpreting themes and patterns contained in the data.
hypothesis	A set of assumptions often couched in the form of tentative propositions which are subject to verification through subsequent investigation. These assumptions are provisionally accepted as a basis of reasoning, experiment or investigation.
ideographic methodologies	Research techniques which use less structured research methodologies aimed at generating qualitative data to facilitate explanation and understanding.
independent variables	Those variables which are responsible for changes in other variables.
inductive research	Research aimed at developing theories and explanations based on observations from the empirical world.
information	Information is data that has been arranged, interpreted and assessed in such a way that it is useful for problem solving and decision making.
internal secondary data	Data which already exists within the organization in some form or another.
internet gateways	Sites that edit sources of information so that the researcher can be directed more immediately to what is relevant and appropriate data.

management information systems	Systems which are designed to collect, store, interpret and utilize information for management decision making.
methodology	The general category of research approach being used in a business research/consultancy study and which relates particularly to the approach to data collection.
moderator	The person who takes responsibility for administering and operating focus group discussions.
nominal data	It is used to describe 'labels' (or categories) such as male/female, occupation and so on; also known as categorical data.
nomothetic methodologies	Research techniques that are based on highly structured research methodologies primarily aimed at generating quantitative data to explain causal relationships.
null hypothesis	An underlying assumption made about a population, the validity of which is the subject of a statistical test.
numeric databases	Databases which contain primarily numerical and statistical information.
observational reactivity	A reaction on the part of those being observed whereby their actions and behaviour are influenced by the process of being observed.
off-line databases	Data which is accessed through diskettes and CD Rom disks.
online databases	Databases which consist of a central data bank which is accessed via a computer or terminal via a telecommunications network.
ontology	A philosophical approach to theory building based on investigating the universal and necessary characteristics of all existence.
operationalize	The process whereby the dependent and independent variables to be researched and empirically measured and tested are defined and specified in such a way that allows both dependent and independent variables to be observed and measured and allows for the variation and manipulation of the independent variables.
ordinal data	Can be ordered, sequenced or ranked.
parameter	Greek letters, for example, μ to denote the mean. Normally used to determine the extreme(s) of a continuum.
population	Measures used to describe a population usually denoted by the full set of items or people under investigation.

primary data	Data that is collected for the first time for the purpose of a particular study (consultancy project) at hand.
qualitative data	Non-numerical data which cannot be, mathematically, statistically, or both – interpreted and analysed.
quantitative data	Data in the form of numbers which can be mathematically and/or statistically interpreted and analysed.
quasi-experiments	Techniques of research aimed at analysing causal relationships between independent and dependent variables, but where full experimental control is not present.
quota sample	A sample selected so that its most important demographic characteristics match those of the population of interest.
random sample	A sample in which every member of the population has an equal chance of being selected.
relevance tree	An approach to identifying and delineating research problems so as to more accurately delineate data requirements.
reliability	The extent to which a data collection or measurement technique yields the same results on different occasions.
research brief	A detailed agreement between consultant and client, preferably written, which encompasses agreement with regard to: research/consultancy objectives, timing and funding, responsibilities and duties, reporting requirements and constraints and restrictions.
research plan	A detailed agreement between consultant and client, preferably written, which encompasses agreement with regard to: research/consultancy objectives; data and information requirements, methods of data collection, methods of data analysis, interpretation and presentation.
sample statistic	Summary measures used to describe a sample, usually denoted by Roman letters, for example, S, to denote the standard deviation.
sample	A part (or a subset) of a population.
secondary data	Information which is already collected and available in some form to the researcher.
set	A term used in action learning for the small groups that meet periodically for the members of the group to describe and discuss the problems they are working on.
special-purpose databases	Databases which focus on specialist/selected areas only.
stratified random	A sample which treats each segment of the population separately.
syndicated sources	Organizations that collect and sell secondary data to different organizations that subscribe to their services.

task oriented	The term indicates that a number of different and independent methods of data collection and analysis have been combined.
triangulation	A term borrowed from navigation and surveying where multiple reference points are taken to check an object's location. The process whereby several methods of research and data collection are used such that the findings from one type of study can be checked against the findings derived from another type.
unitising	Determining the objects of measurement in content analysis.
validity	The extent to which a data collection or measurement technique measures what it is supposed to measure.
verificationism	That school of philosophy of science which suggests that scientists must attempt to verify rather than refute their theories.

Appendix V
Referencing and Advice on Presentation

This information has been compiled by John Colby principally from University of Central England's website, and it deals mainly with the Harvard system of referencing which has now become the unofficial world standard system. It is reproduced, along with other material he supplied, by kind permission of John Colby.

This appendix is written principally with the interests of research students in mind. This text is also aimed at business consultants, so clearly some of the advice that is specifically aimed at students will not apply, although the principles of correct referencing still pertain.

Introduction

Rules for Harvard referencing are often misunderstood and tend to be rather complex. This information tries to show you how you should go about providing references and gives you a recording method so that you do not fall foul of academic regulations and standard conventions.

Perhaps the most frequently asked question is why? Why is all this necessary? The answer is that in order to pass a degree or gain other qualification, well, you have to adopt an academic writing style. This advice also pertains to a consultancy report where due acknowledgement of sources is also required. This type of style is not just so that you have something to do or to confuse you, but to prove that in getting this qualification or in assembling this information you can adhere to the discipline of good writing in a clear, concise style and that ideas you present are backed up by evidence, the evidence being that you have done the research.

A reference quoted correctly gives certain information:

An originator, who wrote or edited the work.
A date – when was it published or accessed.
A name – what's it called?
A description – a book, journal, article, webpage or whatever.
Where was it published and who published it?
Where in the work did you look?

So you prove your research. A correctly researched and referenced academic piece of work will gain higher marks than one that has had the same amount of research done but lacks the references.

A reference is something that you use directly in your work to support your argument. If you quote something directly it must come from a reference.

A bibliography is material that you have consulted but you are not using directly to support your argument – background, if you like.

How can I make sure I do it right?

The following form has been adapted from the University of Central England's website. On this you can record the essential information you need while

Your Name			Date / /	time	:	am		pm	
Originator of referenced work			**Originator Type**						
			One author		Two authors				
			Three authors		More than 3 authors				
			Lecturer		Interviewee				
			Director		Other Party				
Year of Publication		Year First Published		Inventor		Organisation			
			Database		Ordnance Survey				
Edition		ISBN		Geological Survey of Great Britain (England & Wales)					
		ISSN		Geological Survey of Great Britain (Northern Ireland)					
Title			Geological Survey of Great Britain (Scotland)						
			Printed Source						
			Book		Journal				
			Dictionary		Encyclopaedia				
			Bibliography		Index				
			Microfilm		Cartographic				
Series/Volume Title			Newspaper		Magazine				
			Music Score		Review				
			Paper		Invention				
			Academic Source (published) *also see personal comms*						
			Conference		Proceedings				
Editor/Translator/Arranger/Director/Interviewer/Broadcaster			Lecture		Seminar				
			Tutorial		Interview				
			Electronic Source						
			Web Page		Database				
Chapter Title and Number			CD-ROM		DVD-ROM				
			Computer Program		Email Newsgroup				
			Online Journal		Bulletin Board				

Page(s)		Number		Version Number			**Audio and Visual Source**			
				Volume Number		Audio		Audio & Vision	
				Scale/Sheet Number		Radio Broadcast		TV Broadcast	
				Length of work		Video		CD	
				Report Code/Number		DVD		Streaming	
Title/Subtitle of Conference						Tape		Vinyl	
						Film		Audiocassette	
						Monaural sound		Stereophonic sound	
School/Faculty/Station						Surround sound		Live Performance	

Government Source

House of Commons		House of Lords
EU Institution		Royal Commission
House of Commons		House of Lords
Department		Committee
Scottish Parliament		Welsh Assembly
Northern Ireland Assy.		Royal Commission
Act of Parliament		Parliamentary Bill
Statutory Instrument		Official Report
White Paper		Command Paper
Green Paper		Hansard
County Council		Committee
District Council		Town Council

Producer/Submitter/Distributor

Publisher

Place/Location/Repository

Day		Date		Month		Year	

Ensemble

Legal Source

BS Standard		ISO Standard	
Law Report		Patent	

Graphics

Degree Statement and University

Photograph		Figure	
Illustration		Table	
Chart		Diagram	
Map			

Assignee

Personal Communications and Unpublished Sources

Letter		Telephone Call	
Dissertation		Thesis	
Essay		Email	

Committee/Royal Commission/ Govt Department/ EC Institution/ Parliamentary Bill/Statutory Instrument/Law Case/ Monarch

Website address

researching and compiling reports. For your convenience it is reproduced here:

When you 'do' a reference on the top line fill in the date and time, tick the am or pm boxes.

The form is divided into two parts.

The right-hand side is a set of tick boxes, so fill these in as necessary.

The left-hand column contains a few tick boxes, but is mainly self-explanatory.

What is being provided is a format for recording references, reminding you what you need to record. You do not have to fill in every box for every reference.

Research material

Gathering research material is an ongoing process, which gets harder as the volume and complexity of the material increases.

Getting into 'good habits' at the beginning, will benefit you throughout the research gathering process.

How to collect references

- Reference cards – write everything down on reference cards and sort them in order. This is an old tried and tested method that works.
- Use a form similar to the one that has just been cited, and fill in the necessary information and tick boxes. This helps you to remember what you have to collect. You should then file this away as your research.
- Trust to memory and/or luck. This is proven not to work.

Research from the web

If it is likely that you are going to be getting lots of information from web-based sources then ensure that your research records where you look.

If you print out the website then staple the print to the back of the reference form so you don't lose it.

Research from the web can be complex – just make sure you record everything – you can leave it out in your final essay but it may be a pain to find it again if you have left your records incomplete.

The material that now follows shows how to reference in various contexts including referencing from books to journals to broadcast material.

What is ISBN/ISSN?

ISBN   International Standard Book Number
ISSN   International Standard Serial Number

Both uniquely identify the country, language, publisher, cover type (a hardback book will have a different ISBN from paperback) and edition (different editions have different numbers).

However they are written in the original, the correct way for quoting them in a reference is:

ISBN: 0123456789 – that is, omit all hyphens and spaces.
ISSN: 1234-5678 – that is, two groups of four numbers with a hyphen in the middle.

Books and reference works

Book – single author

List of terms

Author's family name/surname *[comma]*
Author's initial(s) [each initial with full stop]
Year of publication in brackets *[full stop]*
Title of work in italics as it appears on the title page (not necessarily as on the book cover) [full stop]

ISBN [colon]
ISBN Number – omit all hyphens and spaces *[full stop]*
Place of publication (see place rules) [colon]
Publisher [full stop]

Format

Author, I.N. (YEAR). *Title of Work*. ISBN: 0123456789. Place: Publisher.

Example reference entry

Karp, A. (1997). *Windows Annoyances*. ISBN: 1565922662. Cambridge: O'Reilly.

Book – two authors

List of terms

First author's family name/surname *[comma]*
First author's initial(s) [each initial with full stop]
'and' or ampersand (&)
Second author's family name/surname *[comma]*
Second author's initial(s) [each initial with full stop]
Year of publication in brackets *[full stop]*
Title of work in italics as it appears on the title page (not necessarily as on
    the book cover) [full stop]
ISBN [colon]
ISBN Number – omit all hyphens and spaces *[full stop]*
Place of publication (see place rules) [colon]
Publisher [full stop]

Format

Author1, I.N. & Author 2, I.T. (YEAR). *Title of Work*. ISBN: 0123456789. Place:
    Publisher.

Example reference entry

Light, G. & Cox, R. (2001). *Learning and Teaching in Higher Education*. ISBN:
    076196553X. London: Paul Chapman Publishing.

Book – three authors

List of terms

First author's family name/surname *[comma]*
First author's initial(s) [each initial with full stop] [comma]
Second author's family name/surname *[comma]*

Second author's initial(s) [each initial with full stop]
'and' or ampersand (&)
Third author's family name/surname *[comma]*
Third author's initial(s) [each initial with full stop]
Year of publication in brackets *[full stop]*
Title of work in italics as it appears on the title page (not necessarily as on the book cover) [full stop]
ISBN [colon]
ISBN Number – omit all hyphens and spaces *[full stop]*
Place of publication (see place rules) [colon]
Publisher [full stop]

Format

Author1, I.N., Author2, I.T. & Author3, I.A.L. (YEAR). *Title of Work*. ISBN: 0123456789. Place: Publisher.

Example reference entry

Hellingsworth, B., Hall, P. & Anderson, H. (2001). *Higher National Computing*. ISBN: 0750652306. Oxford: Newnes.

Book – more than three authors

List of terms

First author's family name/surname *[comma]*
First author's initial(s) [each initial with full stop]
et al. (signifying there are a number of others involved) *[full stop]*
Year of publication in brackets *[full stop]*
Title of work in italics as it appears on the title page (not necessarily as on the book cover) [full stop]
ISBN [colon]
ISBN Number – omit all hyphens and spaces *[full stop]*
Place of publication (see place rules) [colon]
Publisher [full stop]

Format

Author1, I.N. et al. (YEAR). *Title of Work*. ISBN: 0123456789. Place: Publisher.

Example reference entry

Colby, J. et al. (2003). *Practical Intranet Development*. ISBN: 190415123X. Birmingham: Glasshaus.

Book – chapter, article in or part – no editor specified

List of terms

Author's family name/surname *[comma]*
Author's initial(s) [each initial with full stop] (Note that multiple author rules also can apply.)
Year of publication in brackets *[full stop]*
Title of chapter/article/part as it appears on the chapter header page (NOT in italics) *[full stop]*
In (bold type) *[colon]*
Title of work in italics as it appears on the title page (not necessarily as on the book cover) [full stop]
ISBN [colon]
ISBN Number – omit all hyphens and spaces *[full stop]*
Place of publication (see place rules) [colon]
Publisher [full stop]

Format

Author, I.N. (YEAR). Title of Chapter. **In:** *Title of Work*. ISBN: 0123456789. Place: Publisher.

Book – chapter in edited work

List of terms

Author's family name/surname *[comma]*
Author's initial(s) [each initial with full stop] (Note that multiple author rules also can apply.)
Year of publication in brackets *[full stop]*
Title of chapter as it appears on the chapter header page (NOT in italics) *[full stop]*
In (bold type) *[colon]*
Editor's initial(s) [each initial with full stop]
Editor's family name/surname *[comma]*
Note that the rules for initials are reversed for editors and that if there is more than one editor the same rules apply as for multiple authors. It is unlikely that you get more than three editors.
ed or eds {signifying editor or editors} [full stop]
Title of work in italics as it appears on the title page (not necessarily as on the book cover) [full stop]
ISBN [colon]
ISBN Number – omit all hyphens and spaces *[full stop]*
Place of publication (see place rules) [colon]
Publisher [full stop]

Format

> Author, I.N. (YEAR). Title of Chapter. **In:** A.N. Editor, ed. *Title of Work*. ISBN: 0123456789. Place: Publisher.

Example reference entry

> Klemperer, S.L. & Preddy, C. (1992). Seismic reflection profiling and the structure of the continental lithosphere. **In:** G.C. Brown, C.J. Hawkesworth, & R.C.L. Wilson, eds. *Understanding the Earth*. ISBN: 0521427401. Cambridge: Cambridge University Press.

Book – edited – used when you are citing the whole book

List of terms

> Editor's family name/surname *[comma]*
> Editor's initial(s) [each initial with full stop]
> Note that multiple rules also can apply and that 'author rules' for positioning of initials apply, even though you are citing an editor
> ed or eds {signifying editor or editors} [full stop]
> Year of publication in brackets *[full stop]*
> Title of work in italics as it appears on the title page (not necessarily as on the book cover) [full stop]
> ISBN [colon]
> ISBN Number – omit all hyphens and spaces *[full stop]*
> Place of publication (see place rules) [colon]
> Publisher [full stop]

Format (multiples rules apply)

> Editor, A.N. ed. (YEAR). *Title of Work*. ISBN: 0123456789. Place: Publisher.

Example reference entry

> McKerrow, W.S. ed. (1978). *The Ecology of Fossils*. ISBN: 0715612980. London: Duckworth.

Book – translated

List of terms

> Author's family name/surname *[comma]*
> Author's initial(s) [each initial with full stop]
> Note that multiple author rules also can apply.
> Year of publication in brackets *[full stop]*
> Title of work in italics as it appears on the title page (not necessarily as on the book cover) [full stop]

trans (normal text) *[full stop]*
Translator's initial(s) [each initial with full stop]
Translator's family name/surname in normal text *[comma]*
Note that the rules for initials are as for editors and that if there is more than
    one translator the same rules apply as for multiple editors
ISBN [colon]
ISBN Number – omit all hyphens and spaces *[full stop]*
Place of publication (see place rules) [colon]
Publisher [full stop]

Format

Author, I.N. (YEAR). *Title of Work*. trans. A. Translator. ISBN: 0123456789.
Place: Publisher.

Example reference entry

Agricola, G. (1556). *De Re Metallica*. trans. H.C. Hoover & L. H. Hoover. ISBN:
0486600068. New York: Dover.

Book – edition other than first or reprint with alterations

Editions apply where there have been alterations, not just a reprint of the
original. Reprints should be cited as the original date of publication. However,
where there is a 'reprint with corrections' or 'reprint with alterations' treat it as
a new edition and cite the 'number of edition' as detailed below.

List of terms

Author's family name/surname *[comma]*
Author's initial(s) [each initial with full stop]
Year of publication of this edition in brackets *[full stop]*
Title of work in italics as it appears on the title page (not necessarily as on
    the book cover) [full stop]
Number of edition (e.g. 2nd edition)
However if you are citing an altered or corrected reprint say 'reprint with cor-
    rections' or 'reprint with corrections of nth edition' as appropriate [full stop]
ISBN [colon]
ISBN Number – omit all hyphens and spaces *[full stop]*
Place of publication (see place rules) [colon]
Publisher
'first published' and then original date of publication in brackets *[full stop]*

Format

Author, I.N. (YEAR). *Title of Work*, nth edition. ISBN: 0123456789. Place:
Publisher (first published YEAR).

Example reference entry

Roberts, N. (1998). *The Holocene – An Environmental History*, 2nd edition. ISBN: 0631186387. Oxford: Blackwell (first published 1989).

Book – corporate

Any organisation such as a society or government department can be regarded as an author if no individual's name is supplied.

List of terms

Organisation's name *[full stop]*
Year of publication in brackets *[full stop]*
Title of work in italics as it appears on the title page (not necessarily as on the book cover) [full stop]
ISBN [colon]
ISBN Number – omit all hyphens and spaces *[full stop]*
Place of publication (see place rules) [colon]
Publisher [full stop]

Format

Organisation's name. (YEAR). *Title of Work*. ISBN: 0123456789. Place: Publisher.

Example reference entry

Coopers and Lybrand Deloitte. (1995). *International Tax Summaries: A Guide for Planning and Decisions*. ISBN: 0471115576. Chichester: Wiley.

Book – author unknown or not stated

List of terms

Title of work in italics as it appears on the title page (not necessarily as on the book cover) [full stop]
Year of publication in brackets *[full stop]*
ISBN [colon]
ISBN Number – omit all hyphens and spaces *[full stop]*
Place of publication (see place rules) [colon]
Publisher [full stop]

Format

Title of Work. (YEAR). ISBN: 0123456789. Place: Publisher.

Example reference entry

Domesday Book. (1086). ISBN: 01405155356. London: Penguin.

Book – official publication

An official publication is one written by a government department and this includes Green Papers, White Papers, Hansard (the proceedings of the UK Parliament) and other reports. The author is the department concerned; the publisher is (usually) HMSO (Her Majesty's Stationery Office)

List of Terms

Department *[full stop]*
Year of publication in brackets *[full stop]*
Title of work in italics as it appears on the title page (not necessarily as on the book cover) [full stop]
ISBN [colon]
ISBN Number – omit all hyphens and spaces *[full stop]*
Place of publication (see place rules) [colon]
Publisher [full stop]

Format

Department. (YEAR). *Title of Work*. ISBN: 0123456789. London: HMSO.

Book – part of series

List of terms

Author's family name/surname *[comma]*
Author's initial(s) [each initial with full stop]
Year of publication in brackets *[full stop]*
Title of work in italics as it appears on the title page (not necessarily as on the book cover) [comma] – note not a full stop
Series title (and number if applicable) *[full stop]*
ISBN [colon]
ISBN Number – omit all hyphens and spaces *[full stop]*
Place of publication (see place rules) [colon]
Publisher [full stop]

Format

Author, I.N. (YEAR). *Title of Work*, Series title nn. ISBN: 0123456789. Place: Publisher.

Book – one volume of multi-volume work
List of terms

Author's family name/surname *[comma]*
Author's initial(s) [each initial with full stop]
Year of publication in brackets *[full stop]*
Title of work in italics as it appears on the title page (not necessarily as on the book cover) [comma]
Volume number in format vol nn where nn is the number of the volume *[comma]*
Volume title in italics [full stop]
ed or eds {signifying editor or editors} [full stop]
Editor's initial(s) *[full stop]*
Editor's family name/surname (upper and lower case type) *[full stop]*
Note that the rules for initials are reversed for editors and that if there is more than one editor the same rules apply for multiple authors. However if there are no editors specified and all volumes are the work of a single author then omit all references to the editor.
ISBN [colon]
ISBN Number – omit all hyphens and spaces *[full stop]*
Place of publication (see place rules) [colon]
Publisher [full stop]

Format

Author, I.N. (YEAR). *Title of Work*, vol nn, *Title of Volume*. ed. E.I. Editor. ISBN: 0123456789. Place: Publisher.

Book – one chapter of multi-volume work
List of terms

Author's family name/surname *[comma]*
Author's initial(s) [each initial with full stop]
Year of publication in brackets *[full stop]*
Title of chapter as it appears on the chapter header page (NOT in italics) *[comma]*
in (normal type)
Title of work in italics as it appears on the title page (not necessarily as on the book cover) [comma]
Volume number in format vol nn *[comma]*
Volume title in italics *[full stop]*
ed or eds {signifying editor or editors} [full stop]
Editor's initial(s) *[full stop]*
Editor's family name/surname (upper and lower case type) *[comma]*
Note that the rules for initials are reversed and that if there is more than one editor the same rules apply as for multiple authors.

ISBN [colon]
ISBN Number – omit all hyphens and spaces *[full stop]*
Place of publication (see place rules) [colon]
Publisher [full stop]

Format

Author, I.N. (YEAR). Chapter name, in *Title of Work*, vol nn, *Title of Volume*. ed. E.I. Editor. ISBN: 0123456789. Place: Publisher.

Reference work – encyclopaedia

List of terms

Author's family name/surname *[comma]*
OR editor's family name/surname *[comma]*
Author's (or editor's) initial(s) *[each initial with full stop]*
Year of publication in brackets *[full stop]*
Title of article (NOT in italics) [comma]
in (normal type)
Title of work in italics as it appears on the title page (not necessarily as on the book cover) [comma]
Volume number in format vol nn *[full stop]*
Edition number
Edition (the word) *[full stop]*
ISBN [colon]
ISBN Number – omit all hyphens and spaces *[full stop]*
Place of publication (see place rules) [colon]
Publisher [full stop]

Format

Author/editor, I.N. (YEAR). Title of Article, in *Title of Work*, vol nn. nnth edition. ISBN: 0123456789. Place: Publisher.

Reference work – dictionary

Dictionaries have no author as such – so the title of the work takes precedence.

List of terms

Title of work in italics [full stop]
Year of publication in brackets *[full stop]*
Volume number in format vol nn *[full stop]*
  • OR – if you are referencing the complete work define the volume set (e.g. vols 1–32) *[full stop]*

Edition number *[full stop]*
ISBN [colon]
ISBN Number – omit all hyphens and spaces *[full stop]*
Place of publication (see place rules) [colon]
Publisher [full stop]

Format

Title of Work. (YEAR). vol 12. nnth edition. ISBN: 0123456789. Place: Publisher.
Title of Work. (YEAR). vols 1–5. nnth edition. ISBN: 0123456789. Place: Publisher.

Example reference entry

Concise Dictionary of English Etymology. (1996). 2nd Edition. ISBN: 0192830988. Oxford: Oxford University Press.

Reference Work – Bibliography

Bibliographies have no author as such – so the title of the work takes precedence.

List of terms

Title of work in italics *[full stop]*
Year of publication in brackets *[full stop]*
Volume number in format vol nn *[full stop]*
  • OR – if you are referencing the complete work define the volume set (e.g. vols 1–32) *[full stop]*
Edition number *[full stop]*
ISBN [colon]
ISBN Number – omit all hyphens and spaces *[full stop]*
Place of publication (see place rules) [colon]
Publisher [full stop]

Format

Title of Work. (YEAR). vol 13. nnth edition. ISBN: 0123456789. Place: Publisher.
Title of Work. (YEAR). vols 1–5., nnth edition. ISBN: 0123456789. Place: Publisher.

Reference Work – Index

Indices have no author as such – so the title of the work takes precedence.

List of terms

Title of work in italics [full stop]
Year of publication in brackets *[full stop]*

Volume number in format vol nn [*full stop*]
- OR – if you are referencing the complete work define the volume set (e.g. vols 1–32) [*full stop*]

Edition number [*full stop*]
ISBN [colon]
ISBN Number – omit all hyphens and spaces [full stop]
Place of publication (*see place rules*) [colon]
Publisher [full stop]

Format

Title of Work. (YEAR). vol 15. nnth edition. ISBN: 0123456789. Place: Publisher.
Title of Work. (YEAR). vols 1–5. nnth edition. ISBN: 0123456789. Place: Publisher.

 # Journals and Serial Productions

Journal Article – single author

List of terms

Author's family name/surname [*comma*]
Author's initial(s) [each initial with full stop]
Year of publication in brackets [*full stop*]
Title of work as it appears at the head of the article NOT in italics [*full stop*]
Name of Journal in italics [*comma*]
ISSN [colon]
ISSN Number – display as two groups of four digits with a hyphen in the middle [*full stop*]
Volume number and part number, part number in brackets. Sometimes a season is given instead.
Page number(s) as appropriate designated by p. [*p with full stop*] for a single page or pp. [*pp with full stop*] for multiple pages [*full stop*] (*designate multiple pages as a range*)

Format

Author, I.N. (YEAR). Title of article. *Name of Journal*. ISSN: 1234-5678. VN(pn) pp. nn–mm.
Author, I.N. (YEAR). Title of article. *Name of Journal*. ISSN: 1234-5678. VN(pn) p. nn.
Author, I.N. (YEAR). Title of article. *Name of Journal*. ISSN: 1234-5678. Season YEAR pp. nn–mm.

Example reference entry

Galvin, J. (2003). Flash flooding and its relationship to the geology of Surigao del Norte, Philippines. *Open University Geological Society Journal*. ISSN: 0143-9472, 24(1) pp. 23–26.

Journal Article – two authors

List of terms

First author's family name/surname *[comma]*
First author's initial(s) [each initial with full stop]
'and' or ampersand (&)
Second author's family name/surname *[comma]*
Second author's initial(s) [each initial with full stop]
Year of publication in brackets *[full stop]*
Title of work as it appears at the head of the article NOT in italics *[full stop]*
Name of Journal in italics *[comma]*
ISSN [colon]
ISSN Number – display as two groups of four digits with a hyphen in the middle *[full stop]*
Volume number and part number, part number in brackets.
Sometimes a season is given instead *(See journal with single author for example.)*
Page number(s) as appropriate designated by p. *[p with full stop]* for a single page or pp. *[pp with full stop]* for multiple pages *[full stop]* *(designate multiple pages as a range)*

Format

Author1, I.N. & Author2, I.T. (YEAR). Title of article. *Name of Journal*. ISSN: 1234-5678. VN(pn) pp. nn–mm.

Journal Article – three authors

List of terms

First author's family name/surname *[comma]*
First author's initial(s) [each initial with full stop]
[comma]
Second author's family name/surname *[comma]*
Second author's initial(s) [each initial with full stop]
'and' or ampersand (&)
Third author's family name/surname *[comma]*
Third author's initial(s) [each initial with full stop]
Year of publication in brackets *[full stop]*
Title of work as it appears at the head of the article NOT in italics *[full stop]*
Name of Journal in italics [comma]
ISSN [colon]
ISSN Number – display as two groups of four digits with a hyphen in the middle *[full stop]*
Volume number and part number, part number in brackets. Sometimes a season is given instead. *(See journal with single author for example).*

Page number(s) as appropriate designated by p. *[p with full stop]* for a single page or pp. *[pp with full stop]* for multiple pages *[full stop]* *(designate multiple pages as a range)*

Format

Author1, I.N., Author2, I.T. & Author3, I.A.L. (YEAR). Title of article. *Name of Journal*. ISSN: 1234–5678. VN(pn) pp. nn–mm.

Journal Article – more than three authors

List of terms

First author's family name/surname *[comma]*
First author's initial(s) [each initial with full stop]
et al. (signifying there are a number of others involved) *[full stop]*
Year of publication in brackets *[full stop]*
Title of work as it appears at the head of the article NOT in italics *[full stop]*
Name of Journal in italics [comma]
ISSN [colon]
ISSN Number – display as two groups of four digits with a hyphen in the middle [full *stop]*
Volume number and part number, part number in brackets. Sometimes a season is given instead *(See journal with single author for example.)*
Page number(s) as appropriate designated by p. *[p with full stop]* for a single page or pp. *[pp with full stop]* for multiple pages *[full stop]* *(designate multiple pages as a range)*

Format

Author, I.N. et al. (YEAR). Title of article. *Name of Journal*. ISSN: 1234-5678. VN(pn) pp. nn–mm.

Newspaper article

List of terms

If author is stated:
    Author's family name/surname *[comma]*
    Author's initial(s) *[each initial with full stop]*
    Year of publication in brackets *[full stop]*
    Title of article NOT in italics *[full stop]*
If author is not stated:
    Title of article NOT in italics *[full stop]*
    Year of publication in brackets *[full stop]*
Name of newspaper in italics *[comma]*

Day and full date of publication *[comma]*
Page number(s) as appropriate designated by p. *[p with full stop]* for a single page or pp. *[pp with full stop]* for multiple pages *[full stop]* *(designate multiple pages as a range)*

Format

Author, I.N. (YEAR). Title of Article, *Name of Newspaper*. XXXday, nth month YEAR, p. m.

Example reference entry

Harris, S. (2003). Anger as Cash Crisis Brings Call for Pay Freeze on Teachers, *Daily Mail*. Saturday 12th July 2003, p. 9.

Magazine article

List of terms

Author's family name/surname *[comma]*
Author's initial(s) [each initial with full stop]
Year of publication in brackets *[full stop]*
Title of article NOT in italics *[full stop]*
Name of magazine in italics *[comma]*
Date of publication *[comma]*
Page number(s) as appropriate designated by p. *[p with full stop]* for a single page or pp. *[pp with full stop]* for multiple pages *[full stop]* *(designate multiple pages as a range)*

Format

Author, I.N. (YEAR). Title of Article, *Name of Magazine*. Month YEAR, p. m.

Example reference entry

Evans, J. (2001). Enigma Trail, *Classic fm Magazine*. June 2001, pp. 44–46.

Reports

List of terms

Author's family name/surname *[comma]*
Author's initial(s) [each initial with full stop]
Year of publication in brackets *[full stop]*
Title of report in italics *[full stop]*
ISBN [colon]
ISBN Number – omit all hyphens and spaces *[full stop]*
Place of publication (see place rules) [colon]

Publisher *[comma]*
Report code and number (in brackets) [full stop]

Format

Author, I.N. (YEAR). *Title of Report*. ISBN: 0123456789. Place: Publisher, (REP-CODE & number).

Reviews

List of terms

Author's family name/surname *[comma]*
Author's initial(s) [each initial with full stop]
Year of publication in brackets *[full stop]*
Title of review in italics *[full stop]*
Review of (these words)
Identification of the work being reviewed *[full stop]*
Name of Journal in italics *[comma]*
Volume number and part number, part number in brackets. Sometimes a season is given instead
Page number(s) as appropriate designated by p. *[p with full stop]* for a single page or pp. *[pp with full stop]* for multiple pages [full stop] (designate multiple pages as a range)

Format

Author, I.N. (YEAR). *Title of Review*. Review of Work being reviewed. *Journal Name*, VN(pn) pp. nn–mm.

Electronic and internet sources

It is vital that you cite Internet and Electronic sources correctly. This is an area that researchers are using more and more so that when you rely on the source it is very much in your own interest that you can prove from where it comes. The issue of referencing electronic sources of information is fluid. The field is developing so that any standards become out of date rapidly. Some electronic sources may quote an ISSN or ISBN – in which case quote them as for printed matter just after the title.

Website document (webpage)

List of terms (Multiple author/editor/originator/provider rules apply)

If there is an author or originator state them
Author's family name/surname *[comma]*

Author's initial(s) *[each initial with full stop]*

If the person submitting the text is stated, give them as well

Either the date that is given on the site or the year you accessed it in brackets *[full stop]*

Title of page in italics *[full stop]*

Or if no author or originator is stated

Title of page in italics *[full stop]*

Either the date that is given on the site or the year you accessed it in brackets *[full stop]*

Type of Medium = [online] *[full stop]*

Version if appropriate *[full stop]*

Available from *[colon]*

Full website address

[Open Square Bracket]

Accessed *[colon]*

Date, month, year

[Close square bracket] [full stop]

Format

Author, I.N. (YEAR). *Title of Page.* [online] Available from: http://website.com/directory/filname.html [Accessed: date month year].

Example reference entry

Colby, J. (2003). *United Kingdom Web Accessibility Congress* [online] Available from: http://www.cie.uce.ac.uk/ukwac/index.html [Accessed: 14th July 2003].

Suspect Sources

Be aware that not all Internet sources are entirely accurate. Some are so erroneous as to be derisory. For an example of this see http://nov55.com/index.html where the author claims in one section that all the soil on earth was not created from the weathering of rocks and biological activity but fell down from space where a planet exploded in the asteroid belt. The author claims to be serious. In cases such as this question the veracity of the content of the source by an appropriate note in square brackets at the end of the reference, and follow it with a full stop.

Example suspect reference entry

Novak, G. (2003). *Geology of Soil Origins.* [online] Available from http://nov55.com/geol.html [Accessed 18th July 2003]. [Source inaccurate].

CD-ROM, DVD-ROM or Online entire bibliographical database

List of terms

Database name in italics *[full stop]*
Year of publication in brackets *[full stop]*
Medium – [CD-ROM], [DVD-ROM] or [online] in square brackets *[full stop]*
Range of dates applicable in round brackets *[full stop]*
Place of publication (see place rules) [colon]
Producer name and (Producer) *(the word)* *[full stop]*
Available from *[colon]*
If online as below, otherwise distributor name and address
- Full website address
- *[Open square bracket]*
- Accessed *[colon]*
- Date, month, year
- *[Close square bracket]* *[full stop]*

Format

Database Name. (YEAR). [Medium]. Date range. Place: Producer (Producer).
Available from: Distributor and details or [website and accessed date].

Journal or Newspaper article from CD-ROM, DVD-ROM or Online database

List of terms

Author's family name/surname *[comma]*
Author's initial(s) [each initial with full stop]
Year of publication in brackets *[full stop]*
Title of article NOT in italics *[colon]*
Name of Journal or Newspaper in italics
Medium – [CD-ROM], [DVD-ROM] or [online] in square brackets *[comma]*
Volume number *[colon]*
Date, month, year *[comma]*
Page number(s) as appropriate designated by p. *[p with full stop]* for a single
   page or pp. *[pp with full stop]* for multiple pages *[full stop]* *(designate multi-
   ple pages as a range)*
If online as below:
Full website address
[Open square bracket]
Accessed *[colon]*
Date, month, year
[Close square bracket] *[full stop]*

Format

> Author, I.N. (YEAR). Title of Article: *Name of Journal or Newspaper*. [Medium], Volume number: Date month Year, pp. nn–mm.

Electronic Journals

Use this format also for electronic conferences and bulletin boards

List of terms (multiple author/editor/originator/provider rules apply)

> Author's family name/surname *[comma]*
> Author's initial(s) [each initial with full stop]
> Either the date that is given on the site or the year you accessed it in brackets *[full stop]*
> Title of page not in italics *[full stop]*
> Title of Journal in italics *[full stop]*
> Type of Medium = [online] *[full stop]*
> Version if appropriate *[full stop]*
> Available from *[colon]*
> Full website address
> [Open square bracket]
> Accessed *[colon]*
> Date, month, year
> [Close square bracket] [full stop]

Format

> Author, I.N. (YEAR). Page Title. *Journal Title*. [online]. Version. Available from: http://website.org [Accessed: date month year].

Computer Program

List of terms

> If the originator is given:
> Originator's family name/surname *[comma]*
> Originator's initial(s) *[each initial with full stop]*
> Title of program in italics
> Version Number in round brackets *[comma]*
> [Computer Program] in square brackets *[full stop]*
> Date in brackets if given *[full stop]*
> Availability Information for example, distributor and address.
> End with a *[full stop]*

Format

Originator, I.N. *Program Name*. (Version Number), [Computer Program]. (YEAR). Availability.

Example reference entry

Read and Write (Version 6 Gold), [Computer program]. (2003). textHELP Systems Ltd. Enkalon Business Centre, 25 Ranoldstown Road, Antrim, N. Ireland, BT41 4LJ.

Government Publications (UK Legislature)

Act of Parliament

List of terms

Name of Act *in italics*
Year of publication in italics and in brackets *[colon]* – the year is an integral part of the name of the Act, so no full stop after the name
Monarch (e.g. Elizabeth II) *in italics [full stop]*
Chapter number in italics [full stop]
ISBN [colon]
ISBN Number – omit all hyphens and spaces *[full stop]*
Place of publication (see place rules) *[colon]*
Publisher [full stop]

Format

Name of Act (YEAR): *Monarch. Chapter NN.* ISBN 1234567890. Place: Publisher.

Example reference entry

Disability Discrimination Act (1995): Elizabeth II. Ch 50. ISBN: 0105450952. London: HMSO.

Parliamentary Bill

List of terms

Great Britain *[full stop]* (words required)
Parliament *[full stop]* (words required)
House of Commons or House of Lords as appropriate *[full stop]*
Year of publication in brackets *[full stop]*
Name of Bill in italics [full stop]
ISBN [colon]
ISBN Number – omit all hyphens and spaces *[full stop]*

Place of publication (see place rules) [colon]
Publisher *[comma]*
Bill number (in brackets) *[full stop]*

Format

Great Britain. Parliament. House of Commons. (YEAR). *Name of Bill*. ISBN: 0123456789. Place: Publisher, (Number).

Command paper

List of terms

Great Britain *[full stop]* (words required)
Name of Committee or Royal Commission Title *[full stop]*
Year of publication in brackets *[full stop]*
Command paper title in italics *[full stop]*
ISBN [colon]
ISBN Number – omit all hyphens and spaces *[full stop]*
Place of publication (see place rules) [colon]
Publisher *[comma]*
Paper number (in brackets) *[full stop]*

Format

Great Britain. Committee or Royal Commission. (YEAR). *Name of Command Paper*. ISBN: 0123456789. Place: Publisher, (Number).

Non-Parliamentary or Departmental Publication

List of terms

Great Britain *[full stop]* (words required)
Name of Government Department *[full stop]*
Year of publication in brackets *[full stop]*
Publication title in italics [full stop]
ISBN [colon]
ISBN Number – omit all hyphens and spaces *[full stop]*
Place of publication (see place rules) *[colon]*
Publisher *[comma]*
Series name/number (in brackets) *[full stop]*

Format

Great Britain. Department Name. (YEAR). *Name of Publication*. ISBN: 0123456789. Place: Publisher, (Series).

EU publication

List of terms

European Community *[full stop]* (words required)
Name of EC institution *[full stop]*
Year of publication in brackets *[full stop]*
Publication title in italics [full stop]
ISBN [colon]
ISBN Number – omit all hyphens and spaces *[full stop]*
Place of publication (see place rules) [colon]
Publisher *[comma]*
Series name/number (in brackets) *[full stop]*

Format

European Community. Name of EC institution. (YEAR). *Name of Publication.*
ISBN: 0123456789. Place: Publisher, (Series).

White or Green Paper

List of terms

Government Department *[full stop]*
Year of publication in brackets *[full stop]*
Title of paper in italics *[full stop]*
Paper number *[full stop]*
ISBN [colon]
ISBN Number – omit all hyphens and spaces *[full stop]*
Place of publication (see place rules) [colon]
Publisher [full stop]

Format

Department Name. (YEAR). *Title of Paper*. ISBN: 0123456789. Place: Publisher.

Hansard

List of terms

Great Britain *[full stop]* (words required)
Parliament *[full stop]* (words required)
House of Commons or House of Lords as appropriate *[full stop]*
Year of publication in brackets *[full stop]*
Official Reports *[full stop]* (words required)
Parliamentary Debates (Hansard) *[full stop]* (words required)
ISBN [colon]

ISBN Number – omit all hyphens and spaces *[full stop]*
Place of publication *(see place rules) [colon]* (will be London)
Publisher *[full stop* (Will be HMSO)*]*

Format

Great Britain. Parliament. House of Lords. (YEAR). Official Reports. Parliamentary Debates (Hansard). ISBN: 0123456789. London: HMSO.

Specific Citation from Hansard

List of terms

MP's (or Member of Upper House) family name/surname *[comma]*
MP's (or Member of Upper House) initial(s) *[each initial with full stop]*
In (bold text)
Great Britain *[full stop]* (words required)
Parliament *[full stop]* (words required)
House of Commons or House of Lords as appropriate *[full stop]*
Year of publication in brackets *[full stop]*
Official Reports *[full stop* (words required)*]*
Parliamentary Debates (Hansard) *[full stop]* (words required)
ISBN [colon]
ISBN Number – omit all hyphens and spaces *[full stop]*
Place of publication *(see place rules) [colon]* (will be London)
Publisher *[full stop]* (will be HMSO)
Date in full (date/month/year) *[colon]*
Column and item number *[full stop]*

Format

Mpname, M.P. **In** Great Britain. Parliament. House of Commons. (YEAR). Official Reports. Parliamentary Debates (Hansard). ISBN: 0123456789. London: HMSO. Date month year: Column Number Item Number.

House of Commons or House of Lords Paper

List of terms

Great Britain *[full stop]* (words required)
Parliament *[full stop]* (words required)
House of Commons or House of Lords as appropriate *[full stop]*
Year of publication in brackets *[full stop]*
Name of Paper in italics *[full stop]*
ISBN [colon]

ISBN Number – omit all hyphens and spaces *[full stop]*
Place of publication *(see place rules) [colon]* (will be London)
Publisher *[comma]* (will be HMSO)
Paper number (in brackets) [full stop]

Format

Great Britain. Parliament. House of Commons. (YEAR). *Name of Paper*. ISBN: 0123456789. London: HMSO. (Paper Number).

Statutory instruments

List of terms

Statutory Instrument name *in italics [full stop]*
Year of publication in brackets *[full stop]*
Statutory Instrument Number *[full stop]*
ISBN [colon]
ISBN Number – omit all hyphens and spaces *[full stop]*
Place of publication (see place rules) *[colon]*
Publisher [full stop]

Format

Statutory Instrument Name. (YEAR). S.I.Number. ISBN: 0123456789. Place: Publisher.

Material from Scottish Parliament and Welsh and Northern Irish Assemblies

This will also apply to any regional assemblies as they come into being.
   Treat as for UK Government publications changing sources as appropriate. Check on who is performing the publication.

Material from councils of Parish, Town, District, County, Unitary Authority

Treat as for books or journals or any other publication as appropriate.

Material from e-Government sites, EU, National, Regional or Local government

Treat as normal websites.

Material from any other Government or United Nations

Treat as normal publication.

 Legal, Patents and Standards

Law Reports

List of terms

> Case in italics *[full stop]*
> Year in SQUARE brackets if there is no volume number, ROUND brackets if there is. *[full stop]*
> Volume number, if applicable *[full stop]*
> Abbreviation for name of report and first page of report *[full stop]*

Format

> *Name1 v. Name2.* [YEAR]. Necessary Abbrev.
> *Name1 v. Name2.* (YEAR). Volume Number. Necessary Abbrev.

Patent

List of terms

> Inventor(s) – the names formatted as for authors, but quote all names. *[comma]*
> Assignee [full stop] (this may be a person or a company)
> Year in brackets *[full stop]*
> Title of Patent in italics [full stop]
> Patent number *[full stop]*

Format

> Inventor, I.N., Assignee. (YEAR). *Patent Title.* Patent Number.

Standards (BS or ISO)

List of terms

> BS or ISO as appropriate
> Standard number [colon] Year [comma] (note that the year is not in brackets)
> Title of Standard in italics *[full stop]*

Format

> BS/ISO nnnn: YEAR, *Title of Standard.*

Theses and Dissertations

Thesis

List of terms

Author's family name/surname *[comma]*
Author's initial(s) [each initial with full stop]
Year of presentation in brackets *[full stop]*
Title of thesis in italics *[full stop]*
Unpublished (this probably applies)
Degree Statement (e.g. PhD Thesis) [full stop]
Degree Awarding Body (i.e. the name of the university) [full stop]

Format

Author, I.N. (YEAR). *Title of Thesis.* Unpublished PhD Thesis. University.

Dissertation

List of terms

Author's family name/surname *[comma]*
Author's initial(s) [each initial with full stop]
Year of presentation in brackets *[full stop]*
Title of dissertation in italics *[full stop]*
Unpublished (this probably applies)
Degree Statement (e.g. BSc Dissertation) [full stop]
Degree Awarding Body (i.e. the name of the university) [full stop]

Format

Author, I.N. (YEAR). *Title of Dissertation.* Unpublished MSc Dissertation. University.

Unpublished Material

Unpublished works

Unpublished works can be found in (usually) University or other specialist libraries. They may be theses or dissertations, in which case the forms for these should be used, or may be original source material.

List of terms

Author's family name/surname *[comma]*
Author's initial(s) [each initial with full stop]

Year of presentation in brackets *[full stop]*
Title in italics *[full stop]*
Unpublished
Description (e.g. essay) [full stop]
Place of lodgement (i.e. which library) [full stop]

Format

Author, I.N. (YEAR). *Title of Work.* Unpublished essay. Repository.

 # Microform

Microfiche/Microfilm

Microfilming techniques save space. You need only specify the medium if such item is a rarity, otherwise use the standard for the original material that is involved. This specification is for a newspaper article with the source type included.

List of terms

If author is stated:
Author's family name/surname *[comma]*
Author's initial(s) *[each initial with full stop]*
Year of publication in brackets *[full stop]*
Title of article NOT in italics *[full stop]*
If author is not stated:
Title of article NOT in italics *[full stop]*
Year of publication in brackets *[full stop]*
Source type *(e.g. microfiche)* in square brackets
Name of newspaper *in italics [comma]*
Day and full date of publication *[comma]*
Page number(s) as appropriate designated by p. *[p with full stop]* for a single
    page or pp. *[pp with full stop]* for multiple pages *[full stop] (designate multi-*
    ple pages as a range)

Format

Author, I.N. (YEAR). Title of Article [microfiche] *Name of Newspaper.* XXXday,
    nth month, YEAR, p. n.
Title of Article. (YEAR). [source type] *Name of Newspaper.* XXXday, nth month,
    YEAR, pp. nn–mm.

Conferences, seminars and lectures

Seminar or lecture presentations or lecturer's notes

List of terms

Lecturer's family name/surname *[comma]*
Lecturer's initial(s) [each initial with full stop]
Year of presentation in brackets *[full stop]*
Title of lecture or seminar NOT in italics *[comma]*
Title of course and code in brackets NOT in italics *[full stop]*
Place of lecture *[comma]*
Full date of lecture (day, date, month and year) *[full stop]*

Format

Lecturer, I.N. (YEAR). Title of Lecture, Course and code. Place, Xxxxday date month YEAR.

Example reference entry

Colby, J. (2003). Ethics, Internet Systems T3I. University of Central England, Thursday 1 May 2003.

Study Guides

List of terms

Institution *[comma]*
School or Faculty *[full stop]*
Year of presentation in brackets *[full stop]*
Title of study guide NOT in italics *[comma]*
Title of course and code NOT in italics *[full stop]*
Term or semester dates or reference, year *[full stop]*

Format

Institution, School or Faculty. (YEAR). Study Guide Title, Course Title and code. Term or Semester dates or reference YEAR.

Notes taken by yourself at seminars or lectures

List of terms

Lecturer's family name/surname *[comma]*
Lecturer's initial(s) [each initial with full stop]

Year of lecture in brackets *[full stop]*
Lecture Notes *[full stop]*
[Open square bracket]
Description of the lecture note *[comma]*
Full date of lecture (day, date, month and year)
[Close square bracket] [full stop]

Format

Lecturer, I.N. (YEAR). Lecture Notes. [Description of Lecture Note Xxxxday n month Year]

Published conference proceedings with author or editor(s)

List of terms

Author's or editor's family name/surname *[comma]*
Author's or editors initial(s) *[each initial with full stop]*
NOTE: Multiple authorship/editor rules apply.
NOTE: If the name cited is the editor, include (ed) *[full stop]*
Year of publication in brackets *[full stop]*
Title of Conference *in italics [colon]*
Subtitle in italics [comma]
Location of conference *[comma]*
Date of conference (date range, month and year) *[full stop]*
ISBN [colon]
ISBN Number – omit all hyphens and spaces *[full stop]*
Place of publication (see place rules) [colon]
Publisher [full stop]

Format

Author/Editor, I.N. (YEAR). *Conference Title: Conference Subtitle*, Location, date1–date2 month YEAR. ISBN: 0123456789. Place: Publisher.

Paper from published conference proceedings with author and or editor(s)

List of terms

Author's or editor's family name/surname *[comma]*
Author's or editors initial(s) *[each initial with full stop]*
Year of publication in brackets *[full stop]*
Title of paper NOT in italics *[colon]*
In (bold text) *[colon]*
Title of Conference *in italics [colon]*

Subtitle in italics [comma]
Location of conference *[comma]*
Date of conference (date range, month and year) *[full stop]*
If there is an editor as well as an author, insert editor with normal rules at this point
ISBN [colon]
ISBN Number – omit all hyphens and spaces *[full stop]*
Place of publication (see place rules) *[colon]*
Publisher *[comma]*
Page number(s) as appropriate designated by p. [p with full stop] for a single page or pp. [pp with full stop] for multiple pages [full stop] (designate multiple pages as a range)
  • Note: Multiple authorship/editor rules apply.

Format

Author/Editor, I.N. (YEAR). Title of Paper: **In:** *Conference Title: Conference subtitle*, Conference Location, date1–date2 month YEAR. A.N. Editor, ed. ISBN: 0123456789. Place: Publisher, pp. nn–mm.

Unpublished papers at conferences, meetings, etc.

List of terms

Author's or editor's family name/surname *[comma]*
Author's or editors initial(s) *[each initial with full stop]*
Year of publication in brackets *[full stop]*
Title of paper NOT in italics *[colon]*
In (bold text) *[colon]*
Title of Conference *in italics [colon]*
Subtitle in italics *[comma]*
Location of conference *[comma]*
Date of conference (date range, month and year) *[full stop]*
Unpublished Conference Proceedings *[comma]*
Repository where document can be found *[full stop]*
Page number(s) as appropriate designated by p. *[p with full stop]* for a single page or pp. *[pp with full stop]* for multiple pages [full stop] (designate multiple pages as a range)
  • Note: Multiple authorship/editor rules apply. Insert editor in appropriate place.

Format

Author, I.N. (YEAR). Title of Paper: **In:** *Conference Title: Conference subtitle*, Conference Location, date1–date2 month YEAR. A.N. Editor, ed. Unpublished Conference Proceedings, Repository. pp. nn–mm.

Interviews

Interview – published

List of terms

Interviewee's family name/surname *[comma]*
Interviewee's initial(s) [each initial with full stop]
Year of communication in brackets *[full stop]*
Title of the interview (if any) *[colon]*
Either
    Interview with
    Interviewee's name (forename/lastname) *[full stop]*
    by
    Interviewer's name (forename/lastname) *[full stop]*
Or
    Interview by
    Interviewer's name (forename/lastname) *[full stop]*
Publication medium – follow the rules outlined for the publication medium in which the interview was published.

Format

Interviewee, I.N. (YEAR). Title: Interview with Ian Interviewee by The Interviewer. (then publication medium)
Note. It is correct that the interviewee's name is mentioned twice – it does depend on the title in the publication. The first mention of their name is the *attribution* which is always required, the second is mentioned only if it forms part of the title or subtitle in the publication.

Interview – personal

List of terms

Interviewer's family name/surname *[comma]*
Interviewer's initial(s) [each initial with full stop]
Year of communication in brackets *[full stop]*
Interview [full stop]
[Open square bracket]
Interview with
Name of interviewee (forename/lastname) *[comma]*
Full date of interview (date, month and year)
[Close square bracket] [full stop]

Format

Person, N. (YEAR). Interview. [Interview with Named Person, dd mmm, YYYY].

Personal Communication

Personal communications can be of many forms – be sure to record whatever details are necessary to back up any argument you make in your submitted work.

Letters, telephone calls and email

Some sources on referencing state that items of this nature should be cited only and not quoted in references. If you need to reference something like this, ask your tutor for advice.

List of terms

Other party's family name/surname *[comma]*
Other party's initial(s) [each initial with full stop]
Year of communication in brackets *[full stop]*
[open square bracket]
Telephone call with, letter from or email from
Name of other party (forename/lastname) If an email include email address *[comma]*
Full date of telephone call, letter or email (day, month and year)
[close square bracket]

Format

Person, I.N. (YEAR). [Telephone call with Other Party. date month Year]
Person, I.N. (YEAR). [Letter from Other Party. date month Year]
Person, I.N. (YEAR). [Email from Other Party. other.party@somewhere.com, date month Year]

 # Graphics and tabular data

Cartographic Material

List of terms

If originator/author is known:
Author's family name/surname *[comma]*
Author's initial(s) *[each initial with full stop]*
Year of publication in brackets *[full stop]*
Title of work *in italics* as it appears on the title page or fold *(not necessarily as on the cover) [full stop]*
If originator is not known:
Title of work *in italics* as it appears on the title page or fold *(not necessarily as on the cover) [full stop]*
Year of publication in brackets *[full stop]*

Scale of map (e.g. 1:25,000) *[full stop]*
ISBN [colon]
ISBN Number – omit all hyphens and spaces *[full stop]*
Place of publication (see place rules) *[colon]*
Publisher [full stop]

Format

Author, I.N. (YEAR). *Title*. Scale. ISBN: 0123456789. Place: Publisher.

Example reference entry

Moule, T. (1990). *The County Maps of Old England*. Scale: Various. ISBN: 1851704035. London: Studio Editions.

Ordnance Survey Maps

List of terms

Ordnance Survey *[full stop]*
Year of publication in brackets *[full stop]*
Title in italics *[comma]*
Sheet number (e.g. sheet 100) *[full stop]*
Scale (e.g. 1:50,000) *[comma]*
Series in brackets (e.g. Landranger series) *[full stop]*
ISBN [colon]
ISBN Number – omit all hyphens and spaces *[full stop]*

Format

Ordnance Survey. (YYYY). *Title of Map*, sheet nnn. Scale, Series. ISBN: 0123456789.

Example reference entry

Ordnance Survey, (2000) Telford, Ironbridge and The Wrekin, sheet 242. 1:25,000, Explorer Series. ISBN: 031921873.

Geological Survey Maps

List of terms

Corporate Body *[full stop]*
Common Corporate Bodies
   Geological Survey of Great Britain (England and Wales)
   Geological Survey of Great Britain (Scotland)
   Geological Survey of Great Britain (Northern Ireland)

British Geological Survey
Year of publication in brackets *[full stop]*
Title and type designation in italics *[comma]*
Sheet number (e.g. sheet 100) *[full stop]*
Scale (e.g. 1:50,000) *[full stop]*
ISBN *[colon]*
ISBN Number – omit all hyphens and spaces *[full stop]*

Example reference entries

British Geological Survey (1989). *Sutherland Solid Geology*, Sheet 58°N–06°W, 1:250 000.

Geological Survey of Great Britain (England and Wales). (2001). *Falmouth Solid and Drift*, sheet 352, 1:50,000. ISBN: 075180830X.

Illustrations

Cite the source from which the illustration is referenced, whatever it is. The example given here is for a single author book

List of terms

Author's family name/surname *[comma]*
Author's initial(s) [each initial with full stop]
Year of publication in brackets *[full stop]*
Title of work in italics as it appears on the title page (not necessarily as on the book cover) [full stop]
ISBN *[colon]*
ISBN Number – omit all hyphens and spaces *[full stop]*
Place of publication (see place rules) *[colon]*
Publisher *[comma]*
Page number designated by p. *[p with full stop]* then the number *[comma]*
Select one of (use the abbreviation designated) and quote a number – then *[full stop]*
Illustration – illus
Figure – fig
Photograph – photograph
Chart – chart
Diagram – diag
Table – table
Map – map

Example reference entry

Cunliffe, B. (2001). *Facing the Ocean*. ISBN: 019969110X. Oxford: Oxford University Press, p. 114, fig 4.4.

Broadcast and non-broadcast visual material

Because of the diverse nature of this medium no real standard can be applied. You may in some cases cite an author or director, or maybe just the title. The general principle should be to cite as much as the information you can obtain in order for someone else to be able to trace the origin. You should cite the publisher if the medium is a recording of some sort, or if it is a broadcast you should give both the station and the time and date of the broadcast. Internet broadcasts and streaming video are also covered in this category.

Television, film and video, audio visual

Television Broadcast
Film
Video (tape)
Video (CD)
Video (DVD)
Video (Streaming)
Audio–visual material (more than one medium)

List of terms

If a named person is identifiable:
Director's or Originator's family name/surname *[comma]*
Director's or Originator's initial(s) *[each initial with full stop]*
Year of publication in brackets *[full stop]*
Title of work *in italics [full stop]*
If a named person is not identifiable:
Title of work *in italics* [full stop]
Year of publication in brackets [full stop]
Publisher or broadcaster *[comma]*
Select one of material type (and give date and time if necessary)
Television Broadcast
Film
Video (tape)
Video (CD)
Video (DVD)
Video (Streaming)
Audio–visual material [full stop]
If the material is in an archive, also specify the archive location.
If the type of material is important then you should cite that, e.g. VHS tap, DV tape etc.

Format

Director, I.N. (YYYY). *Title of production*, Publisher/Broadcaster, material type Xxxday, n month Year.

Music and sound

Sound recording – Audiocassette, Vinyl, CD, DVD, Video used for sound

List of terms

If the originator is identifiable then:
Originator's family name/surname *[comma]*
Originator's initial(s) *[each initial with full stop]*
Year of publication in brackets *[full stop]*
Title of work in italics *[full stop]*
If the originator is an unidentifiable group then:
Title of work in italics *[full stop]*
Year of publication in brackets *[full stop]*
Place of publication (see place rules) *[colon]*
Publisher [full stop]
Publisher's reference number *[full stop]*
Stereo, mono or surround *[colon]*
Then the medium:
Audiocassette
Vinyl Recording
CD
DVD
Video *(if you are using it primarily as a sound recording)*
Then length of work (usually in minutes)
Then [full stop]

Format

Originator, I.N. (YEAR). *Title of work*. Place: Publisher. Ref Number. Sound type: Medium. Length.

Example reference entry

Coasters, The. (1958). *Sorry But I'm Gonna (sic) Have to Pass*. New York: WEA International Inc. A4591C. Stereo: Audiocassette, 3 min.

Sound broadcast – Radio, Television

List of terms

If the originator is identifiable then:
Originator's family name/surname *[comma]*
Originator's initial(s) *[each initial with full stop]*
Year of broadcast in brackets *[full stop]*
Title of broadcast in italics *[full stop]*

If the originator is an unidentifiable group then:
Title of broadcast in italics *[full stop]*
Year of broadcast in brackets *[full stop]*
The station (this will usually give the medium) [full stop]
The day, date, month, year and time as appropriate *[full stop]*

Format

Originator, I.N. (YEAR). *Title of Broadcast*. Station. Xxxday n month YEAR Time.

Example reference entry

Six o'Clock News. (2003). Radio 4. Monday 7 July 2003 18:00.

Music Score

List of terms

Composer's family name/surname *[comma]*
Composer's initial(s) [each initial with full stop]
Year of publication in brackets *[full stop]*
Title of work as it appears on the title page in italics *[colon]*
Describe the instruments or voices for which the music is intended *[full stop]*
If there are arrangers or editors given, mention these according to the editors' rules given elsewhere. Use 'Scored by' or 'Arranged by' or (ed.) as appropriate *[full stop]*
Place of publication (see place rules) [colon]
Publisher [full stop]

Format

Composer, I.N. (YEAR). *Title of Work:* Ensemble required. Place: Publisher.

Example reference entry

Bach, J.S. (1938) *The Passion of our Lord According to S. Matthew:* SATB Choir and Orchestra. E. Elgar & I. Atkins eds. London: Novello. (First Published 1911).

Miscellaneous

Multiple references

If an author you are citing has several works in a year, then add a letter (a), (b), (c) and so on after the year for every instance.

Capitalisation rules

Titles have all words with initial capitals except minor prepositions and articles (e.g. of, the, by)
People have initial capitals letters for their last family name and capitalised
initials.

Place rules

Applies to publisher's location.
If there is more than one location, quote the first.
If there is doubt about the country – quote it. For example either:
Birmingham (UK)
Birmingham (Alabama, US)
If there is a UK office of the publisher, quote that. For example:
   Publisher gives offices in New York, London – quote London.

Secondary referencing

A secondary reference is a quote from a work that you have not read in a
   work that you have read.
This is cited by the following method:
Author's family name/surname [comma]
Author's initial(s) [each initial with a full stop]
Year of publication in brackets [full stop]
cited in (these words)
The full reference for the host work as defined in this booklet.

Quoting page numbers

Page number(s) are quoted if appropriate at the end of the reference (where
   not otherwise designated in the examples below) by p. [p with full stop] for
   a single page or pp. [pp with full stop] for multiple pages [full stop] (designate multiple pages as a range).
However if you are quoting specific pages from a reference it is usually better to quote this in the in-text citation rather than in the reference itself,
   except where the rule is defined in the examples.
It is recommended that you do include page numbers in citations to tightly
   specify where you have read the material.

Dates and times

Dates are necessary for online references and for sources that need to be
   defined by time, like newspapers, broadcasts, and so on.
Because a Briton would understand a date like 02/05/03 as the 2nd May 2003,
   and American would think it was 5th February 2003. So to be unambiguous

it is suggested that you use the date month year format, so the previous example should be rendered as 2nd May 2003.

Occasionally it is also necessary to specify the day of the week as well – these are marked in the text of this booklet.

What if there is no date?

Where the date should be in your reference, in brackets put (no date) or (undated).

Use of ibid and sic and other Latin

ibid – Latin abbreviation for 'ibidem', in the same place. If you are citing a number of references from the same work, you would give the reference as:

Karp, A. (1997). *Windows Annoyances*. ISBN: 1565922662. Cambridge: O'Reilly. And then make sequential citations in your work as:

Karp (1997) p34.

ibid p. 47.

ibid p. 68.

This does not work if the citations from the same work are not sequential in your work.

sic means thus – so if someone has made a misspelling in the title of their work, keep it in, but indicate that you have noticed it:

e.g. University of Brimingham *(sic)*

et seq – onwards – usually used for page references p.89 et seq

i.e. – id est – that is. Saying something in different words to clarify its meaning. *Do not confuse its usage with e.g.*

e.g. – exempli gratia – for example. Giving an example of something to clarify the meaning of what you have said. *Do not confuse its usage with i.e.*

n.b. – nota bene – notice what follows. Use in context to amplify points you are making.

op cit – opere citato – literally in the work cited. Used to refer to a work cited earlier in the chapter or paper.

et al – et alii – and others. Used when more than three authors have written the work you want to use.

Principles of citation

When writing, if the author's name occurs naturally in a sentence, you might say:

In a study on network design, Oppenheimer (1999) said …

But if you have to interrupt the flow:

A recent study on network design (Oppenheimer, 1999) shows that …

If there are two authors with the same name with publications in the same year, also quote each of the author's initials.

Page or chapter numbers can also be quoted, for example (Oppenheimer, 1999 pp.248–263)

If an author has several works in a year, then list the suffix letter as well

A recent study on network design (Oppenheimer, 1999b) shows that ...

Quoting page numbers

Page number(s) are quoted as appropriate, designated by p. [p with full stop] for a single page or pp. [pp with full stop] for multiple pages.

How much can I quote?

Only quote enough to support your argument. As an example:

If it is a description, just cite the reference (Colby, 2003).
If it is a definition, put the actual words of the definition into your work.

When you do quote, include your quotations in quotation marks. If it is a long quotation (over two lines) then put it in separate paragraph and indent both sides of the paragraph.

Appendices and how to use them

Appendices are useful sections of a piece of work where you can sensibly present some of the material you have collected – if it is relevant.

Do not be tempted to stuff it full of everything just to expand a word limit. Conventionally, appendices are not counted in the word limit of an academic piece of work.

Do not put mainstream argument material in the Appendices – it is the wrong place for such material and it might get missed and so spoil your argument.

Notes on conclusions, executive summaries and abstracts

The report's conclusion

Conclusions come at the end of a report. They are where any decisions or recommendations that you make are discussed, and any 'next steps' that will be required are discussed. A conclusion is **not** a summary of the whole report, it is the **major output** of the report and should be your strongest point. A busy executive or manager should be able to read the executive summary and conclusion and be able to have a good understanding of what the report covers, what is decided, and what the executive (or someone else) needs to do next.

Executive summary

An executive summary is positioned at the beginning of a report or dissertation or thesis, but it can only be written once the rest of the report is completed. The executive summary needs to be a piece of work that can stand alone. The formal work should make sensible reading without the executive summary, and the executive summary should be able to be read in isolation without recourse to the rest of the report and still be a legitimate document.

The executive summary condenses the whole work into one or two pages of text, usually of around 250–500 words. It should set the scene, why the work was commissioned and who is the intended audience. It should then outline the rest of the work. Whilst it is difficult to give precise definitions, as a rule of thumb each page of the report should be condensed to one or two simple sentences.

The idea of an executive summary is that people who are too busy to read the whole report can read the executive summary as well as the conclusions, and from this be able to get the main thrust of the arguments presented. Because of this, the executive summary should not contain any material that is not mentioned elsewhere in the report, though if a particularly relevant reference by someone well respected in the field can provide a good start or finish to the executive summary, this is acceptable.

Abstracts

An abstract usually refers to academic texts, theses, papers and dissertations, but you may be specifically asked to produce one for a formal report. The purpose of an abstract is identical to an executive summary, but condensed down to usually a single paragraph. An abstract may also have a 'key words' section associated with it, so that if archived electronically, the report can be indexed (and later searched) against these key words.

Why is a first draft important?

Creating a first draft, for reviewing and revising the document before submitting is a stage that is sometimes overlooked when a report deadline is due. This is an essential stage. Whatever ideas or arguments we may have in our head, we may not be able to get these concepts down on paper first time round. Reviewing a first draft to produce a final version is essential, and when this review is completed by someone else, this is known as a peer review. Allowing 1–2 days between finishing the draft and then reviewing it helps to 'clear your head'. You will read what is actually there, not what you expect to see that is, put yourself in the place of the intended audience.

What is a peer review?

A peer review is simply asking someone else to read the report, and make comments on the style, language and grammar used. The person who is conducting the peer review does not need to know the background or purpose of the report (though this should be clear from the executive summary and introduction of the report) but simply acts as a fresh pair of eyes to ensure that any silly mistakes have been corrected. Examples of the type of thing that a peer reviewer will pick up include:

Spotting the wrong use of their, they're and there,
sentences which are not complete,
two, to and too used incorrectly,
know and now confused,
switching of style from the present to past tense, and the use of active and
   passive voices,
undefined terms, use of abbreviations and jargon

Presentation style

The presentation of a report in industry is paramount to how well the report is received. It is an unfortunate fact that the presentation style of the report can sometimes have a greater bearing on the final impression of the work received than the content of the report. Therefore, the following general advice is given to guide the writer towards what may be acknowledged as a 'good' presentation style. In addition to these style points, always ensure that the report is printed on good quality paper (80 g.s.m. minimum) and that the toner or inkjet cartridge is producing good, clear results.

Presentation tips

Do s	*Don't s*
Use a standard font such as Arial (preferably) or Times New Roman	Select an obscure font that attempts to be quirky
Use a font size of at least 11 point, and preferably 12 point	Select a font size that is too small or too large to be read easily
Use a line spacing of at least 1.5 lines. This allows comments to be added to the report	Try to save paper by reducing the line spacing to (e.g.) 0.8 lines, as this leads to 'word bleeding'
Use the standard margin settings in Word documents. This allows for room for any binding/stapling	Use a 1 cm margin. If combined with standard line spacing this allows no room for comments/notes
Use the header area at the top and bottom of the page to put your name, student ID, report name and the page number	Leave the page header blank. If the report is dropped and the cover sheet mislaid then there may be no way of identifying the work or re-ordering the pages
Use emphasis styles such as **bold**, or *italics* with ***extreme*** care	USE CAPITALS TO EMPHASISE or use a combination of *styles* that are *not* appropriate. Underlining also causes difficulties for people with less than perfect sight, so it should not really be used in a report

Essential report structure

The following summary lists what you should include in a 'standard' formal report:

Title
Table of contents
Executive summary
Introduction
Main body
Findings
Conclusion
References and bibliography
Appendices

Index